PENGUIN BOOKS

HOW TO HAVE MORE THAN ENOUGH

Dave Ramsey knows what it's like to have—and lose—it all. By the age of twenty-six, he had accumulated a personal real estate portfolio worth more than $4 million; by the age of thirty, he was so far in debt he was forced to declare personal bankruptcy. Ramsey rebuilt his financial life and has spent the last decade counseling hundreds of thousands in his seminars; his thirteen-week course, Financial Peace University; and in more than ten thousand hours on the radio as the host of the nationally syndicated radio show *The Dave Ramsey Show*. He is the author of the bestsellers *Financial Peace* and *The Financial Peace Planner* as well as a sought-after speaker and seminar leader in churches and corporations throughout the country. He and his wife, Sharon, and their three children live in Nashville, Tennessee.

How to Have MORE Than Enough

A Step-by-Step Guide
to Creating Abundance

DAVE RAMSEY

PENGUIN BOOKS

PENGUIN BOOKS
Published by the Penguin Group
Penguin Group (USA) Inc., 375 Hudson Street, New York, New York 10014, U.S.A.
Penguin Group (Canada), 90 Eglinton Avenue East, Suite 700, Toronto,
Ontario, Canada M4P 2Y3 (a division of Pearson Penguin Canada Inc.)
Penguin Books Ltd, 80 Strand, London WC2R 0RL, England
Penguin Ireland, 25 St Stephen's Green, Dublin 2, Ireland (a division of Penguin Books Ltd)
Penguin Group (Australia), 250 Camberwell Road, Camberwell,
Victoria 3124, Australia (a division of Pearson Australia Group Pty Ltd)
Penguin Books India Pvt Ltd, 11 Community Centre, Panchsheel Park, New Delhi – 110 017, India
Penguin Group (NZ), cnr Airborne and Rosedale Roads,
Albany, Auckland 1310, New Zealand (a division of Pearson New Zealand Ltd)
Penguin Books (South Africa) (Pty) Ltd, 24 Sturdee Avenue,
Rosebank, Johannesburg 2196, South Africa

Penguin Books Ltd, Registered Offices: 80 Strand, London WC2R 0RL, England

31 33 35 37 39 40 38 36 34 32

PUBLISHER'S NOTE
This publication is designed to provide accurate and authoritative information
in regard to the subject matter covered. It is sold with the understanding
that the publisher is not engaged in rendering financial, accounting, or other
professional service. If financial advice or other expert assistance is
required, the service of a competent professional person should be sought.

LIBRARY OF CONGRESS CATALOGING IN PUBLICATION DATA
Ramsey, Dave.
How to have more than enough: a step-by-step guide to creating abundance /
Dave Ramsey.
p.   cm.
Includes index.
ISBN 0 14 02.8193 2
1. Finance, Personal. 2. Finance, Personal—Religious aspects—Christianity. I. Title.
HG179.H632   2000
332.024—dc21   00–024969

Printed in the United States of America
Set in New Caledonia

To my family, where we get to share
our lives of **More Than Enough**:
Sharon, my beautiful wife and partner,
and my children, Denise, Rachel, and Daniel.

To those thousands of our readers and listeners
who have made the painful decision to change their lives,
their family tree, and their entire community.

Money is worth nothing to the man
who has more than enough.
—George Bernard Shaw

Acknowledgments

First, I'd like to acknowledge my family for giving up their dad and husband for the hours spent one summer on this project. Next, Ken Abraham, who saved this book with his dedication and breathed life into these words. Thanks, Ken. As always, we acknowledge our Lord and Savior, the true author of *How to Have More Than Enough,* Jesus Christ.

Contents

How to Have
More Than Enough

Store Manager, to Aisle One, Please!

1984:

IT'S ONE O'CLOCK in the morning and I'm tossing and turning in bed . . . again. Like most nights that I've endured for the past several months, all I can think about are my massive debts and the fact that I am going broke. Fast.

Even in the darkness, I can feel my face turning red from embarrassment, and although I have the covers pulled up around my chin, my body alternately shivers with chills and then breaks out in a sweat. Lying next to me, my wife, Sharon, stirs in her sleep. My wife—the woman who loves me, who has stood by me, believed in me, and who has trusted my financial decisions completely, even when I couldn't explain what I was doing with our money or why I was doing it. My wife, the mother of our two beautiful little girls who are sleeping down the hall from us, two innocent cherubs who believed that Daddy was so smart.

How could I have done this to them?

I'm dog-tired, but I can't sleep, so to keep from rousing Sharon further, I slip out of bed and go to the living room, where I turn on the television. Earlier in the evening, I had used the TV to bore myself into a drowsiness that I had hoped would lead to sleep. No such luck.

Now, at this hour, I'm not looking for quality content, or even an electronic sleeping pill. I just want the TV on so the noise will distract my racing thoughts.

I don't want my mind to drift back to what's happening in my life, but I can't seem to prevent it, either. The mental and emotional fatigue brought on by our financial stress has finally caught up with me. I feel drained in every way. My body aches; my stomach churns like a washing machine, my brain pounds with a throbbing that Tylenol can't cure. My self-image has plummeted through the floorboards. I don't have any energy left with which to fight.

The pressure of not being able to pay my bills brings on unbelievable fear. I don't want to have to face it, but like my body, the fear refuses to lie down and go to sleep. It is almost palpable. I can feel it, taste it, smell it. It slips past my defense mechanisms like an ominous fog in a B horror movie. It envelops me; wraps its slimy fingers around my throat and squeezes. The fear and insecurity wake up a little child inside me. And the child is afraid. Scared stiff.

But I'm not a child. I'm an adult—a husband, father of two, an employer. I am responsible for the lives of others as well as myself. Oh, God, what can I do?

My business is failing, we are losing everything, and I don't know if we can even keep the electricity on, much less keep the house, cars, and all the other "stuff" my wife and I call our life.

Although I haven't had a decent night's sleep in months, I don't dare talk about our financial situation with anyone. All our friends and business associates think we are wildly successful—and for a while, we were. But not anymore.

What has happened to me? I wonder. A few months ago everything seemed great: I had a thriving business buying, fixing up, and reselling houses—"rehabbing," we called it. My profits were soaring; I had a great marriage and family, a lovely home, and drove a sporty-looking Jaguar. Life seemed so great, but now suddenly I am faced with losing everything. What went wrong?

Looking back, it was simple to figure out. I had gotten cocky; I didn't think anything could ever go wrong—or at least, nothing that I wouldn't be able to handle.

I had gotten too far into debt to get out. Everything I owned—from my business to my home to all the stuff we had accumulated—was leveraged to the hilt. And all it took was one bank to call in a ninety-day note for the entire house of cards to come tumbling down.

Have you been there? Most of us have walked through personal or financial, career, spiritual, or physical crises. These times of blinding pain and discomfort cause us to take inventory. We can either give up and lose everything, or realize that we have to change. But change does not come easily. We must consider what we are doing wrong, and make some hard decisions about what we want to do differently.

Amazingly, these times of insecurity can be the times of greatest personal growth. Not until the pain of the same is greater than the pain of change will you embrace change. We need to look at who we are, not just at what we do or who we are married to. We need to examine what we believe and ask questions such as "What am I doing with my life that really matters?" When we start to examine life at its core and really take stock of what we are about, that's when real change can begin.

> *Not until the pain of the same is greater than the pain of change will you embrace change.*

Character cannot be developed in ease and quiet.
Only through [the] experience of trial and suffering
can the soul be strengthened.
—*Helen Keller*

Meet the New Me!

It's the year 2000: "This is Dave Ramsey, and you're on the air. How can I help? What can I do for you today?"

Some sixteen years after my night of torment, my family and I have come a long, long way. Today I host a nationally syndicated radio show which provides advice on personal finance and, as I have learned, about life itself. I head the Lampo Group, an organization that is committed to teaching others how to survive crisis and build wealth. We have counseled thousands of people one-on-one and hundreds of thousands more all across America in our live seminars—helping the hurting and directing the prosperous.

My wife, Sharon, and I live in a beautiful, fully paid for home, along with our two daughters and our son. I've made the journey back from being a bankrupt former millionaire to having more money than I ever dreamed of—this time without taking on any debt. I have a little less hair than I did sixteen years ago, but a lot more wisdom.

In the past decade and a half, I've learned lots of lessons, not only from my own experience, but also from the heartrending experiences of thousands of others whom I have helped as they faced similar crises. In the process, I have become a student of the character traits of successful people, as well as the patterns of unsuccessful people. As my team and I have counseled all these folks—in crisis or in prosperity—I have discovered what works in wealth-building and in "people-building."

Beyond that, over these years, I have been privileged to spend time with hundreds of folks who have successful families and successful businesses, and who are living joy-filled lives. I have also been honored to work with hundreds of people who are my heroes, people who have faced unbelievable odds and have "made it" even when it seemed that there was no way that they could.

How Do They Do It?

What do successful people do when the pressure is on? They find the desperation or the courage, or usually some mix of the two, and do what so few apathetic Americans are willing to do: They take inventory of the person in the mirror, and when they find him or her coming up short, they *change*. They are determined to reach for something better. They decide to play *Rocky* music in the background while they are shaving or putting on their makeup.

They refuse to blame others or circumstances or poor potty training for their situation, and they do something radical: THEY DECIDE TO CHANGE THEMSELVES! They reach deep inside, search until they find the missing elements causing the crisis, and restock the shelves. Most of all, truly successful people—people who are rich in the areas of personal relationships, not just in dollars and cents, stocks and bonds—willfully put themselves on the path where they can discover how to have more than enough.

This is a path that anyone can walk, no matter where you are financially, emotionally, or spiritually. You may be facing a mountain of debts or you may need to pull yourself out of a hole. You may be living a ho-hum, mediocre (boring!) life in which you're meeting all of your basic needs, but not much more than that. Or maybe you seem to have everything—the way I thought I did all those years ago—but you are missing the core from which you can draw energy, which will empower you to have a rich existence in every sphere of your life.

❖ ❖ ❖

> You will never leave where you are until
> you decide where you'd rather be.
> —*Lewis Dunnington*

More Than Enough What?

This book, *How to Have More Than Enough,* is explosive. It is not meant to be read and merely laid aside. It is intended to be read, written in, mulled over, and acted on. This is a book for someone ready and willing to face the pain of personal change, and to grab just a little bigger slice out of the pie. This book is about how you can have more than enough.

By "More Than Enough," I mean not merely having more money, but also having more fulfillment, more happiness from your relationships, more hope, more energy, and more reason for being alive.

In my research, I have discovered that people who have **More Than Enough** inevitably share ten character traits. They are:

1. A GOOD VALUE SYSTEM
2. A VISION FOR THEIR LIVES
3. UNITY WITH THEIR SPOUSE (or a contentment with their singleness), coworkers, church members, team, or kids
4. THE ABILITY TO HOPE
5. A WILLINGNESS TO BE ACCOUNTABLE TO OTHERS
6. A NEED TO LIVE LIFE WITH REAL INTENSITY
7. A LIFELONG HABIT OF WORK, DILIGENCE, AND DISCIPLINE
8. PATIENCE
9. THE CAPACITY FOR CONTENTMENT
10. THE DESIRE TO GIVE TO OTHERS

Before we go any further, let's take a few moments right now to do a bit of self-evaluation. How many of the above ten character traits do you see occurring regularly in your life? Be honest, now. Nobody is grading your paper. You won't get a big bonus check if you answer all the questions correctly. This book is a mirror in which you can see yourself, but it will do you little good if you are not willing to face who you really are. However, as you accurately discover your strengths and weaknesses, you will see the areas in which you want to improve.

So let's get an honest appraisal of where you are right now, and we will repeat the exercise after you are finished reading and working through this book.

On a scale of one to ten (ten being excellent, one being just plain pitiful), circle a number that best rates you in each of the following areas. (Tell your mom, dad, spouse, or teacher that I said it is okay to write in this book—unless you borrowed it from a library. In fact, it is highly suggested.)

I'd say my VALUE SYSTEM is a:

  1   2   3   4   5   6   7   8   9   10

My VISION for my life is a:

   1   2   3   4   5   6   7   8   9   10

My UNITY WITH MY SPOUSE (or contentment with my singleness), coworkers, church members, team, or kids is a:

   1   2   3   4   5   6   7   8   9   10

My ABILITY TO HOPE is a:

   1   2   3   4   5   6   7   8   9   10

My WILLINGNESS TO BE ACCOUNTABLE TO OTHERS is a:

   1   2   3   4   5   6   7   8   9   10

My NEED TO LIVE LIFE WITH REAL INTENSITY is a:

   1   2   3   4   5   6   7   8   9   10

My HABITS OF WORK, DILIGENCE, AND DISCIPLINE are a:

   1   2   3   4   5   6   7   8   9   10

My PATIENCE is a:

   1   2   3   4   5   6   7   8   9   10

My CAPACITY FOR CONTENTMENT is a:

   1   2   3   4   5   6   7   8   9   10

My DESIRE TO GIVE TO OTHERS is a:

   1   2   3   4   5   6   7   8   9   10

There, that wasn't so bad, was it? At the end of the book, we will rate ourselves again and note the similarities and differences. In the meantime, within these pages, I'll explain how each of these characteristics leads to **More Than Enough**. We will take an inventory of these qualities in your life, and I'll then guide you toward achieving them, or improving them, supplying you with plenty of practical suggestions along the way.

Warning!

I feel compelled to warn you in advance that this is not a guide for the weakhearted. If you are lazy, complacent, apathetic, or indifferent—if you think you are just fine the way you are—you may want to pass along this book (assuming that you've already paid for it, of course) to a friend who is interested in getting more out of life. You may not have what it takes to do these exercises and put these elements to practice in your life. This book is designed for people who want to *be* somebody, who want to *do* something significant with their lives, who want to have something engraved on their tombstone that really matters.

This book is also intended to be a catalyst for folks who are at a point of crisis, who are willing to change, and never want to go back to the "same ol', same ol'."

> We must change in order to survive.
> —*Pearl Bailey*

Why Change?

What does all this discussion of change have to do with accumulating piles of cash, investing in things that matter, and changing your family tree? Plenty! Because if you are not presently enjoying more than enough, it is obvious that something has to change. If you keep doing what you have always done, you will keep getting the same results you've always gotten. That's great if what you are doing is producing a **More Than Enough** lifestyle for you and the people you love; but if not, this is your chance to start anew! The place we have to initiate change is within ourselves.

Which of the following statements best describes your attitude toward change? (Check one.)

____ I am extremely open to change.
____ I'm relatively open to change, as long as I can control it.
____ I'm indifferent to change. "Whatever."
____ I'm reluctant, but not totally resistant to change.
____ I am opposed to change. I like my life fine the way it is.

❖ You were so happy. You were safe and secure. Life was wonderful. You were living in paradise; laid-back; taking it easy; floating comfortably on the warm, gentle waves; cushioned from all shocks; insulated and isolated from the pressures of the outside world. Your every need was supplied by someone larger than yourself. You knew little of pain, disturbance, or threats. Yours was a fine existence indeed.

Then one day something happened that shook your world to its foundations. It began quietly, intermittently, almost imperceptibly, sort of a tugging feeling at the center of your being that quickly turned into a violent, jolting earthquake. Suddenly, your security started to collapse around you. The walls seemed to be pressing in upon you. Your body became bent over, your arms and legs felt twisted and crushed. You sensed that you were falling, head over heals, upside down.

Next came the pain, the heat, the pressure, almost too intense to bear. Your head felt as if it were being squeezed in a vise grip. You were pushed, harder and harder, into a dark, narrow chasm. Fear rushed through every fiber of your body. Then suddenly you saw it—the light at the end of the tunnel! Helplessly, your body was thrust toward the light. You thought, *Almost there. Keep going.* Cold, clammy hands were grabbing at you. One reached for your head and pulled. Another latched onto your torso and together they tore you away from the last vestige of safety and security. You felt as though you were going to die as a result of all this pressure, pain, and change.

Actually, you were just born.

From the moment you left your mother's womb, your life has been filled with change and transition. It doesn't go away with the accrual of money, possessions, status, or age. We are all in process, from the instant of conception until the second the Lord calls us home. We'd better get used to change!

It Happens to the Best of Us

Doug flopped down in the chair across from the desk in my office. He stretched his long legs out into the middle of the room, revealing his expensive, Italian-made shoes. He crossed his arms over his stylish, perfectly tailored, imported suit. Although Doug's external appearance was impeccable, I could tell something was troubling him. His face was flushed with color and his lips were pursed.

"What's going on with you?" I ventured. "You look as if you just lost your best friend."

"The company decided to transfer me to our western office," Doug began, "and I'm just not up for any more changes in my life right now. My wife, Marsha, and I recently bought a house, and we've finally begun to make some friends in this town and put down some roots. Now we have to sell our home and move again. We have a new baby, as well as a six-year-old and an eight-year-old. I hate to pull the kids out of school, but I guess we're going to have to do it.

"Worse than all that, I just feel so stirred up on the inside. I feel as though time is running out for me. I'm almost forty years old, still living financially from paycheck to paycheck, with too much month at the end of the money. I haven't accomplished my goals, and I guess I've realized that, for me, the future is now. If I don't do something significant with my life now, and take some steps toward financial freedom, it probably won't happen. But I feel so unstable, so insecure. All of the props are being pulled out from under me. The last thing I needed in my life was another major change—and especially in the area of my career."

Doug is not alone. Whether it is a job transfer or a job termination, it is stressful. Nowadays, the term "job security" is an oxymoron. The workplace is no longer the bastion of stability in our society that it once was. According to Richard Nelson Bolles in his annually updated book *What Color Is Your Parachute?*, the average employee will pursue the painful, often humiliating process of seeking new employment at least eight times in his or her adult lifetime. That means most of us are going to experience an immense amount of change, rejection, and stress regarding our careers and how we acquire and use our money. The way in which we deal with those things can quite literally make or break us.

But I'm Sick of Change!

Dr. Thomas Holmes and Dr. Richard Rahe, of the University of Washington, studied the ways in which various changes affect our physical and psychological health. Their discoveries startled stress researchers. They concluded that "four out of five people who have experienced many dramatic changes in their lives over the past year can expect major illness within the next two years." Furthermore, the researchers discovered that stress-inducing changes were not limited to what we would commonly call negative events. Any condition or experience, even those in which we thoroughly rejoice, such as the birth of a child, can create stress.

The doctors published their findings in what is now well known as the "Life Change Units Scale." On this scale, events in a person's life are given a numerical value according to the amount of stress they cause. At the top of the list are death of a spouse (100 points), divorce (73 points), marital separation (65 points), jail term (63 points), and death of a close family member (63 points).

Further down the list are such stress inducers as business readjustment (39 points), trouble with in-laws (29 points), and change in residence (20 points). Not surprisingly, even Christmas shows a 12-point rating on the stress scale, and you can probably guess that the holiday stress has little to do with a baby born in Bethlehem. (I wonder what the rating would be if the researchers could measure the stress when all those credit card statements show up early in January?)

The researchers concluded that it is dangerous for most individuals to accumulate a high stress score over a short span of time. Generally, a total score of 150 or less over twelve months is fairly normal. Between 150 and 300 indicates considerable stress, possibly injurious to one's health. Holmes and Rahe found that of those who scored between 150 and 300, half would suffer a serious health change in the next year. Of those individuals who scored over 300 on the scale, the illness rate rose to a shocking 80 percent. Clearly, change affects us more than we might admit—especially the resulting financial changes that usually accompany most of the major stress inducers.

How, then, do we embrace our need to change without suffering severe consequences as a result?

You Gotta Believe!

The place where all true and lasting change must start is in our attitude toward ourselves. Dan Scott, a pastor friend of mine, is a master storyteller. He once told a story to my team at our office devotional that caused us to buzz with excitement for weeks over the power to change that a crisis can unleash.

Jean, an adult woman, was still dealing with the abuse she had suffered as a child. The abuse left her with a fearful and tentative approach to life. No matter what she tried, she never seemed to get ahead in her relationships, her career, or anything else, for that matter. Eventually, she lapsed into a deep, prolonged depression. She began to see a therapist and attended group sessions to help her endure her ongoing struggle.

Not long after she started therapy, Jean's doctors determined that her depression wasn't chemically based, but was induced by her inability to get past the horrible events of her childhood. They tried everything they could think of to help her break free from her awful memories, but nothing seemed to work for long. She struggled for many years to overcome her problem; she sought help from numerous therapists, but none could help her make any headway. She continued to be tied to the pain of the past.

One of Jean's few joys in life was spending time with her three-year-old niece and her five-year-old nephew. When she baby-sat for them, she always read them a bedtime story. The children's favorite was a story about the circus: it included the big-top tent, the three rings with the ringmaster dramatically announcing each sensational act, the clowns, the tightrope walkers, the lion tamers, the tumblers, and best of all, the elephants. Oh, those wonderful, huge, powerful beasts, the elephants!

One day, Jean saw an advertisement in the local paper announcing that the circus was in town. She called her sister for permission to take the tots to "the greatest show on earth."

When the big night finally arrived, the kids could barely keep their seats as they took in all the sights, sounds, and smells of the circus. The children's eyes sparkled with delight as they enjoyed cotton candy, peanuts, the hilarious clowns, fireworks, and best of all, those wonderful elephants.

Near the close of the performance, the ringmaster announced that children aged five and under could ride an elephant—for a small fee, of course—after the final act.

"Oh, can we, Aunt Jean? Can we, please?" the children begged.

Aunt Jean smiled and said, "Well, let me think about it . . . ," knowing full well that there was no way she was going to refuse the children this wonderful opportunity to ride an elephant.

"Oh, please, Aunt Jean. We'll go right to sleep tonight, we'll pick up our toys every day from now till forever. . . ."

Aunt Jean laughed. "Okay, it's a deal. Let's go get in line."

As they were awaiting their turn, Jean's nephew noticed a large elephant that was secured by a rope, tied to a tent stake driven into the ground. It wasn't a thick, heavy rope and the stake wasn't large; yet the elephant seemed convinced that the rope and stake were strong enough to keep him tied down. Why, he didn't even try to break free!

The five-year-old was intrigued. He asked the trainer, "Sir, why doesn't that big, strong, powerful elephant try to get away? Doesn't he know that the tent stake couldn't possibly hold him back?"

The trainer said, "That's easy, son. When the elephant was young, and much smaller than he is today, we tied him to a much stronger stake, one that was secured to a heavy steel and cement pillar buried in the ground. Attached to that stake was a heavy chain that we used to keep the elephant tied down. And did he ever hate it! He tried to pull loose, he ran as far as the chain would allow him, jerking on the chain, trying to get free. He reared his trunk high in the air and trumpeted for everyone to hear. He'd get angry, he'd yank on that chain until it almost cut his ankles, but he was not strong enough to break free. Eventually he just gave up. That's when we knew that we had him. From then on, we could use a small stake, and a rope to keep the elephant in place. Every time he feels that rope tug against his ankles, he remembers the pain and he thinks, *Oops! That's about as far as I want to go.*"

Jean watched and listened as the trainer put his arm around the boy's shoulder, and pointed across the field to where the other elephants were secured. "Son, do you see those big elephants over there? Every one of them could easily break free. But inside each of them is a little elephant who doesn't believe he can. And as long as he doesn't think he can, he never will."

The ride went splendidly, the magical night was over, and Jean delivered the kids safely back to their parents. The next morning Jean went for her regularly scheduled appointment with her therapist. As she was signing in at the front desk, she glanced down at the morning paper and was horrified. The banner headline across the front page read: FIRE DESTROYS CIRCUS! The lead story described the disaster, recounting how sometime after midnight, the big top at the circus had ignited. The tent, straw, bleachers, everything erupted in flames. Several workers were injured, and many of the animals had been killed, hurt, or badly burned.

Jean sat down in the waiting room and carefully read the full article. She was particularly interested in finding out how the elephants had fared through the fire. Sure enough, the writer, too, was interested in that important detail. He reported: All the elephants had pulled themselves free and had escaped unharmed.

Relief flooded over Jean. As she sat back in the chair, she remembered the trainer's words about how the elephants could easily break free, but the little elephants inside couldn't believe it. Apparently, in the face of the fire, as the flames leaped all around them, when it looked as though there was no hope, the elephants had somehow mustered the courage to overcome the pain of the past and to break free. Had they remained where they were, holding on to the bitter memories, refusing to take courageous steps into an unknown future, the elephants would have perished in the inferno. But because they had somehow found the strength to change their minds, they changed their destinies.

Tears flowed down Jean's cheeks, and a smile spread across her face as she applied the lessons of the elephant to her own life. Right then and there, she made a decision. She stood calmly, walked to the reception desk, and canceled her appointment with the therapist. *From this day forward,* she decided, *I will stop living in the past. I will face down my fears, and step into the future.* For the first time in years, Jean was free!

❖   ❖   ❖

The human soul cannot be permanently chained.
—*W. E. B. Du Bois*

The purpose of the time you and I will spend together over the course of this book is to wake up and feed the big elephant within us. Each of us has had life experiences that have hurt. Sometimes the pain of those past experiences is so intense, you can still feel it as though it took place yesterday. None of us is immune to that kind of hurt. But the pain of the past can keep us immobilized in the present and rob us of our future—if we allow it to do so.

And most of us have had plenty of other people feed the little elephant, always telling us we aren't good enough, that we can't make it, that we'll never amount to anything of significance. You live on the wrong side of town; you aren't capable enough; you aren't smart enough, rich enough, or powerful enough. But I want to tell you that you can have more than enough! An immense amount of untapped power lies dormant in each of our lives, and in these pages we want to uncover it, ignite it, and allow it to fire us up not just in an hour of crisis, but for the rest of our lives.

Within these pages we will feed that big elephant that represents your untapped potential. To do so, we're going to stop by and pick up a few character qualities from the **More Than Enough** Grocery Store. This store has ten aisles, all filled with goodies. As we explore each of these aisles (character qualities), we will first take inventory, and then restock the shelves where needed. People who have a well-stocked **More Than Enough** Store will be

❖ Helen Keller was blind, deaf, and unable to speak, but that did not keep her from living life to its fullest. She once wrote, "Life is either a daring adventure or nothing. To keep your face toward change and behave like a free spirit in the presence of fate is strength undefeatable."

On a scale of one to ten (ten representing the optimum, one the minimum), circle the number that would best represent how you would rate your life on the "adventure" scale.

1	2	3	4	5	6	7	8	9	10
Boring		Drudgery		Okay		Exciting			Incredible

List two areas of your life that you are genuinely excited about. (For example, *"My relationship with my spouse is terrific."* Or, *"I am making great progress in getting out of debt."*)

1. _____
2. _____

Now list two areas in which you would like to see the "adventure factor" increase in the next six months:

1. _____
2. _____

Just off the top of your head, write down two steps that you can take within the next six months that will dramatically change your life for the better:

1. _____
2. _____

pleasantly surprised at how easy it is to feed their elephant, their untapped potential.

As your big elephant's belief gets stronger and you begin to change and succeed, be ready for resistance. Most of us have people in our lives who aren't ready for change, or who are made uncomfortable by our desire for personal growth. Woodrow Wilson said, "If you want to make enemies, try to change something." Change, even for the better, is hard; it is not always readily accepted, and sometimes your willingness to do things differently may upset other people's applecarts in the process. That's okay. Remember, you can't change anyone else, but you can change yourself!

Hang on! This will be a great ride and well worth any challenge it brings!

TWO

Foundation Failure

*Values really do matter and real values
are the foundation of everything to come.*

Disciplines become your habits; habits become
lifestyles; lifestyles influence your character; your
character becomes your destiny.
— *Stan Mitchell*

YEARS AGO I was in the housing-rehab business. I scoured the city searching
for run-down properties that were available at bargain prices. Most of the real
estate that I purchased was priced inexpensively because the owner wanted to
sell quickly due to a bankruptcy or some other financial calamity. Sometimes
I'd find dilapidated old family estates that had been left unattended for long
periods of time. I'd buy the property, fix it up, and then resell it for a profit—
thus the word "rehab." The idea was to add just enough value to the underval-
ued properties to make them attractive to potential buyers.

One time, a contractor working for me told me that he had a home in which
the foundation had fallen in. Since his homeowners insurance had paid him
for the value of the house, he was willing to sell the property for merely the
price of the lot—between $10,000 and $12,000. When I went to look at the
property, I quickly understood why the contractor wanted to sell—the property
was a total mess. The house was a one-level ranch with a basement. The front
yard was level with the front of the house, but because of a drastic slope

between the front and back yards, the backyard was level with the floor of the basement! The basement contained a garage with doors opening toward the backyard.

Worse yet, something had caused the front wall of the basement to cave in, so the house was perched precariously on the two side ends of the foundation, which held the house up in the air like some oversize tree house with a saggy middle.

Beyond the obvious need for repair, I soon discovered that the house had been vandalized. That brought the price down to $6,000.

As I inspected the house, estimating in my head what it might cost to refurbish the place, despite its bad condition, I was still drooling. I thought, *This is the deal of a lifetime! I'm guessing that $20,000 should cover the repairs, and I figure I can sell this baby for about $65,000. I'm looking at serious profit here!* This was one of the many deals back in those days that I didn't bother to run by my wife, Sharon; *after all*, I thought, *I'm the real estate whiz in this family!*

I bought the house and sent my work crews in, and they rebuilt it. The crews pulled out the old, failed foundation and built a new wall. When the renovations were complete, the house was lowered onto its new foundation; the yard was re-graded and landscaped, and we put a FOR SALE sign up in the front yard.

Eight days later, I scheduled an appointment to show the property. As I drove up in front of the house, I was nearly bursting at the seams. I couldn't wait to show this property to the buyer. *This is almost too easy!* I thought. *A guy should have to work harder than this to make this much money!*

A guy did.

When I got out of the car, I couldn't believe my eyes. My brand-new front wall had caved in almost exactly where it had just been rebuilt. The foundation lay in a crumbled heap of cement blocks and concrete, just as it had been the day I first saw the place. *Is there something spooky going on here, or what?* I wondered.

Not surprisingly, my buyer suddenly had business to attend to elsewhere, now that my newly renovated house was nearly worthless again.

Undeterred, I hired an engineer to tell me how to build a stronger foundation. We rebuilt the house again. We built the foundation again, this time with stronger concrete and bigger blocks. Less than a week later, the foundation caved in again!

I was furious! The engineer and I searched and searched for the answer. Was there something wrong with our brick? Was the bedrock below the wall not strong enough to support the weight? What could cause the foundation to crumble three times in row, all in the exact same spot?

Finally we discovered the problem. A spring existed in the front yard. Because of the yard's drastic slope, in a strong rain all the runoff poured behind the foundation wall until the wall couldn't hold any more. The pressure built up until it was like a dam bursting, blowing the cement blocks right out of the wall.

When the engineer redirected the spring and installed steel-reinforced walls, the foundation finally stayed up. Unfortunately, by that time I was $15,000 in the hole on this deal.

A strong foundation is essential in any house, and it is even more essential in your life. It takes a firm foundation to build financial wealth while you strengthen your family and experience spiritual abundance . . . all at the same time! Furthermore, without a strong foundation, it is nearly impossible to stand when the pressures begin to beat on you like the winds of a category-five hurricane. This is as true of your financial life as it is of your business, personal, and spiritual life. So let's discover how you can establish a firm foundation upon which you can build a secure future.

What Makes a Firm Foundation?

The concrete blocks of your foundation are made up of your *values*.

"Values!" I can almost hear you saying while raising your eyebrows. "What in the world do values have to do with making more money and using it wisely?"

Plenty.

What are values? According to *Webster's Dictionary,* a value is "a principle regarded as worthwhile or desirable."

We all have values, whether we choose to admit it or not. Teenage gangs in the street, thugs in prison, and slimeball drug runners all have a value system. It may be based on being the toughest, or the loudest, or the shrewdest, but it is a value system nonetheless.

Con artists and "shock" artists, Wall Street brokers, and used-car dealers all have values. And you and I have values. The question is: Do we have good values or bad values? Are they the kind of values that will help establish solid financial, emotional, and spiritual security in your life and in the lives of your family members, business associates, and others for whom you are responsible? Are they the sort of values that will lead you to true success?

Those are the kinds of values you will want to incorporate into your foundation—the values that will help you live life to the fullest, values that will help you make a positive addition to your family tree. Values that will support you when times get tough as well as when you are fabulously successful—these are the kind of strong, positive values that you want to lay in your foundation. A foundation built on such strong values will never fail.

Forging Solid Values Isn't Easy

Strong values, principles on which you base your life path, will always cause you occasional short-term pain, but they will allow your life to grow and prosper for years to come. Sure, some people try to cut corners, cheat, skip the tough jobs, and put together a foundation that looks good externally but has no real substance. Similarly, some values will stand for only a short time. They may look good initially, but like the first wall we built, when the pressure comes—and you can be sure it will—the foundation crumbles. Strong values usually take some time and effort to establish, but they will stand the test of time. In fact, the values that lead to the **More Than Enough** life will stand forever.

The Three Little Pigs Principle

❖ You remember those three little oinkers, don't you? One little pig built his house out of sticks because sticks were easily obtained, easy to work with, and could be used to throw up the house in a hurry. The second little pig built his house out of straw because it was cheap. Anything cheap must be a bargain, right? The third little pig spent more time and probably some major money, but he built his home out of brick.

The first two little pigs lost their homes when the big bad wolf came huffing and puffing. The wolf blew down the homes that belonged to the first two little pigs. But the third little pig not only survived all the huffing and puffing; he came out ahead of the wolf, and turned that blowhard into wolfburger.

Like the third little pig, you need to build your life with solid materials and values. Anything short of that and you are bound to lose. You can be certain that the wolf, who represents all those things in life that can and do cause problems, will pay a call on you at some point. When he comes huffing and puffing, will your foundation be strong enough to survive?

Strong, positive values are the foundation on which you can build a strong life. Once the values are in place, it becomes much easier to discover and use the proper tools to overcome the challenges you face while you create and enjoy success and wealth.

1. When we model our lives after the two little pigs who tried to get something valuable for less than it is worth, or to do so with less effort than required, we will always lose—maybe not in the short run, but definitely over the long haul. Briefly describe a time in your life when you tried to get what you wanted, or where you wanted to go, by cutting corners. (For instance, once when I was in college, I tried to make the grade by cheating on a test.)

_____

_____

2. What were the short-term results of your compromise? (Check all that apply.)

    1. _____ None at all that I noticed.

    2. _____ I got in big-time trouble!

    3. _____ I became terribly embarrassed.

    4. _____ I'll never have lunch in that town again.

    5. _____ I was severely punished.

    6. _____ I was never caught, so nobody knew but me.

    7. _____ My reputation was damaged irreparably among certain people whose opinions mattered to me.

    8. _____ I could barely live with myself.

    9. _____ It didn't bother me a bit. I'm glad I did it.

    10. _____ I got exactly what I wanted.

3. What were some of the long-term effects of cutting corners?

_____

_____

_____

Building on What You Have

Most of us don't spend a lot of time thinking about what poor values are and how they affect our lives. We simply adopt them almost imperceptibly. Often we have to knock down the old foundation to replace it with the truly important positive values; but if we have already established strong values, and just need a touch-up, it is foolish to replace the entire foundation. If the foundation is strong, we can simply add some reinforcements and keep building on the good start we have made. Before we get to what values you need, let's explore what values you already hold.

List the five most important values you hold. Remember a value is a principle that you consider worthwhile or desirable. They are principles by which you live your life. For instance, love, respect, honor, caution, hard work, freedom, peace.

1. _____
2. _____
3. _____
4. _____
5. _____

Put a check mark in front of all the following statements that describe your prevailing life view and the main principles by which you live:

____ I try to treat other people the way I would like to be treated.
____ Love is the answer.
____ Don't worry, be happy!
____ Never forget, everyone is beautiful in his or her own way, and everyone is weird in his or her own way.
____ Don't let the "blankety-blanks" get you down!
____ Work hard, play hard.
____ Give something back.

Now list some of your own life principles.
Some of the main principles by which I live my life are:

1. _____
2. _____
3. _____

Are My Values Good or Bad?

A good value is one that helps you to create long-term solutions to the issues you face. It does so while taking into account how your actions will affect both others and yourself.

Look back over your list of values, above. How well do your values pass the "good values test"?

Overall, I'd give myself an (circle one):	A	B	C	D	F	Detention!
Value number 1	A	B	C	D	F	Detention!
Value number 2	A	B	C	D	F	Detention!
Value number 3	A	B	C	D	F	Detention!
Value number 4	A	B	C	D	F	Detention!
Value number 5	A	B	C	D	F	Detention!

Look again at the values you listed above. Does each of your values provide long-term gain with occasional short-term pain? How does each of your values help and encourage others?

If you answered "yes" to the above question, your values are probably extremely good. You are well on your way to building a strong, **More Than Enough** foundation for your life. If you couldn't answer "yes" to any particular value, you may wish to reevaluate whether that is a value that you want as part of your foundation. Keep in mind that it doesn't take a large hole for a wall to break when the pressure begins to build.

Five Essential Values

Five essential values will help you to build and maintain wealth, improve your relationships with your spouse and family members, and enhance your spiritual life. The "fabulous five" are:

1. integrity
2. commitment
3. loyalty
4. compassion
5. responsibility

Each of these values is vital if you want to build wealth and live abundantly, joyfully, and contentedly. Just having one or two of these values won't cut it. Developing four out of five will still lead to a foundation failure. If you want **More Than Enough,** you must resolve now that you are going to go for the whole deal. No shortcuts! No compromises with the mix! These are not whimsical ideas that I just dreamed up to fill some space in a book. These are the values that have shaped, and continue to be incorporated into, the lives of some of the most successful people in history.

The Big "I" Is Not You

The cornerstone of your foundation—the most important block in the whole house—is *integrity*. If you lay a strong foundation in every other respect, but forget to include integrity, your house will eventually come crashing down. To avoid integrity is to welcome failure.

Lots of people have given integrity some fancy definitions, but to me, the simple one is still the best: Integrity is old-fashioned honesty. It is doing things right, and knowing that you can hold your head up high, regardless of what anyone else says or thinks. In a letter to Andrew Jackson, Sam Houston wrote, "I would give no thought to what the world might say of me, if I could only transmit to posterity the reputation of an honest man." Nowadays, all too few of us consider honesty such a valuable legacy.

Integrity is a commitment to truth, but it is more than just *telling* the truth. It is living and acting truthfully. It involves at least three elemental questions that we should ask ourselves in any decision we must make in the area of finances, relationships, career, or conduct:

1. Is this true?
2. Is this what I truly believe I should do?
3. Is what I plan to do consistent with what I am saying?

Notice the correlation between truth, belief, and action. And let's not forget that we must consider how our decisions and actions will impact others.

List two major decisions or questions with which you have been grappling recently, and apply the Integrity Test to your proposed responses. (For instance, I've been considering resigning from the club, and the reason I gave the manager was that I simply couldn't afford it any longer.)

ISSUE NUMBER ONE

The issue you must decide:_____

Your proposed response (what you plan to do):_____

_____

_____

Now apply the Integrity Test (check the appropriate box):

Is this true?   Yes _____   No _____

Is this what I truly believe I should do?   Yes _____   No _____

Is what I plan to do consistent with what I am saying?   Yes _____   No _____

ISSUE NUMBER TWO

The issue you must decide: _____

Your proposed response (what you plan to do): _____

_____

_____

Now apply the Integrity Test (check the appropriate box):

Is this true?   Yes _____   No _____

Is this what I truly believe I should do?   Yes _____   No _____

Is what I plan to do consistent with what I am saying?   Yes _____   No _____

Little White Lies Don't Exist

"Integrity" means that we don't shade the truth, either. It means that we don't practice telling "little white lies," or "convenient truths," offering statements that are in fact true as far as they go, but not necessarily true when all things are considered. For instance, your boss asks you for a report on how sales are going.

"Oh, fine, boss," you reply guardedly. "Our sales are up significantly in the southern territory." You hand him the ledger charting the upward climb of sales in that region. However, you conveniently neglect to mention that returns are coming in from the western territory faster than you can find room to restock them. Did you tell the truth? No, you told a "convenient truth," convenient for you at the moment, but destructive for others in the long run. A half truth is usually a whole lie.

While few people would identify themselves as liars, most of us might admit that we don't always tell the truth. Remember the lady who was wearing the new hat at the party? "What do you think of it?" she asks. "I got it at Saks Fifth Avenue and it was on sale!"

"Oh, it's absolutely stunning," you reply honestly, yet not actually telling the truth.

Uh-huh.

If you really have integrity, you will find a way to avoid lying and at the same time attempt to be sensitive to other people's feelings. For instance, imagine that you accepted an invitation to a party, but on the day of the event, you don't feel like going. What should you do? Because you have integrity, you don't call and say you are ill. Instead you call and apologize for not being able to make it to the party, and thank your host for the invitation. It's as simple as that. No false statements were made and sincere gratitude was expressed.

Integrity also requires us to be truthful in making promises, signing contracts, giving our word, or hiring employees. We cannot do any of those things without first thinking through our commitments carefully, to assess whether we have the ability and resources to follow through on our promises. We dare not confuse good intentions with integrity. How often have you heard the phrase "But I meant well!"

Great. So did the captain of the *Titanic*. Integrity is the intestinal fortitude to do what we say we are going to do, not merely spouting the right words, "putting on the Ritz," or giving a good appearance of doing so. In a very appearance-conscious culture, it is easy to confuse image with integrity. As John Maxwell, one of the great contemporary teachers of leadership, says, "Image is what people think we are. Integrity is what we really are."

Integrity involves making a real attempt to see the end of the promise and your ability to follow through on it. For instance, because you have integrity, you will not buy a car and finance it, thinking, *I can make the payments.* Instead, the person with integrity thinks through the entire situation. *Could I make the payments if I lose my job next week?* Or, *Could I still afford this purchase if I were to be involved in an auto accident and temporarily unable to work?*

What? Too morbid for you? I'm not suggesting that you live your life waiting for an accident to happen. But unfortunately, millions of people live life like there is no tomorrow, and then when something bad happens, or when Mr. Murphy moves into the spare bedroom, they discover that by living on borrowed money, they have already "lived it up" . . . literally! They've lived up their money, plunged themselves into abysmal debt, and now, with no savings in the bank, they have nowhere to turn.

On the other hand, if you have deeply rooted integrity, you will decide not to buy the car until you can save up for it, and pay for it with *cash*, up front. (Okay, you can write a check if you really want to. In fact, you should.) You will buy a previously owned car, and avoid losing the huge amount of money in depreciation that new-car buyers choke down the moment they pull off the new-car lot. Integrity will lead you away from debt and toward investments, because that path enables you to be a person of your word. You're not promising to pay; you already did!

Many people feel that they have integrity simply because they intend to pay. Of course you intend to pay. Only a con artist intends to rip off the bank by borrowing money and not paying it back. Yet thousands of people every day fall into the trap of not being able to pay. Why? Because they didn't truly count the cost when they made the purchase on credit in the first place.

Take the case of Liz, who called in to my radio show the other day. Liz is twenty-six years old and she just bought a car. She wanted to know if she had the legal right to take a new car back to the dealer one month after she had bought it.

"Is the car not running right?" I asked.

"Oh, no. It runs great," gushed Liz.

"Well, is it defective in some way?" I continued to probe.

"I don't think so," Liz replied.

"I'm sorry, I don't understand," I admitted. "If the car runs great and it is not defective, why would you want to take it back?"

"Because the salesmen coerced me into buying it!" she said, sounding for all the world like a four-year-old.

Sales representatives don't coerce their customers; they sell to them. They show customers enough reasons why they need that product, so they will be willing to part with their hard-earned money to get it. Or (and this is a much more common "sales" technique nowadays), the salesperson shows the customer how "easy" it is to acquire the item on "low monthly payments."

The salesperson who sold Liz her new car was not holding a gun to her head. He or she may have done an outstanding job of pushing Liz's hot buttons and talking her into an unwise purchase. But the salesperson is there to sell cars! Liz simply lacked the depth of character to say no to a car she couldn't afford. Once she realized how much that new car was actually going to cost her, she wanted out of the deal. Too late. Integrity is not just a matter of intent, it is taking the time to consider the end of the obligation. If you can't see the end of the obligation, or if you truly don't understand it, then you shouldn't obligate yourself by agreeing to make car payments! (Incidentally, for those of you who have not yet read my books *Financial Peace* and *More Than Enough*, I don't believe in car payments. Oh, I believe they exist, all right. I just won't ever buy another automobile on payments. It's a bad deal for the consumer. To see how you can buy a car without payments, check out my previous books.)

Liz's only alternative now is to sell the car, probably for a loss, and buy one she can afford to drive. Many auto dealers and banks will roll the loss into another short-term loan, but it's sad that Liz is going to be paying what I call "stupid tax," money that we must pay for making unwise decisions, for a long time to come.

Sure, I've bought things that I've regretted, too. I have been pushed, shoved, and talked into making some foolish purchases, or doing some things that I didn't like, or that I was not proud of. Then, like Liz, when I realized how foolish I had been, I wanted out of the deal. But if you and I are going to live the **More Than Enough** life, we have to grow a backbone and incorporate integrity as one of our foundational values. We will honor whatever commitments we have made in the past, but from this day forward, we will avoid making financial commitments we cannot afford, or that are unwise. We will live our lives with integrity.

Integrity filters through every aspect of our lives. From how we deal with the wrong amount of change we received at the grocery store checkout counter to the notepads and pens we bring home from the office for the family to use to the way we fill out our forms to send to the "KGB"—er, I mean, the Internal Revenue Service. Basic honesty is an indispensable stone in the foundation of a **More Than Enough** lifestyle.

Finders Keepers?

Suppose you found a wallet full of money and credit cards on the sidewalk. The owner was easy to identify, but was not someone you knew. What would you do? (Check all that apply.)

____ I'd keep the money and toss the wallet and credit cards in the trash.
____ I'd keep the money and the wallet.
____ It depends on how much money was in the wallet.
____ I'd look for the owner's name and address and send the wallet back, asking for a reward.
____ I'd run an add in the newspaper for a week and if the owner didn't claim it, I'd spend the money.

____ I'd search for some identification, and return the wallet to the owner, expecting no reward but a word of thanks.

____ I'd spend the money and use the credit cards. (Did you know that it is illegal to use someone else's credit card without his or her permission?)

There's really only one choice for the person who wants **More Than Enough.** He or she must return the wallet, money, and credit cards without a hint of a reward. A simple "thank you" will be sufficient reward, and frankly, even if that is not forthcoming, your integrity in doing the right thing will eventually be rewarded one way or another. And you can take that to the bank!

> Whenever you do a thing, act as if all the world
> were watching.
> —*Thomas Jefferson*

Rock-Solid Commitment

Commitment is the second value you must use for your foundation. It is basic "stick-to-itiveness," the character trait that allows us to stick it out no matter what the cost, pain, or sacrifice required or inconvenience endured. Commitment doesn't necessarily mean that you will stick to the same thing for the rest of your life. But it does mean that you will give 100 percent, full concentration and effort, to whatever you are doing for as long as you have pledged or agreed to do it. If you are contracted to work for six months, you give your employer six solid, top-notch months of work. If you promised to be faithful to your spouse and to stay in the marriage relationship "till death do us part," divorce is a word that doesn't enter your vocabulary.

Commitment is the character trait that causes you to do the tough things now, and to look down the road for rest, relaxation, and rewards. It may mean getting up earlier to spend some time in prayer and Bible reading before you start your work. It may mean making more calls in your business, staying up later to deal with a problem at home, or driving all night to be home on the weekend in time to worship God with your family. It means being content with yourself but never being content with anything less than your best effort.

Often, commitment means sacrifice, inconvenience, and perseverance. It means that you don't give up or throw in the towel just because things are not going as well or as quickly or as productively as you had hoped. For instance, dealing with a seven-year-old brat is tough enough, but taking care of a child given to temper tantrums, physical outbursts and attacks, and mealtime messes is even more difficult to handle when the child is deaf and blind. But Anne Sullivan refused to give up on Helen Keller, even when Helen's own parents were ready to hang out the white flag. Anne was committed to helping Helen learn, and stayed with her through thick and thin. Not only did Anne teach Helen Keller to read and write in braille; she remained with Helen all the way through her college education, spelling out each lecture in Helen's hand. Because of Anne Sullivan's commitment, Helen Keller graduated cum laude from Radcliffe College and went on to be an inspiration to millions of people. It is our commitment that gives us the courage and the strength to bear the unbearable, to do what others might consider to be impossible.

It is commitment to a cause or to a goal that convinces you to push and push, and when all your energy is gone, to push some more. It allows us to endure that second job to earn enough money to take our family on a vacation we otherwise could not possibly afford. With commitment we stay and work through problems in our marriages and families, rather than leaving when times get tough and the mushy feelings are long gone. Commitment is bigger than your feelings. It is your soul.

1. What is happening right now in your life that is testing your level of commitment at home? At work? In your faith?

_____

_____

_____

2. Think of somebody that you admire for their commitment to their family, job, or God. List several character traits of that person that you want to emulate in your life:

_____

_____

_____

3. How "committed" would you say you are right now to (check one in each category):

Your immediate family relationships (spouse, children, and parents):
_____ Extremely committed _____ Fifty-fifty _____ Little to none

Your employer or your work:
_____ Extremely committed _____ Fifty-fifty _____ Little to none

Your relationship with God:
_____ Extremely committed _____ Fifty-fifty _____ Little to none

Nothing in life comes simply because you want it. If you have a financial goal or a stake in a relationship, you must remain committed to it. Too many financial failures and too many divorces are products of a simple lack of commitment—when the going got tough, the tough walked away.

The Farm Animal Principle

❖ The hen was bragging about the labor she had put forth to furnish the eggs for breakfast. But then the pig said, "I appreciate your contribution to this fine meal, but take a look at the bacon; now, that's commitment." The pig had to give up his life to provide the bacon, while the hen merely had to lay the eggs. The farm animal principle is an analogy about the degree to which you are committed. It is a good test to use when you are trying to weigh how invested you are in a project, a person, or a business.

The Dollars and Sense of It

In my book *Financial Peace*, I list "seven financial baby steps," steps that every person seeking financial peace and the **More Than Enough** lifestyle can take. These steps will guarantee your financial success, and will also have positive "spillover" effects in your marriage and family relationships. But in order for them to work, it is not enough to read them and agree with them. You must commit yourself to actually *doing* these steps! Look over the list below, and on a scale of one to ten (ten being highly committed, one being hardly committed at all), rate your commitment level as it stands today toward each goal. Please note: We're not asking for a progress report or how far along you are toward achieving these goals. Right now, the question is: "How committed are you to achieving financial peace and **More Than Enough**?" (Hint: It's okay if some areas are higher priorities than others.)

1. Save $1,000 in an emergency fund.
   My commitment level to this step is:
   1   2   3   4   5   6   7   8   9   10   Done!

2. Pay off all your debts except the home mortgage using the Debt Snowball (paying off the least amount owed first, then adding that payment toward paying down the next monthly debt, continuing until all your debts are paid).
   My commitment level to this step is:
   1   2   3   4   5   6   7   8   9   10   Done!

3. Complete your emergency fund by saving three to six months' expenses and maintaining this amount in savings.
   My commitment level to this step is:
   1   2   3   4   5   6   7   8   9   10   Done!

4. Fully fund your pretax retirement savings plans.
   My commitment level to this step is:
   1   2   3   4   5   6   7   8   9   10   Done!

5. Save for your kids' college education.
My commitment level to this step is:
1   2   3   4   5   6   7   8   9   10   Done!

6. Pay off your home early.
My commitment level to this step is:
1   2   3   4   5   6   7   8   9   10   Done!

7. Build wealth and give like crazy!
My commitment level to this step is:
1   2   3   4   5   6   7   8   9   10   Done!

Are you a "stick-to-it" kind of person? How frequently do you complete something you start, whether it is a new project around the house, that letter you wanted to write, or a Christmas Club savings account? How well do you stick to it until you have achieved the goal?

____ always
____ usually
____ sometimes
____ rarely
____ never
____ eventually

Loyalty, a Lost Virtue

Loyalty is the third important value you must have in your foundation if you want to build a **More Than Enough** home and lifestyle. Loyalty is a close cousin of integrity and commitment, and like those qualities, it is becoming increasingly difficult to find these days. But those people who have it inevitably will have **More Than Enough,** if they have the other foundational stones as well.

There's Gold in Dem Dere Arches

❖ If you need a reminder of the importance of commitment, every time you pass by the McDonald's golden arch, or see a McDonald's commercial on television, let it be an inspiration to you. Ray Kroc sold paper cups to support his family in the 1920s. Eventually, his commitment to excellence propelled him upward in the company's sales force, and after seventeen years, he became one of the top sales representatives of the company. But Kroc wasn't satisfied with merely getting along. He wanted **More Than Enough**.

He took a risk, left the paper cup company, and started a new business selling milk shake machines, concentrating his attention on a new type of machine that could mix more than one shake at a time. Several of Kroc's machines were in use at a bustling hamburger joint in San Bernardino owned by the McDonald brothers. When Ray saw how effectively the McDonalds were using his machines, he suggested that they open similar restaurants in other locations. The brothers were less than enthusiastic about the idea, so at fifty-two years of age, Ray Kroc became the founder of a fledgling hamburger chain known as McDonald's. Since then, literally billions of burgers have been served up at Ray's chain of restaurants.

One of Ray Kroc's favorite quotes is by an unknown author, but it sums up the McDonald's founder's passionate commitment to having **More Than Enough**:

Press on. Nothing in the world can take the place of persistence. Talent will not; nothing is more common than unsuccessful individuals with talent. Genius will not; unrewarded genius is almost a proverb. Education will not; the world is full of educated derelicts. Persistence and determination alone are omnipotent.

Loyalty is so rare nowadays, many suffer from a lack of it and don't even realize what they are missing. Loyalty means to be faithful to a cause, a person, or an entity. For instance, when we pledge allegiance to the flag, we are pledging our loyalty to our nation. We are saying that we believe in this cause, we are committed to it, and we will faithfully uphold its principles.

Sign Your Life Away

Each year in the United States, on July 4, we have a celebration ostensibly to applaud the men who signed the Declaration of Independence on July 4, 1776, and to celebrate our freedom. We sometimes forget what a price those early patriots had to pay for our freedom, even after the declaration was signed. Of the fifty-six men who put their names on the line, many did not live to see the freedom they fought for. Five were captured by the British in the ensuing Revolutionary War, and were tortured until they died. Nine others died in the war itself, either from gunshot wounds or severe hardship. At least twelve had their homes occupied by the enemy soldiers, and then looted and burned. Two signers of the declaration lost their sons to the war. One had two sons captured. Others simply died of natural causes and did not survive the ordeal they had committed themselves to wage. Yet they remained loyal to the cause because they knew freedom was worth it.

Thomas Paine wrote this poignant, insightful statement in 1776:

What we obtain too cheap, we esteem too lightly; 'tis dearness only that gives everything its value. Heaven knows how to put a proper price upon its goods; and it would be strange indeed, if so celestial an article as Freedom should not be highly rated.

Sadly, many people nowadays look at such statements as just so much jingoism, rah-rah hogwash. Not surprisingly, as we have compromised our loyalty to God, and to our country, we have accordingly lowered our level of loyalty in our family relationships and in our employment.

According to Dan Miller, one of the leading career counselors in the nation, the average length of employment lasts 2.8 years. Why is there such a high turnover rate in jobs? A dynamic and rapidly changing economy is certainly an influence, but by far the main reason for job turnovers is lack of loyalty to the company. Ironically, this lack of loyalty on the part of employees to the company has often been fueled by a lack of loyalty by the company to the employees.

Too many companies jerk their workers' lives around, turning them inside out and upside down without so much as a thought. The result is a worker who feels no sense of loyalty to the company or the cause that the company represents.

This attitude has been exacerbated by an ever-growing number of seminars and books teaching us how we can have it all, how we can win by intimidation while we look out for number one. One perennial favorite declares:

"It's O.K. to be greedy. . . .

"It's O.K. to be Machiavellian (if you can get away with it).

"It's O.K. to recognize that honesty is not always the best policy (provided you don't go around saying so).

"And it *always* O.K. to be rich."

The author goes on to say, "*How* you become a success is, of course, your business. Morality has very little to do with success."

And regarding loyalty?

> Nobody *expects* you to be 100 percent loyal at heart, but it is one of those values that must be publicly displayed if you're going to get ahead. . . . Nobody minds ruthless, egocentric careerism and self-interest, provided they are suitably screened. If you can undermine your boss and replace him, fine, do so, *but never express anything but respect and loyalty for him while you're doing it.*

These statements were published more than twenty years ago! As a result, we now have an entire generation (or two!) that has adopted these false "values" into their lifestyle. Loyalty is out. Oh, it's okay to pretend that you are loyal while you undermine your boss, but real loyalty, the kind that we used to take for granted, the kind of loyalty where people could depend on one another to be true to each other, has been replaced with a pseudoloyalty that bows at the feet of "egocentric careerism"!

Would you want to marry someone who lives by this fake loyalty? You'd be foolish if you did so knowingly. Would you want that sort of loyalty from your best friend? Hardly. Yet many people have settled for such a low level of faithfulness for so long, we've forgotten what real loyalty is like.

Loyalty doesn't meant that we will always agree with each other or that we won't occasionally feel some friction. But it does mean that it will take something major to loosen the glue of loyalty that cements us together. Too often we drop an organization, a friend, a church, and even a spouse for almost any offense. But real loyalty means that you have the character to "hang in there" with your friends or groups through hard times and through costly and embarrassing mistakes.

What Goes Around Comes Around

One of the interesting aspects of loyalty is that you usually reap what you sow. With most things in life, although you don't always get what you deserve, you usually get what you expect. But with loyalty, you often get back more than you anticipated. When you express loyalty to friends, family, loved ones, employees, school companions, or teammates, you will often find that you get loyalty in return from others—often more strongly than you have given it yourself.

Here is an example. A professional golfer fell on hard times late in his career. He couldn't keep the ball in the fairway, and frequently found himself struggling just to make the cut rather than the leader board. But he had a long relationship with a particular equipment company, advertising their golf clubs and clothing for years. During his heyday, he turned down one lucrative offer after another to advertise competitors' equipment. He believed in his original sponsor's products, so he refused all others. When the old pro could no longer keep up with the younger generation of players, despite the fact that he had not won a tournament for a number of years, the company to whom he had been loyal decided that they would keep him on as a figurehead, providing him a salary in excess of half a million dollars per year! His loyalty to his sponsors resulted in his sponsors being even more lavishly loyal to him.

List three people in your life who have been unequivocally loyal to you. (Keep in mind, they may not always have agreed with you, but they have been loyal to you.)

1. _____
2. _____
3. _____

Now list three people to whom you have been unequivocally loyal:

1. _____
2. _____
3. _____

What relationships or causes (if any) would you be willing to die for?

1. _____
2. _____
3. _____

How would you rate your loyalty to your employer or to your workplace? (Check as many as apply.)

____ I'll be loyal to my employers and my workplace so long as they are loyal to me.
____ I am extremely loyal to the company.
____ I couldn't care less about my company as long as I keep getting a check.
____ I believe in what my company is doing and I work to the best of my ability to fulfill the company's goals.

___ It's a job, a means of making money.

___ If another opportunity presented itself, I wouldn't think twice about jumping ship.

___ I have no sense of loyalty to my employer. I do the job and go home.

In the workplace, loyalty means that you put in the extra effort to make the deadline for an important project. At home, loyalty means that you support your spouse and kids—you wake up early on a Saturday to take your son to Little League practice, you share the chores, and you find ways to ensure that each member of the family has the opportunity to realize his or her own dreams.

Compassion

> *Others will not care how much we know*
> *until they know how much we care.*

Compassion is the heartfelt ability to sense and be motivated by another's pain. It is caring for others, sympathizing, and empathizing with them in their struggles; and helping to heal their hurts when and where we can. Compassion, if it is genuine, is not simply syrupy sentiment. It is not simply gaining more knowledge about someone's needs. It is actively getting involved in the world, and especially in our neighborhood, family, and churches. The old saying is true: "Others will not care how much we know until they know how much we care."

In our "gerbil-in-a-wheel" run-run culture we tend to limit ourselves to superficial relationships. Who has time to get involved in the problems of other people? We are all so busy dealing with our own situations. Consequently, as my friend Dave Cavender says, "We have become high-tech and lost the high touch." Time-saving inventions are nice, but when you start wishing that you will reach someone's voice mail so you don't have to deal with them personally, you should recognize the red flags. You are limiting yourself to a superficial relationship.

Often, it's not that we don't want to enter into someone else's pain; we simply don't have (or don't want to take) the time to invest in each other. When we ask, "How are you doing," all too often we are afraid someone will answer honestly and really tell us what is going on in their lives—which, of course, would take some of our precious time.

Let's face it. Compassion is time-consuming. To be sensitive to somebody else's struggle besides our own, and to become involved in someone else's life—whether it is helping them through a mess or celebrating a success—take time and energy. Yet I have noticed that most truly successful people are some of the most compassionate. In most cases, they have had to struggle through some valleys or conquer some mountains themselves. They know all too well what it's like to feel helpless and hopeless.

Sure, there's always the scrooge who says, "I made it by the sweat of my brow, so don't expect any help from me!" But those who discover a **More Than Enough** lifestyle are often the first to offer a hand up, rather than a handout, a warm hug instead of a cold shoulder.

When Julie Harris and Ethel Waters were performing on Broadway in *The Member of the Wedding*, Julie was plagued with self-doubt. A perfectionist by nature, Julie's doubts led to self-condemnation and stole the joy from what should have been a marvelous experience.

One night she felt so disgusted with herself, she was reluctant to return to the stage for curtain calls. On the way back to her dressing room, she met Ethel Waters, the star of the show.

"What's troubling you, Julie?" Ethel wanted to know.

Julie was about to mumble, "Oh, nothing," when suddenly she realized that Ethel really cared. Julie broke down and confessed to Ethel her fears and deep feelings of insecurity. The great Ethel Waters stopped right there and took the time to encourage young Julie.

"The Lord is with you, honey," Ethel told Julie. "If you want the strength and confidence you need, all you have to do is hold out your hand and ask."

For the remainder of her career, Julie Harris never forgot that moment, or Ethel Waters's warm compassion and concern.

When you see homeless people on the street begging, or you drive up to a corner where a disheveled-looking fellow is holding a sign, WILL WORK FOR FOOD, what is your reaction? (Check all that apply.)

____ I work for food, too.
____ That person must have fallen on some tough times. Maybe I should help him out.
____ Can't the police do something about these panhandlers?
____ If I don't help this person, I can't expect anyone to help me if I am ever down-and-out.
____ If I open my wallet, this person might try to rob me.
____ He's only going to use the money to buy more drugs or alcohol anyhow, so why should I help him?
____ Maybe I can get him some food and some help.

Meekness, Not Weakness

Some people have difficulty expressing compassion because of their own insecurities. They falsely assume that being compassionate is a sign of weakness. If they dare to display concern for others, their status with their peers or superiors will be diminished. Nothing could be further from the truth. While compassion and meekness are traits often found in the same person, they are indicators of strength rather than weakness. Author Warren Weirsbe said: "Meekness is not weakness, it is power under control."

Having compassion and gentleness as part of your foundational values allows you to function from a position of power. Expressing compassion shows that you are okay with yourself, and that you have the strength and ability to slow down long enough to actually put someone's interests ahead of your own. If you are insecure, your energy is tied up in yourself and you become extremely introspective (and usually quite selfish), because you are unable to see outside of yourself. As the late singer Keith Green said, "It's so hard to see when my eyes are on me!" If you want **More Than Enough,** you must develop the habit of taking the time to "feel for others," even when you aren't feeling so great about yourself.

What does compassion have to do with financial matters? Compassion leads to giving; it affects your vision, goals, and performance. Think of the great business leaders you have known, read about, or heard about. Most of them are very compassionate people, and most of them are great givers. Whether it is singer Whitney Houston donating to a college, television mogul Ted Turner donating to the United Nations, or Microsoft multibillionaire Bill Gates contributing to the educational programs across the United States, inevitably, those who find **More Than Enough** want to give something back to help others.

Compassion Must Be Learned

Compassion cannot be taught; it must be learned. Usually, before we truly learn compassion, we must go through some tough times. Perhaps you have suffered a financial loss; maybe you have had to deal with debilitating heart disease or cancer; maybe you have lost a loved one, or been through a divorce, bankruptcy, or some other personal tragedy. No doubt you have learned the true meaning of compassion from these experiences.

List three "tough times"—three incidents in your life that have helped to teach you the true meaning of compassion, and note how those incidents have helped you to become more sensitive to the needs of others.

1. _____

2. _____

3. _____

Compassion Does Not Mean Codependent

Some people, however, have confused compassion with codependence. Compassion allows you to encourage and give to others, while it gives you the tools to move to a better place. Codependence gives you excuses: someone else or something else is causing you to be the way you are. If we are not careful, in an attempt to be compassionate, we can actually foster codependence if we do not guard our own emotions. Take Sherry, for example.

Sherry and her husband wanted desperately to help their twenty-three-year-old daughter and son-in-law, who had run up $8,000 in credit card debt. Out of the kindness of their hearts, and with no accountability attached, Sherry and her husband paid off the debt to "help the kids." The kids, unfortunately, didn't change their overspending habits. They continued to spend irresponsibly and, worse yet, ran up over $15,000 in bad checks and bad-check charges. Again Sherry and her husband stepped in and paid off the mess, but this time Sherry placed a condition on their help. "The only way we will help is if you allow me to take over the handling of your money until you two get straightened out financially."

Although Sherry's intent was to help bring some order and accountability to the young couple's financial situation, she confused compassion with codependence. A couple of twenty-three-year olds giving Mom their paychecks and allowing her to pay their bills and give them an allowance does not foster financial independence! While Sherry and her husband are extremely compassionate, they continue to enable their daughter and son-in-law to live like dependent little children, rather than married young adults.

The most compassionate action Sherry and her husband could take would be to teach her daughter and son-in-law how to take care of their own finances. Sherry should show them how to balance their checkbook, make a plan for paying their bills, and stick to a budget. After several weekly meetings with both of them, she should hand the responsibility back to them. Once they are standing alone, she should continue to meet with them to hold them accountable for doing the necessary work involved in managing their money. Giving her daughter the tools to run her own financial life is compassion; doing the work for her is codependence.

> *If you give a man a fish he eats for a day, but if you teach him to fish he eats for a lifetime.*

Responsibility

The fifth foundational stone in your **More Than Enough** home and lifestyle is responsibility. As an adolescent, I attended an experimental middle school in which students were encouraged to work at their own pace. The school established minimum standards, but the idea was that if encouraged to do so, many students would achieve far above "grade-level" work. Some students excelled and some didn't, just as in other aspects of life, but I never forgot the school motto: Freedom with Responsibility.

Sadly, an incentive-numbing cultural socialism has crept into our American way of life. We want all the goodies, but we want somebody else—the government, the company, other friends or family members—to pay for them. We think, for example, that just because a credit card company sends us a credit card with a low interest rate as an introductory offer, we can run up charges on it, even though we know we don't have the money to pay the bills. We think that just because the car salesman says we qualify for financing on a $20,000 car, we must have that car, when in reality, we should be buying a used car for $5,000. We think that parenting is about sitting in front of the TV night after night with our kids—as if that represents real interaction with our children. We think that buying our spouse presents means that we have a good marriage—when, in fact, if we aren't communicating or sharing our lives with our spouse, all the presents in the world will be meaningless in the long run.

How often have you heard these words in recent years: "I take full responsibility. . . ."

What does it mean to take full responsibility? Does it not mean that you are willing to right a wrong, repay those you have robbed, fix what has been broken, replace what was destroyed? Does it not mean that we will do the right thing in the first place?

Taking responsibility for our actions has gotten to be a bad joke. Instead, we are obsessed with immediate gratification. We want love without commitment, rewards without sacrifice. Most young couples want the same lifestyle or better than their parents had after thirty years of work, struggle, and pain, when they come home from the honeymoon. And due to the plethora of easy credit opportunities, they can often get it . . . they just can't keep it. Because to get and maintain a **More Than Enough** lifestyle, you must pay the price by taking responsibility for your own actions and living responsibly within your means.

When we refuse to take responsibility, we rob ourselves and those around us. Personal responsibility—taking advantage of the freedom and opportunities we have—is a value that **More Than Enough** folks cherish.

Put a check mark in front of each of the phrases that describes your attitude toward taking responsibility for your life:

_____ You can't fight city hall.
_____ There's no such thing as a free lunch.
_____ Success is a roll of the dice.
_____ We're all just victims of the system.
_____ You get out what you put in.
_____ You can't win for losing.
_____ Life is a calculated risk. Go for it!
_____ If it's going to be, it's up to me.

List some of the responsibilities that you are encouraging your children to take (for example, *I want my younger children to put away their own toys; I want my teenagers to pay their own auto insurance; I want all of my children to establish and maintain their own personal savings accounts*):

1. _____
2. _____

3. _____

4. _____

List some of your responsibilities toward your children (for example, to know where they are when they are out with friends, to stimulate their imaginations through creative input, to model responsible behavior in relationship to food, alcohol, drugs, and care for your body):

1. _____

2. _____

3. _____

Old-Fashioned Is Back in Style

These five foundational values of the **More Than Enough** lifestyle may seem old-fashioned to some people—especially to those who don't care to live by such standards. Frequently, these values are spoken of in condescending terms by our modern news media, movie critics, and radio and television commentators. The public is led to believe that people who build their lives on these "old-fashioned" foundational values are ignorant, deceived, or disingenuous. Much of our "entertainment," for instance, ridicules people who uphold high values such as integrity, commitment, loyalty, compassion, and responsibility. The impression is repeatedly given that standards of civil conduct are only important to the shallow or the dull-witted when in fact people with rock-solid values seem to have more joy in their lives, more fulfillment, and **More Than Enough** when it comes to finances, family, and a rich future.

Establish Some "No Matter Whats"

To help you solidify and build on these five foundational values, you need to establish some "no matter whats" in your life, some statements that declare unequivocally, "I will not compromise this value, *no matter what*. This is what I hold dear."

What kind of "no matter whats" should you have as part of your personal credo? Only you can decide, but let me give you an example from my own business. I have a "no matter what" in the area of my personal endorsements of products we advertise on my radio program. I will not personally endorse a product or company whose values are contrary to my own. No matter what. No matter how big they are, no matter how much clout they have, no matter how much money they offer me.

I recently canceled an endorsement contract worth over $150,000. Why? The internet service provider that I was endorsing decided to do a joint venture with *Playboy*. The internet provider offered three months of free pornography as part of the package subscribers to the service received upon signing up. On the surface, the joint venture was a "good business" decision for the internet provider because *Playboy*'s website boasts a high number of visitors. But money isn't the standard by which I measure my decisions. Pornography is the fastest-growing addiction in America today. Among the families that my staff and I counsel, porn is destroying more marriages than any problem we see in our counseling offices, not to mention that it is highly degrading to women (and to men)! I could not in good conscience endorse an internet provider that purposely designs to suck more people down into the cesspool of pornography . . . no matter what.

Could I have used the $150,000? Sure . . . couldn't you? But I walked away from the money because I refuse to endorse a company that does not share my values. *No matter what.*

Many of us resist such personal discipline and self-imposed codes of conduct. That's a mistake. People who have few if any "no matter whats" in their lives often lack the strength that these values provide—strength to get through the bad times, and power to build a great life financially, emotionally, and spiritually. I must warn you: You will be challenged and possibly ridiculed when you establish character qualities and no matter whats in your life. Having values can cost you. A firm foundation, however, is definitely worth it, and it is the only way to the **More Than Enough** life.

You must have consistency of character to win, lead, and produce in your relationships and your wealth-building. Zig Ziglar says: "What you do off the job influences what you do on the job. Life values at home, not family values, will make you successful wherever you are, as a CEO, salesperson, clerk, etc. There is no such thing as 'family values,' 'school values,' or 'business values,' because the same values or qualities that permit you to succeed at home will make you successful in the rest of your life. Check the records: Virtually all great failures are character failures. Consistency is the key to long-range success. Values matter."

List some of the "no matter whats" in your life (for example, I will not be unfaithful to my spouse, no matter what; I will love my children, no matter what; I will not give up my faith in God, no matter what):

1. _____
2. _____
3. _____
4. _____
5. _____

> Show class, have pride, and display character.
> If you do, winning takes care of itself.
> —*Coach Paul "Bear" Bryant*

Our goal in this book is not just to talk about the character qualities that build winners, but to help you move up on the scoreboard. In the previous chapter, I promised that we were going to go down ten aisles (ten key character qualities) in the **More Than Enough** Grocery Store. We are going to make sure your shelves are stocked to feed the big elephant, your untapped potential. This aisle has been the aisle of "values."

How full are your shelves when it comes to values?

___ Overloaded

___ Comfortably filled

___ In need of restocking

___ Getting sparse

___ Empty

In each of the chapters that follow, select the area of life that you are in and complete the exercises that apply to you. You may qualify for more than one category. For instance, if you are married with children, you will want to complete all the family sections. If you are married without children, perhaps the husband-wife exercises will be sufficient. Or perhaps you may want to focus on the finance section, or do one section all the way through the book and then come back and complete others. Whatever you decide to do, the important thing is to apply yourself honestly to completing these exercises, as they will help you to implement the skills described in each chapter.

Aisle One—Values

1. Business Section

TAKING INVENTORY

How familiar are you with your company's statement of core values? (Note: This may take the form of a mission statement, a code of ethics, or some other written document.)

___ Very familiar ___ I think I know what we stand for ___ Uncertain

If you are not certain of your company's values, to whom can you turn or where can you go to find that information? _____

When will you seek out that information? (Give yourself a specific date or time limit.)

_____

Do you have a personal statement of values on how you will conduct business within your company?

___ Yes ___ No

List three of your core values, principles that govern the way you do business on a daily basis:

1. _____
2. _____
3. _____

What are some "no matter whats" that govern your dealing with clients, coworkers, and staff?

1. _____
2. _____
3. _____

Which of the following losses have you suffered because of a lapse of integrity in your business (either in your own conduct or someone else's conduct within your immediate sphere of influence at your workplace):

___ lost money
___ potential deals disrupted or destroyed
___ future business opportunities impaired
___ lost team members
___ gossip
___ disloyalty
___ inordinate lack of compassion
___ theft
___ severed ties with potential new customers or clients
___ other (you fill in the blank):_____

Your "To Do" List

If you are in management, assign a small group of team members to create a statement of values and a mission statement that reflects those values.

Develop a personal statement of values, some "no matter whats," and a personal mission statement that includes your view of why you do what you do.

Make a separate list of values regarding how you choose to deal with clients and why.

Establish some guidelines for your team members concerning how you expect them to treat each other and your customers.

For example, perhaps there should be a no-gossip rule in your firm. Establish a rule that requires that all workplace problems, frustrations, and disputes be handled directly with the person in question or with a superior in management. Negative workplace issues should never be spread among coworkers. To assure that this rule is taken seriously, you must establish and publish what the consequences will be if it is broken. You may want to make violation of the rule an offense that can lead to dismissal. A rule such as this is important because gossip destroys relationships, which leads to less cooperation among coworkers, less productivity (or poor-quality products), and less profits.

❖ ❖ ❖

2. *Marriage Section*

TAKING INVENTORY

List several of the values you hold most dearly in your marriage (for example, faithfulness, truthfulness, or honesty):

1. _____
2. _____
3. _____

What are some "no matter whats" that govern the way you and your spouse treat each other? (For instance, I will never strike my mate, no matter what.)

1. _____
2. _____
3. _____

Which of the following have negatively impacted you in your marriage relationship?

____ hurt feelings
____ fights and/or strong disagreements
____ harbored resentments over unfulfilled expectations
____ gossip
____ disloyalty
____ lack of compassion
____ disputes arising from integrity issues
____ disagreements over the handling of money within your marriage
____ other (you fill in the blank):_____

Your "To Do" List

Create a statement of values for your marriage.

Based on that statement of values, establish some "no matter whats" that you maintain in your marriage. For example, we will not go to bed mad or let the sun set on our anger.

Make a separate list of specific things that each of you values and that you will attempt to do for each other. For example: I will always call if I am going to be late. Or, We will always agree on your monthly spending before the month begins.

Establish some rules for dealing with in-laws. Hint: These guidelines should also flow from your statement of values. Example: I will always affirm my spouse in a dispute with our parents.

3. Parenting Section

TAKING INVENTORY

What are some of the core values by which you and your spouse will parent your children?

1. _____
2. _____
3. _____

What values of yours do you most want your children to emulate?

1. _____
2. _____
3. _____

What values do you expect your children to hold in regard to the way they treat each other and people outside your immediate family?

1. _____
2. _____
3. _____

What are some "no matter whats" that govern the way you deal with your children?

1. _____
2. _____
3. _____

Which of the following have negatively impacted your relationship with your children?

____ hurt feelings
____ fights or arguments
____ harbored resentments
____ broken promises
____ disloyalty
____ lack of compassion
____ sibling rivalries
____ absentee father
____ other (you fill in the blank):_____

Parents' "To Do" List

Create a statement of values for your parenting.

Based on that statement of values, list the ten most important values that you want to instill in your children.

Make a separate list of specific things that you can do to help instill those values in your children. For example: I will set an example by living the values I am trying to teach my children. Or, I will read to them from the Bible or the *Book of Virtues* when the children are young and discuss the ideas in each section.

Think about the impact your parents had on you. What positive values did they instill in you? Which of these values do you want to pass down to your children? What are some things your parents did that you hope to change in your own parenting experience? List ways you plan to make those changes.

4. Singles' Section

TAKING INVENTORY

List several of the core values by which you have decided to live your life.

1. _____
2. _____
3. _____

What are the most important values that govern your relationships with members of the opposite sex?

1. _____
2. _____
3. _____

List several "no matter whats" that govern your life as a single person. (For example, I will be content with who I am, no matter what. Or, I will not allow myself to be used, no matter what. Or, I will not go in debt, no matter what.)

1. _____
2. _____
3. _____

Which of the following have negatively impacted you?

____ hurt feelings
____ fights or arguments with someone with whom you have been living
____ harbored resentments over your marital status
____ gossip
____ disloyalty
____ lack of compassion
____ disputes arising from integrity issues

_____ dating issues
_____ money matters
_____ maintaining high sexual values
_____ ill treatment in the workplace
_____ loneliness

Singles' "To Do" List

Create a statement of values for yourself.

Based on that statement of values, establish some "no matter whats" that you will maintain. For example: I will not allow myself to compromise my moral values, no matter what.

Make a separate list of specific things that you value and that you will attempt to do for yourself and others.

Make some decisions about love, marriage, premarital sex, and other single issues now—so you will not be so vulnerable in the heat of the moment.

5. Financial Section

TAKING INVENTORY

What values do you most frequently find yourself drawing upon in regard to the handling of money matters?

_____

_____

What values do you most highly regard in other people who are involved in your financial dealings?

_____

_____

What value or character flaw have you often seen missing in yourself or other people that has cost you money?

_____

Think of a time when someone whose values were inconsistent with your own cost you a sizable sum of money. How could that situation have been avoided, corrected, or better handled?

_____

_____

If the person who was most responsible for your loss came to you seeking advice, what important steps would you suggest that might strengthen that person's value system?

_____

_____

Your Financial "To Do" List

Develop several "no matter whats" that govern the way you handle your money. (For instance, I will never get involved in a business deal I cannot explain, no matter what," or, "I will always live on less than I make, no matter what.")

Write at the top of your checkbook the three values that matter most to you in regard to your money.

THREE

Vision: Binoculars Looking at Your Future

SOME PEOPLE wake up every morning and say, "Good morning, Lord!" Others wake up and say, "Good Lord! Morning?"

Those of us with a **More Than Enough** lifestyle can't wait to see the dawn of a new day, because we know that each day is a fresh opportunity, another chance to do something and be something great. We look forward to seeing what good things are going to come our way each day. Men and women with a **More Than Enough** attitude can't wait to get started because they know where they are going! They have firmly established their values and they are building a prosperous life on them.

Your foundational values are the building blocks of the **More Than Enough** lifestyle, but where you go with them . . . ah! That's where vision comes in.

> *Vision without values is a pipe dream; vision with values is a recipe for dreams coming true.*

What Is This Thing Called "Vision"?

Vision is the picture you establish and maintain in your mind of where you want to go in life. Simply put: You go where you look! Without vision you will flounder about aimlessly because you won't know where or what your true destination is. You won't know where you are going, and you won't be able to tell if or when you ever get there. That is no way to live! In fact, Proverbs 29:18 says, "Where there is no vision, the people perish." That doesn't mean that they just drop over and die. Much worse! Without a vision a person tends to meander through life as a wandering generality until he or she simply wears down or wastes away. In contrast, those of us with **More Than Enough** live each day on purpose because we are passionate about fulfilling our vision. We are passionate about getting to where we want to be and doing what we believe we are meant to be doing.

Which phrase best describes your attitude when you woke up this morning?

_____ Good morning, Lord!
_____ Good Lord! Morning?

Think back over the past week. Which phrase best describes your attitude on each day?

Good morning, Lord!	Good Lord! Morning?
_____ Sunday	_____ Sunday
_____ Monday	_____ Monday
_____ Tuesday	_____ Tuesday
_____ Wednesday	_____ Wednesday
_____ Thursday	_____ Thursday
_____ Friday	_____ Friday
_____ Saturday	_____ Saturday

From looking back over your attitude check for each morning of the past week, what general conclusions can you draw about how you start each day? (For instance, I can tell that I am reluctant to go to work on most days. Or, I am really excited about what new opportunities are coming my way.)

_____

_____

Which phrase are you more prone to think or say?

___ Thank God, it's Friday!   ___ Thank God, it's Monday!

Tunnel Vision

❖ Anyone who has ever landed at the Greater Pittsburgh International Airport and then traveled by car toward the Steel City knows what an incredible sight it is. The city is almost inaccessible except by bridge or by tunnel. As you travel down Greentree Hill and drive into the Fort Pitt tunnels, you feel as though you are entering a long brick hallway. It seems to take forever to travel through the mountain that separates the city from the suburbs. Suddenly as you emerge from the tunnel, the city of Pittsburgh bursts forth in a panoramic view of unparalleled beauty. The tunnel leads to the light.

While some people going through the tunnels see the light as a glorious fresh start, others see the light at the end of the tunnel as that of an oncoming train. It all depends on your vision of where you are heading.

Still others have a skewed vision. As motivational speaker Clifford G. Baird says: "We can end up looking at life through a straw, instead of seeing things the way they are." **More Than Enough** people look at life the way we want it to be!

Your Vision Affects Your Attitude

People with vision can see where they want to go, and they refuse to give up until they get there, regardless of the obstacles. Glenn Cunningham was just such an individual. At the age of five, he suffered severe burns on his legs. His doctors believed that Glenn's case was hopeless, that he was crippled and destined to spend the rest of his life in a wheelchair. "He will never walk again," the doctors said. "No chance."

The doctors had thoroughly examined Glenn's legs, but their elaborate medical instruments could not measure the most important element in Glenn Cunningham—his spirit. Glenn refused to accept the doctors' negative prognosis. Instead, he determined within himself that he would walk again unassisted.

Lying in bed, his skinny legs all red and covered with scar tissue, Glenn vowed, "Next week I'm going to get out of this bed. I'm going to walk."

And he did just that! But it wasn't easy.

Glenn's mother recalls how she watched through the window as Glenn struggled to reach out to take hold of an old plow in the yard. Grasping the handles so hard the veins in his hands looked as though they were ready to pop, Glenn forced his gnarled legs to function. And with every step—each one coming with the price of searing pain—he came closer to walking without assistance.

Then one day, it happened. Glenn walked on his own. Inspired now, he worked even harder. A few months later, he was trotting, then before long, he was running at full speed. Once Glenn succeeded in running, he became even more determined.

"I always believed that I could walk," he declared, "and I did! Now I'm going to run faster than anybody has ever run."

And did he ever! Glenn Cunningham became a miler, who, in 1934, set the world's record, running the mile race in 4:06, an incredible accomplishment for any athlete, let alone a young man who would supposedly never walk again.

What Is Your Vision?

Ask most people what their vision for their life is and you will probably receive a variety of dirty looks. Either that, or they will answer in vague, ambiguous terms such as, "Oh, I'd like to have a good life." Or, "I want to be a better person," or, "I'd really like to make a difference in this world." These are nice answers, but are often meaningless. The truth is, many people do not have a vision for their lives. They don't expect to go anywhere or to do anything significant in life, so they make few plans and even less preparations. They are the floaters. Laid back on their rubber rafts, they are floating out to sea.

Without a vision or a direction, they are content to be controlled by the whims of the water and the wind. Naively, they are enjoying what they think is a free ride, oblivious to the fact that they are vulnerable to every violent change in the weather. They hope to end up on "Fantasy Island." More than likely, they'll soon find themselves in the Twilight Zone!

To help you formulate your vision, think in more specific terms about some of the following areas:

If money were no object, what would you really like to do with your life?

_____

_____

_____

Where do you see yourself five years from now?

_____

_____

What will your annual income be in ten years?

_____

_____

How much money will you have in savings at that time?

_____

_____

How will you be enjoying your leisure time?

_____

_____

What will your physical health be like at that time?

_____

_____

What will you be doing to enhance your spiritual life and to help others?

_____

_____

What does your life look like twenty years from now? _____

_____

What does it sound like?

_____

_____

Where will you be living at the time?

_____

_____

Who will be there with you?

_____

_____

What activities will you spend most of your time doing?

_____

_____

Taken together, the answers to the above questions will make up your vision for your life, where you want to go, who you want to be, what you want to be doing, and who you want to bring along with you on the journey. For most of us, our vision of ourselves is intimately connected to our dreams and goals.

Your Vision Affects Your Income

Studies of people who earn $100,000 or more each year and have maintained that income level for a number of years reveal an interesting character trait.

These six-figure earners all think in five-year blocks (or more) of time. They are relatively unconcerned about *today* except in the sense of how today is a building block toward their vision, which may not be fully realized for another twenty years. Six-figure earners think about the long-term implications of every move they make and don't make those moves unless they move them one step closer to their vision.

Folks who are at the bottom end of income brackets and stay there tend to share the character trait of short-term thinking, making decisions based on short-term results.

How's your vision? Are you thinking long term or short term? The following quiz will help you find out (check all that apply to you):

____ I am renting to own my VCR.
____ I am saving and investing in mutual funds.
____ I pawn items of personal property frequently for cash.
____ I frequently use cash advances obtained from credit cards.
____ I view bad times in business as temporary setbacks and a time to learn.
____ I invest in mutual funds, but I move the money in and out of the funds as I need it.
____ I work for the weekend.

If you have your eye on the horizon rather than on your immediate situation or circumstances, chances are that you have good vision. You are a saver and a patient investor who understands that it will take at least five years before you see any real increase in your investments. However, if you are using up your money on pleasure-based immediate gratification, you are probably a short-term thinker. You are either broke now or you will be broke soon if you don't change your way of looking at things.

Vision and Your Dreams

Okay, relax. Nobody is watching. It's just us, here, so allow your imagination to run free for a while. Allow yourself to dream about what you really want out of life. You used to be good at daydreaming, allowing your mind to paint grandiose pictures, thinking about the fabulous life you were going to have, the great relationships you planned to establish, your success in business or in your chosen career, the home you wanted, and the good you wanted to do in the world. Then real life pinched at your idealism, somebody or something stomped on your vision, and squelched your dreams.

But for a few minutes, allow yourself to think back to when you were a teenager, or an idealistic college student, when you dared to dream of greatness for yourself and those people around you. Remember how grand your life was going to be?

What were some of those dreams you once held dear to your heart? List several of them below. It's okay to include the silly ones, too. Or the most grandiose, or the most fantastic. (For instance, "I dreamed that I would be a great musician," or, "I dreamed of marrying Prince Charming and living a fairy-tale sort of life.")

_____

_____

_____

_____

_____

Now, go back and put a check mark by all of the dreams that you listed above that you have actually achieved to date.

What do you notice about the dreams you once had and the dreams you have achieved?

_____

_____

If there are dreams that you listed above but haven't achieved, which of the following statements might apply? The reasons I didn't achieve my dreams include (check all that apply):

____ Unrealistic expectations.

____ I gave up too soon.

____ The deck was stacked against me.

____ It was a silly notion, anyhow.

____ My values have changed, and the dreams I once held have changed with them.

____ Other people.

____ I had nobody to help me achieve my dreams.

____ My upbringing.

____ Lack of education.

____ Lack of money.

____ I simply ran out of steam.

____ The government.

____ I got in with the wrong crowd.

____ Foolish financial mistakes.

____ Poor decisions on my part.

Of all the dreams you listed above, which one would you still most like to see fulfilled in your life?

_____

What steps can you take to help make that dream come true?

_____

_____

_____

_____

_____

List three people who may be willing to help you fulfill your dream. (Note: They can help, but you must do it!)

1. _____
2. _____
3. _____

Growing Up Is Hard to Do

All too often, as we grow older, we grow more cynical, skeptical, and caustic. Whereas we used to approach life ambitiously, now we tend to sit back and watch others vigorously pursue their visions and dreams.

Granted, growing up is a pain. Many of us were constantly informed of our limitations, and informed of all the logical reasons why we couldn't do what we believed we wanted to do. As we watched the years rapidly slipping away (they seem to go faster the older we get!), we also slowly but surely saw our dreams slipping away, evaporating right before our eyes. We settled into an "I-guess-this-is-the-best-I-can-expect" attitude. "This is as good as it gets!" we spouted boisterously, but insincerely, to others who have had their dreams stolen from them as well. Before long, we adopted the attitude that "life is just unfair." Which, of course, it is! But that doesn't mean you must give up on your dreams!

Dream On!

If you want to have **More Than Enough,** you must realize that as you are growing, you must keep dreaming. The good news is that your dreams are even more attainable now than they were in your youth. As a grown-up, you now have a much better understanding of what it takes to achieve your dreams, and most likely you now have the means of realizing your dreams. Connect your dreams to the means of achieving them and they become part of your life's vision! Once you have the vision, you can begin making specific plans as to how you will fulfill your dreams; you can accurately define and measure what it will take to make your dreams come true.

❖ When Arnold Schwarzenegger decided that he wanted to make the transition from world-class bodybuilding champion to actor, he was turned down on three counts. First, he was told his body was too big and muscular for him to be a movie star. (How would you like to have been the fellow who had to tell Arnold *that*?) Second, he had a foreign accent and often spoke in broken or poor English. Third, his advisers suggested that he change his name: "This is America, Arnold. Schwarzenegger just doesn't make it. Redford, Gibson, Hoffman, or Hanks, maybe, but Schwarzenegger . . . never!"

Arnold was undaunted. He set about the task of trimming his body down so it wouldn't look excessively muscular (oh, to have such a problem!). He did so by adjusting his eating and exercising habits. At the same time, he began to study the English language and struggled to improve his enunciation. Arnold stood his ground, however, when it came to changing his name. Instead, he vowed to make Schwarzenegger a household name.

Today, Arnold is much more popular for his movies than he ever was for his bodybuilding. He's no ninety-pound weakling, and his movies don't exactly tax his vocabulary, but he's doing what he wants to do with his life. His name? Whether it is a household name might be debatable, but Maria Shriver, whose family name (Kennedy) is familiar to most Americans, wanted it to be a part of her household. She consented to marry Arnold. Don't ever let anyone steal your dreams!

Go back to page 68 and look at your list of dreams. Which of them got buried somewhere as you grew up and became more "realistic"?

1. _____
2. _____
3. _____
4. _____

From your earlier list, note some of the dreams that were stolen from you or squelched through the negative attitudes, "advice," or demeaning words of other people in your life.

1. _____
2. _____
3. _____

List one or two of the above dreams that are more attainable, now that you have grown older and wiser.

_____

_____

_____

What's Holding You Back?

Have you always wanted to write a book or record a song? Have you always had a secret dream to travel to Africa on a safari? Or to take an Alaskan cruise? Have you always wanted to restore a beat-up '57 Chevy? Have you wanted to create and run your own business? Have you always wanted to own a home on the lake or the beach? Have you always dreamed about becoming a missionary?

What's holding you back from doing what you have always dreamed of doing? Don't allow yourself to be duped into believing that you can't do it! You *can* accomplish your dreams! But just in case you are feeling a bit discouraged, or too overwhelmed by your circumstances even to try to achieve your dreams, let me tell you about my friend David Ring.

David is an internationally known evangelist who speaks at more than two hundred events every year. He has a wonderful wife, and a bevy of beautiful children. He is highly esteemed throughout the Christian community and is one of the most motivating speakers you will ever hear. Audiences ranging from one hundred to ten thousand people sit on the edge of their seats waiting to hear what David has to say. A masterful orator, David can have an audience laughing one minute and move them to tears in the next.

So what's so unusual about that? you may be wondering. *Most successful motivational speakers nowadays can do something similar.*

True, but did I mention to you that David lost his father at age eleven and his mother at age fourteen? And did I tell you that David has grown up with a severe case of cerebral palsy?

When David walks onto a stage, he limps, dragging his leg along the floor. As he turns the pages of his notes, he does so with a curled hand, and with fingers that refuse to cooperate. When David speaks, his audience must listen very attentively, because his speech has been slurred by the cerebral palsy, forcing him to mouth each word carefully, and occasionally causing him to stutter. When David gets excited, his speech becomes even more strained.

Yet despite their compassion for David, his audiences don't hang on every word simply because David has a physical disability and a speech impediment. The audiences don't want to miss a word because David has tremendous wisdom to impart. He has turned an adversity into an advantage.

He has had to work harder to fulfill his vision of being a preacher, but his dream has come true!

So What About Your Dream?

List several of your current dreams that you want to see fulfilled as part of the vision you have for your life.

_____

_____

_____

_____

What obstacles must you overcome to begin fulfilling the vision for your life?

_____

_____

_____

Which one of the above obstacles will you attack first and how do you plan to do it?

_____

_____

You're Never Too Old to Get Started

You may be thinking that you are too old to fulfill your vision, that you have wasted too much time, squandering away the years instead of moving toward your true aspirations.

But you are never too old to start doing things right! Check your heart. Is it beating? Put your hand on your chest. Are you breathing? If your heart is pumping and you are still breathing, you have an opportunity to fulfill your grandest dreams. George Burns won his first Oscar at eighty years of age! Golda Meir was seventy-one when she became prime minister of Israel. At the same age, Michelangelo spent months lying on his back, painting the frescoes in the Sistine Chapel in Rome. George Bernard Shaw was ninety-four when one of his plays was first produced for the theater. Grandma Moses didn't even start painting until she was eighty, and she completed more than fifteen hundred paintings before she died, 375 of them after she had turned one hundred years old!

So enough of this age excuse!

"But I don't have the money to do what I want to do!" I can hear you saying.

Neither did Harlan Sanders. At sixty-five years of age, Sanders was broke and trying to live on his meager social security check of $102 per month. That same year, he decided to open a fledgling business selling chicken fried in his special batter. You may have tasted it, since Colonel Sanders's chicken franchises, known as Kentucky Fried Chicken (KFC), are now a worldwide entity, and the good Colonel died a millionaire.

It's never too late! You are not too old. You still have an opportunity to turn your vision into reality. The only question is: When are you going to get started?

Your Age Is the Best Age

Some people allow time to scare them away from what they really would like to do in their lives. A friend of mine complained, "Dave, I really hate my job."

"Then why don't you try a different job?" I suggested.

"Oh, no! I couldn't do that," he exclaimed. "It's too late for me."

"What do you mean 'it's too late'?" I asked him.

"I can't change jobs this late in life. I mean, after all, I'm thirty-six years old!"

"So, big deal! So you're thirty-six, so what? What do you want to be?" I pressed.

"Well, to tell you the truth"—he dropped his eyes and hesitated before slowly and softly continuing—"I feel that God is calling me to be a preacher."

"Fantastic!" I burst out, and began slapping him on the back. "That's great! And I know you'll be a good one, too."

My friend looked dismayed at my delight. "Oh, no, Dave," he said. "I can't be a preacher," he said dismally.

"What do you mean *you can't be a preacher*?" I practically shouted. "You just got done telling me that the Lord has called you to preach. Why can't you be a preacher?"

"I'm thirty-six years old, Dave."

"Yeah, I heard you before—so what?"

He seemed annoyed at my persistence. "Do you know how long it will take me to become a preacher? Why, I need four years of college, and then three more years of seminary . . ."

"Yes?" I urged him to continue.

"That's seven years! I'm thirty-six. Do you know how old I will be by the time I get to be a preacher? I'd be forty-three!"

"Oh! I see." I feigned a sudden enlightenment. "Hey, buddy. Let me ask you a question."

"Okay."

"How old will you be seven years from now if you *don't* become a preacher?"

"Forty-three," he answered quickly, without even referring to a calculator.

"Well, then, if you're going to be forty-three in seven years anyhow, you may as well go for it. Wouldn't it be better to be doing something you want to do—something that you feel God put you on the face of this earth to do—seven years from now, rather than being stuck in a job you hate, living a life that will never accomplish your vision and dreams?"

"I never thought of it that way," he brightened.

> This is the only chance you will ever have on earth
> with this exciting adventure called life. So why not
> plan it, and try to live it as richly as possible?
> —*Dale Carnegie*

Your Turn

How old are you today? ____

How long do you think it will take for you to prepare to accomplish your vision? ____

In months, and years, it will take me _____ to acquire the training, education, or resources that will set me on the path toward fulfilling my vision.

What steps are required for you to get started?

1. _____
2. _____
3. _____

Set a date. Specifically, when will you take the first step toward fulfilling your vision?

"On (Month) _____ (Day) _____, (Year) _____, I will take the first step toward fulfilling my vision by (describe what you will do):

_____

_____

The Dream Principle

❖ Walt Disney said, "If you can dream it, you can do it."

If you can't dream, or you are unwilling to try to turn your dream into your vision, you will be destined for mediocrity. Alternatively, the moment you establish a lofty vision and start moving in the direction of it, your life will take on an entirely new meaning and excitement level. Now is the time to renew your vision. Create a plan and start making it happen!

Improving Your Vision

You may or may not need bifocals to improve your vision, but certain elements of a **More Than Enough** lifestyle are indispensable if you want to keep your life vision working for you rather than against you.

1. Your life needs balance. You should include large doses of hard work, but be sure to include large doses of relaxation, as well. Where do you see yourself on the scale between work and relaxation?

Work _____ Relaxation

2. You need to read, especially nonfiction books that will help you focus on your goals and help you to achieve them. It's also valuable to read some good fiction simply for the entertainment value. Resist the urge to "dumb down" in front of a television set or a computer on-line service as your sole source of entertainment.

List three nonfiction books you have read within the past year.

1. _____
2. _____
3. _____

List one novel you have read recently.

1. _____

3. You must be financially stable. If you are weighed down with debt, you will have awful difficulty moving forward, no matter how strong your vision is. You must get completely out of debt as soon as possible to avoid wasting your most creative time and energies on digging yourself out of a self-imposed pit. If debt is still in your financial picture, start the Debt Snowball immediately. (See my book *Financial Peace* for an in-depth discussion on how the Debt Snowball can eradicate debt.)

Believe it or not, many people have little idea just how deeply they are in the financial pits until they begin to total up *all* of their debts. How much debt are you carrying right now? (Include auto loans, credit cards, mortgages, student loans, finance company loans, personal loans from friends and family members, and any other debts you might have.)_____

4. Whether you work in your home or at another location, whether you work for yourself or for another employer, make sure to give it your all when you are on the job. But be sure to allow time in your schedule for your family and for yourself. A **More Than Enough** life is much more than mere work. Few are the men or women who on their deathbed cry out, "I wish I would have worked longer or harder!" Yet many men and women have had to look back from death's door and wistfully wish that they had invested more of their best time in their family and in themselves. Complete the following sentence: To keep a proper balance between work and personal time, I plan to _____

5. To make sure your vision remains an important part of your life, you need a sense of destiny, a driving force that moves you toward your vision. To know that it is important for you to achieve your vision will help you to seek to fulfill your dreams, rather than just mull them over in your mind.

One hundred years from now, how much will it really matter whether you achieved your vision or not?

	It will be rather	It won't matter	It won't
___ A great deal.	___ important.	___ much.	___ matter at all.

Putting the Why in the What

If you are like most people, you will need some extra motivation in order to achieve your vision. Author Rob Gilbert defines motivation as "having a strong *why.*" You can do almost anything if you have a big enough "why." On the other hand, if the "why" is too small, or unimportant, your chances of achieving anything of true value diminishes commensurately. Now, here is a surprise: In most cases, you will need more than mere money to motivate you.

Okay, I'll wait for a moment while you stop laughing. I can almost hear you chortling as you say, "Dave, you've got to be kidding! Obtaining more money is what the game is all about! It's what I work for, so I can buy more nice things for my family, so I can do more, give more. Money makes my world go round."

Sorry to burst your bubble, but people who work merely for money will never be satisfied and they are usually terribly miserable. That's why taking a new job simply to make more money will never lead you to a **More Than Enough** lifestyle. If there is no personal fulfillment in the job, no significance to what you do, all the money in the world will still leave you empty and wanting more. People who live out their vision will recognize that *"why"* we do what we do is by far the greatest motivator for *what* we do. Furthermore, if the *why* is important enough, the *how* will come. *Why* will find a way to make it happen.

Take the case of Randy Leamer. Randy's youngest daughter was slowly dying due to kidney failure. She needed a new kidney, and Randy—like most dads—was ready and willing to give up one of his kidneys to save the life of his darling daughter.

But the doctors refused to do the transplant because Randy was overweight. They gave him eight months to lose one hundred pounds. "If you can lose that amount of weight in that short amount of time, we might be able to do the operation," the doctors told Randy matter-of-factly.

Randy took the doctors at their word and set out to lose the one hundred pounds. Despite losing the battle of the bulge for years, Randy suddenly found the motivation he needed to shed the pounds even before the allotted time was up, and in the process he also discovered the willpower to keep the weight off. "It wasn't even that difficult to lose the weight," Randy said later, "because I had the greatest incentive in the world—to save my daughter's life." When the "why" is important enough, the "how" is not a problem. You'll find a way.

What are some of the "whys" in your life that motivate you? (Check all that apply.)

    ____ God
    ____ your spouse
    ____ your children or extended family members
    ____ church
    ____ financial goals
    ____ community concerns
    ____ pride
    ____ love

> ❖ Mike, a traveling salesman, keeps a small photograph of his wife and daughter glued to the frame around his laptop computer. "On the long nights when I am away, staying at a hotel, and running spreadsheets till the wee hours of the morning, when I look at that photograph, it reminds me why I do what I do. Money alone could never keep me on the road. But the people in that picture give me the strength to face another day when I'd rather call the boss and say, 'I quit.'"

Having a big enough "why" is important in every area of your life. Have you been trying to save money? Do you want to invest for your family's future? The "why" will provide the motivation for the "how." If, like Randy Leamer, your daughter's life depended on your taking some radical action, you'd find a way to do it. Say you had to save $10,000 this year so your child could have a lifesaving operation. You'd do whatever was necessary, starting by working on your budget to squeeze every extra dollar you can find out of it. Then you'd sell so much stuff that the dog would be hiding under the bed, thinking that he's next!

No doubt you would work extra hours, or perhaps an extra job to bring in more money. Whether it took you working overtime at your present employment, or finding a temporary second (or even third) part-time job, you'd do it because your "why" was important—to earn the money for your daughter's operation.

Do you have to be in a life-or-death situation before the "why" becomes large enough to motivate you? Let's hope not! But if your "why" is too small, you will be less focused, less driven, and less likely to plan and implement the means of increasing your productivity. On the other hand, when your "why" is important enough to you—regardless of whether others deem it important—it will motivate you to go the distance, and to do whatever it takes.

In each of the following areas of your life, list the "why" that is large enough to motivate you to improve in that area.

The why that most motivates me in my FINANCIAL area is:

_____

The why that most motivates me in my CAREER is:

_____

The why that most motivates me in my INTELLECTUAL GROWTH is:

_____

The why that most motivates me in my SOCIAL LIFE is:

_____

The why that most motivates me in my SPIRITUAL LIFE is:

_____

The why that most motivates me in my COMMUNITY INVOLVE-MENT is:

_____

> *If you measure success in service,*
> *money will flow to you in truckloads.*
> —More Than Enough

Remember, money is a selfish motivator that will not keep you moving when the noonday sun burns bright on your forehead and you are looking for an excuse to quit. If you develop goals that are outside yourself for serving others, then those will translate to money. . . . In our firm, we measure sales in dollars, but we always discuss the goals in terms of numbers of families served. How many radio listeners do we have? How many books have helped folks? How many lives were changed at a seminar? If you measure success in service, money will flow to you in truckloads.

The "Why" Makes What You Do Special

Once a journalist happened upon a construction site where he noticed a group of bricklayers going about their jobs. As the journalist observed, he became intrigued by the various manners in which the workers performed their duties. For instance, one fellow moved as slowly as possible and looked extremely bored with his work.

"What is it that you are doing here?" the journalist asked.

The bricklayer glared back at the journalist, looking disgusted that anyone would ask a question with such an obvious answer. "What do you think I'm doing?" he bristled. "I'm laying bricks."

The journalist noticed another worker who seemed to be enjoying his job more than the first man. He had more enthusiasm and seemed to work with more skill. When the journalist asked this man what he was doing, the worker squared his shoulders and replied, "I am building a wall."

A third man caught the journalist's attention. This worker was a joy to watch. One could almost imagine a symphony playing in the background as the craftsman fluidly picked up each brick, prepared it with mortar, and swung it into position. With tremendous pride, he smoothed the extraneous mortar around the edges of each brick, careful to make sure that each brick was placed with precision. It looked as though he thought the entire building would stand or fall according to the way he did his work.

When the journalist asked the third man what he was doing, he stood up with pride and smiled broadly. "I am building a magnificent cathedral to the glory of the Lord," he replied.

Same building, same job description, what the men were doing was the same, but the men had different "whys," and that changed the way they approached their daily work.

Which are you doing in your field of endeavor?

____ Laying bricks, stupid!
____ Building a wall.
____ Doing something magnificent for God.

Creating and working toward your vision means finding a purpose—a dream—that you care so passionately about that you are willing to do whatever it takes to achieve it. Philosopher William James said, "The greatest discovery of my generation is that a human being can alter his life by altering his attitude of mind."

When you adopt the attitude of the bricklayer who was building a great cathedral, you will have altered your frame of mind in such a way that you will be ready to put your vision into action.

Get Ready to Fly!

Take a few moments, and turn back to page 73, where you listed several of your current dreams that you would like to see fulfilled before somebody engraves your name on a tombstone. As you review your dreams, ask yourself this question: "Isn't it time that I do something to start making these dreams come true?" Granted, you may not be able to call an immediate halt to life going on around you. You can't simply unplug your current life like a sink full of dirty water and let it go down the drain. You've made some commitments and you must honor them. But today is the day to start filling that sink with fresh water, to replace the dirt from the past. Today is the day to start taking steps in the direction that will achieve your dreams. To do that, you must establish realistic, attainable goals.

> *Goals are the building blocks that make a vision come true.*

Write Your Own Ticket

Setting realistic, attainable goals provides a step-by-step plan that you can follow toward fulfilling your dreams and achieving your vision. Goals are the building blocks that make a vision come true. Goals become the "how" that flows from your "why." Your goals will become the footpath over which you can traverse the troubled waters all around you as you move in the direction of your vision. They are how the job is going to get done. But in order for your goals to work, they have to meet certain specific criteria.

How to Set Goals That Work

1. They must be *your* goals, not those of your parents, your friends, or even your spouse. Your goals must emanate from you. You must own them. Other people can give you suggestions, but if the goal is to lead you to success, it must become your own passion.

2. Goals that work must be measurable. It often helps to measure your goals numerically. For instance, *On a scale of one to ten, how far am I along in the process of reaching this goal?* Money is also a good standard of measurement, but be sure that it is not your only means of determining whether you are moving toward your goal.

3. Goals must be *written*. The older I get, the more I realize that the most crumpled piece of paper is often better than the best of memories. Beyond that, something powerful happens when you actually write out your goals. Writing them helps to clarify them, and gives you a chance to see them more realistically. Besides, once they are written down, you can keep the goals in front of your eyes much more easily. Write the goals on a notepad, use refrigerator magnets to hold a copy of your goals, write your goals on a "sticky note" on your computer, on the dashboard of your car—write it anywhere it is legal and keep it before you constantly.

4. Goals that really work are the ones you place a time limit on. To say that you have a goal of finishing your college education is noble, but it is pure drivel unless you say something such as, "I will finish my degree program by June of next year." Even weekly or daily goals should have a finish line.

Take a few minutes right now to think about some of your goals, both short-term and long-term. Which of your goals will best move you toward fulfilling your life vision?

_____

_____

_____

_____

Do you have a goal of putting some money aside in savings each month so you can afford to pay cash for that trip to Europe that you have always wanted to take? How much will you need? How much do you think you can save each month specifically for that trip? Be realistic, now. It will only be discouraging if you set extremely high goals for yourself and you are unable to reach them. Put your goal just slightly out of reach so you will have to struggle and work to attain it, but don't put it so far beyond you that attaining it is an impossibility. When will you start saving? Write out the goal and all the details you can include. How many months will it be before the goal is reached?

Do you want to take some instructional classes in carpentry so you can build the gazebo you have always wanted to build in your backyard? Where are the classes offered and when? How much does the course cost? Who will care for the kids while you are "in school"? When will the classes be completed? These are the kinds of questions you must write out and answer for each of your major goals.

Do you want to open a small business of your own? Great! With whom do you need to consult at the local level? Which local business owners might offer to help you by providing information or answering some of your questions about doing business in their area? Make a list. When will you start? What is your grand-opening date?

Have you always wanted to compete in a marathon? When is the next one to be held? What are the entry requirements? When is registration? What sort of training do you need, how soon should you begin, and how many months in advance must you train? Should you join the local health club to begin training in an environment in which it might be easier to measure your progress?

Notice how specifically we are honing in on each goal. Vague generalities rarely ever turn into realized goals, so the more detail in which you can describe your goal and how you plan to achieve it, the better!

Choose one of the goals that you feel is important to your overall life vision and let's break it down into achievable, measurable, realistic steps, which you will accomplish within a specific length of time.

An important goal in fulfilling my life vision is: _____

_____

To reach this goal, I will need to acquire, develop, or improve the following: _____

_____

Beginning _____ (month, day, year), I will take the following action toward reaching my goal: _____

_____

I will continue this process until _____

_____

I will achieve this goal by _____ (month, day, year)
I will know that I have reached this goal because _____

_____

You Get to Make the Choices

Let's be honest about this goal-setting business. Most realistic goals are not that difficult to attain, if all you have to do in life is set your goal and go for it. But who has that sort of luxury? Not me. Most likely you don't, either. That's why if you are going to achieve certain goals, you must decide which of your goals are most important right now. Many good goals are simply not priorities at certain stages of our lives. For instance, a goal of a $350,000 home in the suburbs is lofty, but it is not a priority for a young married couple just starting out in life together. They'd be much better off saving for and buying a less exorbitantly priced home and working toward some of their other mutual goals.

Similarly, you must be prepared to postpone or give up completely competing goals to achieve the ones that really matter to you. For instance, if your goal for this year is to improve your marriage relationship, you will need to spend more time with your spouse. You may have to forgo some of your more aggressive career and financial goals, as well as your intellectual pursuits, so you may apply yourself to reading books about marriage, attending marriage seminars, or simply doing fun activities with your mate. But the trade-offs will be worth it! And eventually, the other goals will be easier to attain because you and your spouse will be working together rather than against each other.

However, if your goal is to be a millionaire within the next two years, it is unlikely that you will be able to spend bunches of time trying to build a better marriage during the next twenty-four months. The myth that we can have it all and do it all at the same time is just that—a myth! Your goal of a better marriage and your goal to become a millionaire within the next two years will compete for your time, energy, and attention, and by trying to do both, you will run the risk of accomplishing neither. I don't mean to rain on your parade, but there is no such thing as a "get rich quick pill." The best way to get rich (and possibly the only way to get rich, apart from winning a lottery or receiving a windfall) is by working hard, taking your time, and setting your priorities.

You'll need to decide which goal is more important to you, and set your priorities based on that decision. Most of us who have discovered the **More Than Enough** lifestyle would choose a better marriage over more money any day. Why? Because with a better marriage you will have the added strength and insight of your spouse, which will give you a stronger financial sense so you will be able to make more money and use what you earn more wisely.

Does that mean it is impossible to work on your marriage while working on your career goals? Absolutely not! Quite the contrary. You need to be working on specific goals in each area of your life. But what it does mean is that instead of becoming a millionaire in two years, it will take you more time to reach your financial goals. But when you get there, if you have been working on your marriage along the way, you'll still be having fun. How sad it would be to reach the goal of becoming a millionaire and lose your spouse and family in the process.

Let's say that you want to get out of debt within the next twelve months. To be debt-free within a year is a noble goal, easily measurable with a set time limit. So far, so good. But let's assume that you also want to be an excellent parent. You must recognize that these two goals may not be compatible. Ridding yourself of debt may require you to work extra hours, or to take on a part-time job, robbing you of precious time with your children. How can you solve this dilemma?

Frankly, you may not be able to satisfy everyone in this case. You may need to lower your parenting expectations so you can take on the extra income-producing work for a short period of time in order to achieve a long-term goal of financial independence. You may need to miss a few of your kids' ball games or recitals. Not all of them, of course, and you must not make a habit of missing those special moments with your children. But for a limited period of time you may not be able to attend every single event, but you are working so you can be there for your kids for the rest of their lives.

Or you may want to extend the amount of time necessary to get out of debt, keeping your original goal of being debt-free but working fewer hours for a longer period of time. There are no magic formulas for these decisions. Whatever route you choose, you should thoroughly discuss the situation with your spouse and children so everyone understands that this is a temporary inconvenience that is a trade-off for permanent improvement. The family needs to know that they may have to give up vacations and other luxuries and live on an extremely tight budget while you are working your way out of debt. But because everyone is consulted, it becomes a team effort, and makes the situation more tolerable. You are working together, sacrificing together, for a common goal.

One caution: People who want **More Than Enough** never sacrifice their family relationships over the long run. When a short-term situation demands that sacrifices must be made, be sure to involve the entire family in the decision-making process.

It's amazing what we can endure if we know the cause is worthwhile and the pain is only for a limited amount of time. Moreover, it is relatively easy to accomplish a goal if you believe it can be achieved, and that the amount of time that it will take to reach the goal is reasonable.

For most of us, saving $100 per month is a realistic, achievable goal. Saving that amount every month for forty years might not bother us, either. Saving $500 per month, however, is tougher, but the savings in time may be enough to make it a worthwhile and attainable goal. Ask yourself, "Would the pain and sacrifice it takes to save that extra amount of money each month be worth it to fulfill my financial vision fifteen years sooner?" How about the effort required to save an additional $500 per month so you could achieve your goal five years sooner? Is that worth it to you?

Only you can answer these questions, and what is right for one family may not work for another. But recognizing that the trade-offs exist, and are required, will help you develop a more realistic, attainable plan to reach your goal. One of the main reasons people give up on achieving their goals is that they did not count the cost correctly at the outset.

Becoming a Millionaire

❖ To become a millionaire by saving money at a 12 percent interest rate, it will take you:

Forty years if you save $100 a month.
Twenty-five years if you save $500 a month.
Twenty years if you save $1,000 a month.

If your vision doesn't cost you something, it is a daydream.

—*John Maxwell in*
21 Irrefutable Laws of Leadership

List some of the possible short-term trade-offs you may have to make to accomplish your long-term goals, the stepping-stones to fulfilling the vision for your life. For instance, I can drive an older, less expensive car for a year longer so I can save money for our family's new house. *Or,* I may have to bag my lunches for a few months so I can save some money to buy Christmas gifts.

_____

_____

_____

_____

Your spouse, family members, and coworkers will not commit to the **More Than Enough** lifestyle unless they can see a pep in your step and a gleam in your eye. These qualities are the result of having a vision that energizes your life, that motivates you to tackle the tough jobs, and rewards you with incredible joy and satisfaction when the goal is achieved. Remember, your values are the foundation on which your vision is formed. Your values will help you to prioritize your goals and will give you the stability and strength with which you can start to achieve your vision.

Aisle Two— Vision and Goals

1. Business Section

TAKING INVENTORY
What is your company's or business's vision?

_____

Is this vision written and placed where you and other employees can see it?

___ Yes   ___ No

On a scale of one to ten, how frustrated are you at your company's lack of vision?

1   2   3   4   5   6   7   8   9   10
Very frustrated   Slightly irritated   Doesn't bother me

How frequently do you suffer a loss of energy or motivation due to your company's lack of direction?

___ Often   ___ Occasionally   ___ Frequently   ___ Constantly

Who decides the majority of your goals at work?

___ I do.
___ My boss or immediate superior.
___ Outside influences.
___ My spouse.

Write out a personal vision statement for your involvement in your company or business. This statement should be a vision that you can pour your life into with real excitement.

_____

_____

_____

Your "To Do" List

Divide your personal vision statement into step-by-step goals, each with specific time limits and methods of measurement.

List three goals you have regarding your company or business:

1. _____
2. _____
3. _____

What can you begin doing on your next workday that will start you moving in the direction of achieving each of the above goals in the fastest and most efficient manner?

1. _____
2. _____
3. _____

Note: Business and career goals should always contain a monetary measuring stick, but you must make certain that these goals also contain personal achievement and relationship-building elements. If your above goals were measurable only by money, list them again, this time including the sorts of comments you'd like to hear at your retirement party.

2. *Married Section*

TAKING INVENTORY

Describe your vision of a great marriage. (For instance, in a great marriage, both partners are working to outdo one another in serving the other person.)

_____

_____

Your "To Do" List

On separate sheets of paper, your spouse and you should answer the following questions:

1. What is your spouse's vision of a great marriage?
2. What is your spouse's personal vision for his or her life?

(Hint: If you don't know what your spouse's personal vision is, this will make a great topic for an after-dinner conversation or a topic to discuss after all the kids are tucked into bed. After all, you need to know where you want to go if you ever hope to get there together!)

After you have completed questions one and two, swap papers with your spouse. As you read what your spouse regards as a vision of a great marriage, do not become overly sensitive or defensive. Accept your spouse's ideas with openness and a sincere desire to enter into his or her world.

Notice the aspects of your spouse's vision of a great marriage that differ from yours.

How have these differences of opinion created stress or conflict in your marriage?

_____

_____

How are your priorities similar to those of your spouse?

_____

_____

How are your priorities dissimilar to those of your spouse?

_____

_____

How often do your differing priorities cause strife between you and your spouse?

____ Frequently   ____ Occasionally   ____ Rarely

Take some time to discuss with your spouse how each of you can help enable the other to achieve his or her personal vision of marriage.

Create a shared vision for your marriage. This vision will flow from your shared values which you examined in the previous chapter, so take time to review those values before beginning to write down your joint marriage vision.

Discuss with your mate some ways you can help each other reach your individual goals as well as the goals you have set for your marriage. For example, you and your mate may need to set up a time to go over your calendars together, just to make sure you are aware of each other's schedules. Do you have a set time when you will do the monthly budget together (for instance, on the first or last day of the month, or the day the bank statements arrive)? When will you meet together for no other reason but to prepare this coming month's budget?

_____

By planning your schedules and your money matters together, you and your spouse will discover that you are getting much better at communicating your priorities.

3. Parenting Section

TAKING INVENTORY

Describe your vision of the ideal parents._____

_____

_____

Have you and your spouse agreed on a vision of what successful parenting should be like?

____ Yes   ____ No   ____ We've not discussed it recently

Have you communicated your vision of parenting to your children?

__ Yes   __ No

List some important elements of parenting that you want your children to understand about you and your mate.

_____

_____

_____

List some goal that you have encouraged your children to set (according to the age-appropriateness of the goal):

1. _____

2. _____

3. _____

Parents' "To Do" List

If you have not already done so, create a joint statement of your parenting vision.

List some of the attributes you and your spouse want your children to have by the time they graduate high school.

1. _____

2. _____

3. _____

4. _____

5. _____

Discuss the above list with your children, sharing with them your vision for their lives. Be careful that you do not give the impression that they have no choice or control over their own vision for their lives. Simply express to them your heart's desire for them. Begin doing this with your children from an early age, as it will impart to them a tremendous sense of self-worth.

Help your children to set some of their own goals.

Select two goals with them, and write them down. Be sure that you help your child to establish time limits for these goals. For example, "I will make the honor roll this next grading period." Or, "I will make my bed every day next week."

Discuss with your children the importance and value of having realistic, specific, measurable goals often. Give them examples, and be sure to reward their successes when they reach their goals. Remember, for these goals to be effective they must be goals that your child adopts as his or her own. You can help guide them, but allow the children to take ownership of the goal.

4. Singles' Section

TAKING INVENTORY

What is your personal vision statement that directs your path through life?

_____

_____

List several step-by-step goals that will be important in the fulfillment of your vision:

1. _____
2. _____
3. _____

List three of the most significant people in your life whose input concerning your future you greatly respect:

1. _____
2. _____

3. _____

Who is there in your life with whom you might be able to establish a mentoring relationship: a person from whom you can learn and whose example you may want to emulate?

_____

Who has the most influence over the decisions that most directly impact your vision for your life? (List according to the level of influence, one being the most influence.)

    ____ my parents
    ____ God
    ____ my peers
    ____ my closest friends
    ____ my boss
    ____ society
    ____ my pastor

Singles' "To Do" List

If you have not already done so, write a personal mission statement that reflects your values and vision for your life.

List several goals that will help fulfill your vision. (These goals may include your health, finances, career, and social involvements, among others.)

1. _____
2. _____
3. _____

Describe your vision of marriage or singleness:

_____

In your personal vision, do you see yourself as most likely remaining single with the outside possibility of marriage, or do you see yourself as probably getting married, with the outside possibility of remaining single?

How does your marital status influence the goals you listed above?

5. Financial Section

TAKING INVENTORY

On a scale of zero to ten, how much of an impact is your vision currently having on your wealth-building process?

0   1   2   3   4   5   6   7   8   9   10
None at all   A moderate impact   It is the guiding principle

In what ways will clarifying your vision help you to prosper financially within the next three years?

_____

_____

_____

List three specific financial goals you plan to achieve within the next twelve months.

1. _____
2. _____
3. _____

Are these goals totally consistent with your vision?

____ Yes   ____ No   ____ Uncertain

(If you are not sure that a goal is consistent with your vision, go back and revise it, or consider it to be less than a priority.)

Your Financial "To Do" List

Schedule an appointment within the next three months with a professional financial adviser for a "financial checkup." Have your adviser examine whether your financial savings and investment program is helping you to achieve your vision and goals.

Discuss with a friend or a financial adviser how you plan to move to the next financial level, without compromising your values and your vision.

FOUR

Unity—A Tangled Rope Is Just Loops

HAVE YOU EVER seen a flock of geese flying through the sky in a V formation? What an incredible sight! But have you ever wondered *why* those large birds fly together, rather than each one going off in his or her own direction? Scientists who study such things have discovered an interesting phenomenon. As each bird flaps its wings, the force not only lifts and propels the bird forward; it creates an uplift for the bird immediately behind it. Flying in the V formation allows the flock to fly farther with less effort. Scientists estimate that by sticking together, the flock can travel 71 percent farther than the distance each bird could fly alone. Not only do the birds fly farther, they do so more quickly and much more efficiently. If a goose slips out of formation along the way, the impact is immediate. Suddenly the bird feels an immense drag and resistance due to trying to go it alone, and it quickly tries to get back in formation so it can take advantage of the lifting power of the other birds.

We're No Birdbrains!

If a flock of geese can figure out that there is power in unity, how much more do *we* need to discover the excitement, encouragement, and support that working together with other people toward a common goal can bring! Two heads really *are* better than one! Working together in unity creates an incredible synergy which leads to **More Than Enough**. Inevitably, being unified in your workplace, in your marriage, with your children, in your church, and in your community will result in your having more creativity, productivity, and power in your life.

Unity is a powerful force. People who share a common direction can get where they are going much more quickly than those who are going through life as Lone Rangers. (In fact, even the Lone Ranger had Tonto to help him out of tough spots!) We really do need each other. Besides, traveling together is just more fun. Sharing emotional, intellectual, physical, and spiritual resources with like-minded friends, family members, and coworkers always makes the journey more interesting. If we have the good sense of a goose, we'll recognize the value of staying in formation with those people who are headed in the same direction we are.

List several people in your life with whom you are currently working together for a common cause.

In my profession, I am working in unity with:

1. _____
2. _____
3. _____

In my community, I am working in unity with:

1. _____
2. _____
3. _____

In my church and spiritual life, I am working in unity with:

1. _____
2. _____
3. _____

In my personal life, I am working in unity with:

1. _____
2. _____
3. _____

The Largest Obstacle to Unity

The most difficult obstacle to overcome as we attempt to create unity is the person we see in the mirror each morning. Most of us are tempted to think, *I am so important; you are less important, and most other people I know are not important at all.* Of course, we'd never say that—we just live that way! But egotism and unity are contradictory terms. It is impossible for a self-centered egotist to truly function in unity with others, because he or she thinks the whole world revolves around himself or herself. "Other people exist merely to meet my needs or to make me happy" is the unspoken but all too real attitude of the self-centered person.

Unfortunately, the reason so few of us experience the power, productiveness, and sheer pleasure of pulling together with a team is that we make our *selves* and our egos the top priorities. But if you are ever to enjoy the sort of unity required for a **More Than Enough** lifestyle, the "you" in "unity" must be silent. Most of the problems you will encounter in trying to develop unity with your spouse or your coworkers or your fellow citizens in the community can be traced back to selfishness on the part of somebody. You don't want that somebody to be *you!*

Take John and his wife, Marilyn. They are arguing over how they will spend John's $10,000 bonus check. Let's listen in on their conversation:

JOHN: I think we should use the money to buy that new "Sailfish" I was telling you about. Just think about how much fun we could have this summer with that boat!

MARILYN: But John, honey, we really need some new living room furniture.

Buying a boat seems frivolous to me, especially when our sofa and chairs are so old and tattered that I am embarrassed when any of our friends stop over. I've been waiting for years to redecorate that room. This bonus will give us enough money to finally do it.

JOHN: I know that, honey. And I appreciate your feelings. But really—it's my bonus. I worked hard for it. I earned it, and I think that I should be the one to decide how we're going to spend it.

Does Marilyn and John's conversation sound familiar? Not much unity going on, is there? Notice that neither of them is expressing much thought and consideration for the desires, vision, or goals of the other person. It was all about me, *me*, *ME*! "I want what I want." That is unbridled selfishness.

In your opinion, how could John and Marilyn have handled the situation in such a way as to create unity in their marriage? What should they have done differently in regard to the bonus money?

_____

_____

_____

Let's listen in to Marilyn and John a bit more:

JOHN: I have to say, Marilyn, I am not eager for us to spend my bonus check on new furniture. I understand your discomfort with the idea of buying a new boat. I hear you loud and clear. What do you say that we put our heads together and come up with something that we both agree on?

MARILYN: That's a good idea. And maybe we can set aside part of your bonus as a savings toward the boat and the furniture, too.

JOHN: Now you're talking!

That's the way unity in a relationship works. It means that each person lays aside his or her own selfish desires for the good of the relationship as a whole. It's amazing what we can accomplish when we are willing to help others achieve their dreams. Motivational master Zig Ziglar put it well when he said, "You can get everything in life you want if you help enough other people get what they want."

What do you see as the important elements in how Marilyn and John chose to handle the matter of John's bonus check?

_____

_____

_____

Get Time on Your Side

❖ Next to money, the way we use our time is one of the most telling indicators of what we consider to be important in life. Make this a rule: "Other than emergencies, I will not do anything to change our family schedule without consulting my spouse first."

Untangled Knots

When I was about ten years old, I took a water-skiing trip with a neighbor boy and his family. My friend and I had a great deal of enthusiasm, but not a lot of wisdom. Since we had more energy than the adults, and we really wanted to be the first to ski, we hurriedly threw on our life preservers and tossed the ski rope off the back of the boat into the water. We plunged into the cool water and swam to the ropes.

Unfortunately, we had been in such a hurry to get up on the skis, we had been careless about the manner in which we had tossed in the rope. In next to no time, we had a tangled mess of rope in tow behind the boat.

The interesting thing about ski ropes is that they may tangle mighty fast, but it seems to take forever to get them untangled! Especially when two excited ten-year-olds are the ones doing the detangling. The more my friend and I tried to twist, turn, and untangle the rope in the water, the more elaborate a mess we created.

Finally, the patient boat captain (otherwise known as my friend's dad) gave us a rope-untangling lesson. I've never forgotten the simple yet profound truth he taught us. When a ski rope that is attached to the boat starts to tangle, it usually does so in the middle rather than at the ends. The tangle is simply a series of twists, turns, and loops. So the trick to getting out the knots while the rope is in the water is to keep in mind that every twist leads back to another. If you try to untangle the knot where you find it, you will have an enormous task on your hands, and the rope will continue to tangle even more while you are working on it. One mess will loop into another, tangling up the entire rope and taking even more time to extricate, all the while robbing you of fun-filled skiing opportunities. With patience and perseverance, however, you can push or pull the rope back through the knots all the way to the end of the rope, and thus untangle the mess.

Achieving unity or causing disunity works in much the same way as those ski ropes. We need to understand that we are in this "tangle" together, and that most of the problem is looped back toward us, often as a result of our selfishness. Sometimes the loop gets twisted even worse because the more we try to defend our own interests, the more we tighten our grip on our part of the rope, pulling against progress rather than uniting to work together for positive solutions. With some patience and a willingness to lay down your self-orientation for the good of the group, the work of untangling the knots can be done easily and everyone will be better off as a result.

Remember, the chief opponent of unity is often looking back at you in the mirror. You may not always have the power to create unity in your workplace or in your marriage and family relationships, but you always have the power to destroy the unity that already exists. All you have to do is start "looking out for number one."

Describe the balance between being an ambitious, aggressive self-starter who works well alone, and the added effectiveness of working together on a team.

_____

_____

_____

Although unity is incredibly powerful, it is also extremely fragile. It can be easily broken. For instance, one of the things that almost instantly destroys unity, whether in the home, workplace, or community, is gossip. When the unity is broken, the next to go are usually respect, trust, and confidence. When that happens, anger, indifference, or disdain sets in, along with mistrust and suspicion. Let me show you how easily this can happen.

Sam and Dave shared a room at a hotel where their company had sent them to attend a large business convention. One night at dinner, Sam flirted with a young woman from another company. After dinner, Dave politely excused himself and returned to the hotel room so he could catch up on some reports. The hour grew late, and there was still no sign of Sam. "Why, that sly fox!" said Dave as he crawled into bed.

The following morning, Dave awakened to discover that Sam had not returned to their hotel room at all the previous evening. With no sign of Sam, Dave spent the coffee hour before the first morning session "sharing" his scoop of interoffice gossip with the other members of the company team at the convention.

Later that morning Sam showed up. It turned out that Sam had indeed spent the night with the young woman he had met at dinner. He and Sally had remained behind in the hotel restaurant to talk after the others had long since returned to their rooms. Suddenly Sally began to experience heart palpitations. When she explained her discomfort to Sam and revealed that her mother had died of a heart attack, they both agreed that it might be wise to have a doctor check Sally. They quickly drove to the nearest hospital emergency room, where the doctors kept Sally under observation all night long. Sam stayed with Sally, all right, but it wasn't the illicit romance that Dave had suggested to his and Sam's colleagues.

When Sam learned what Dave had insinuated to their coworkers, he was furious. He and Dave had worked together for more than three years, and he was absolutely shocked that Dave could suggest that he had done something immoral.

For several months following the incident, Sam and Dave's relationship remained strained. Coworkers noticed the chill in the air any time the two men were in the same room, so their fellow employees avoided being in close proximity to Sam and Dave for long. The men rarely looked at each other and spoke only in curt blasts. Questions and innovative ideas went unspoken because of the awkwardness other workers felt in the presence of the two estranged men.

Sam simply refused to trust Dave anymore. Despite Dave's feeble attempts at an apology—"Hey, old, buddy, you know I was just teasin', don't you?"—Sam was hurt, angry, and resentful that his friend and colleague had insinuated that he had done something "naughty." Dave's miscreant mouth destroyed the unity in his and Sam's working relationship, caused tension, division, and discord among their coworkers, and fostered further mistrust among the company team. Productivity in the company eventually dropped, and layoffs ensued.

What do you think Dave should have done when Sam did not return to their room that evening?

_____ Call his (Dave's) wife and say, "Honey, you aren't going to believe this one. . . ."
_____ Report Sam to his superiors.
_____ Go out looking for his friend.
_____ Wait up for Sam to make sure he was okay.
_____ Wait until midnight and then call the police.
_____ Inform the next person up in the company hierarchy of his concern.

Rather than creating discord by gossiping, Dave's wisest move would have been to inform the next person up in the company chain of command. This is a general rule of thumb in business that helps guard the company unity: Hand negative information up the ladder and positive information laterally or down the chain of command. If you have a gripe, a complaint, or a concern, take it up with your manager. Do not send negative comments down through your company ranks. It will serve no good purpose and it will disrupt your corporate unity. Seek to build a company culture that values unity above petty voices.

List three things that your boss or coworkers are doing right.

1. _____
2. _____
3. _____

What are some ways that you can believe the best about each other as you bring the best out of each other? (For instance, I can compliment the work of at least one colleague each day before the close of the day's work.)

_____
_____
_____
_____

A Key to Business Growth

In a business setting, unity means teamwork. If your goal is to get a quality product to market at a fair price on a tight schedule, you will need the combined efforts of every person on your staff—from the designers to the marketing people to the sales force and the shipping department. No one person can do the job alone. You must set your company goals and then each person in the team must do his or her part to achieve the success everyone desires. Once you enjoy a measure of success, if it is properly acknowledged (such acknowledgment need not always be financial incentives), it motivates the team to work together on the next project. Each person is recognized as a valuable part of the team and every individual is made to feel that his or her contribution to the end result is vital. This sort of group effort, focusing on unity of purpose, plans, and results, will cause most viable businesses to prosper far beyond what the sum total of the individuals could produce by working in isolation.

Putting yourself first is usually the short-range view. In what ways can you consciously attempt to put others first in your business?

_____
_____
_____

Who are you really working for? _____

_____

_____

Teach Your Children the Value of Teamwork

No parent sets out to raise a selfish child, but that is what our children will become if we neglect to teach them how to work together in unity with others. Think about it—you never have to teach a child to be selfish. That comes all too naturally. But you will spend eighteen years (and sometimes more!) teaching your children to be considerate of others. Start early with your children to instill within them the desire to seek unity with their siblings or friends. For instance, it is vital that you teach your children to share their games or toys. The simple act of sharing reminds a child that there are others in his or her world who matter, too.

Similarly, a family can do projects on which all the members can work together, whether it is building a backyard tree house or raking the autumn leaves. Certainly, a young child shouldn't be allowed to use power tools or other dangerous items, but even a toddler can bring Daddy the hammer. Even a young adolescent can saw a straight line on a board, or help paint the structure once the construction is completed. Look for ways to involve your children in the activity. You will not only build a tree house or rake some leaves, but you will be building self-esteem in your child.

Involve your children in group activities at your church, in school, and in the community. The trend nowadays is to allow kids to become more and more isolated, spending hours on end in front of computer screens or video games. This is a dangerous trend. Why? Because in the real world, kids need to learn how to function as part of a team. That's why groups such as the Boy Scouts, Girl Scouts, Little League baseball, soccer leagues, ballet dance groups, and school sports teams are valuable resources you should take advantage of. Participating in one or more of these groups will help teach your children the value of teamwork, working together toward a common goal to achieve success that all can enjoy. It will also foster a sense of camaraderie with their peers.

What group activities are your children involved in at church, school, or in the community that are helping them to learn teamwork and concern for others?

_____

_____

_____

List several potential activities from which you believe your children would benefit and learn more about functioning in unity with others.

1. _____
2. _____
3. _____

Unity in Your Marriage

One of the most important places to experience unity is in your marriage, in your relationship with your spouse. We've all heard it said, "Behind every successful man there is a supportive wife . . . and a shocked mother-in-law!" No doubt something similar could be said concerning many successful women.

Nevertheless, success in the workplace pales in comparison to discovering **More Than Enough** in your home. And a unified marriage is among the most important elements necessary to having **More Than Enough**. Unity in marriage does not mean that you and your partner submerge your personalities or give up your individual identities, ideas, and choices. Nor does it mean, however, that two "independent" people simply live together in the same house. Unity in marriage means that two previously "independent" people have made conscious choices to commit themselves to each other, to live together as

"Not Without Anna"

❖ The international competition had drawn the best of the best from all over the world. The focus and concentration showed on each of the warrior's faces as they lined up to begin the race.

The track judge raised the starter's gun and fired. The race was on! The competitors burst out of the blocks with all of their might. They rounded the first bend and then, to the horror of everyone in the stands, the unthinkable happened. One of the runners stumbled and fell, the hard track abrasively ripping her flesh open, causing a gaping wound. With blood spattering as she continued to tumble, the young woman screamed in pain.

The other runners heard the shrill, ear-piercing cries of their fellow competitor. Several of them turned to look back, slowed down, and then stopped cold in the center of the track. One by one the other female athletes stopped as well. They turned en masse and ran back to the young woman who had fallen. They gathered around her on the ground. One young woman held the fallen competitor in her arms. Another, a young woman with Down's syndrome, pursed her lips and blew on the fallen racer's bloody knees, hoping to make them feel better. Slowly and gently, the young women athletes lifted their friend from the ground, helping her stand.

Then an amazing thing happened. The racers locked arms and walked the remaining distance around the track together, crossing the finishing line as one unit, while the spectators in the stand stood to their feet, cheering with all their might!

As you may have guessed, this event was part of the Special Olympics, and although the incident would not be televised on many sports wrap-up shows, it was indeed a special moment in sports history.

During an interview after the race, one of the young competitors was asked why the runners went back to help their friend. The athlete looked at the interviewer with a marvelous, naive incredulity and replied, "When Anna fell, we had to go back. We couldn't win without Anna!"

That's the unity we want to see worked out in our lives. We can't win without each other.

Equal but Separate Often Leads to Divorce

❖ Many modern couples have been duped into believing that they are better off to maintain separate checking accounts and maintain their independence in other financial matters. Wrong! Separating your money in the name of independence robs you of the unity you want to develop in a great marriage. Separating your money puts you in the spiritual and emotional position of separation: You remember, what you do right before divorce.

---

husband and wife, sharing everything with each other—including their money—supporting and encouraging one another, sharing both the struggles and the victories of life together. "The two shall become one" is not merely a biblical truth, it is a powerful "secret" for any couple wanting to discover **More Than Enough**.

Why do you think some people are reluctant to put their money where their mouth is in marriage by combining all their financial resources with those of their spouse?

_____

_____

Which of these elements do you think might cause you and your spouse to want to maintain separate financial accounts? (Check all that apply.)

____ worries that the marriage will not work
____ loss of personal identity
____ greed
____ past mistakes
____ power issues (or attempts to wield power over your spouse through the control of your money)
____ different priorities than those of your spouse

___ freedom to spend what I want without accountability

___ misunderstanding of your spouse's strong points and weak points

___ fear that your spouse will mishandle your money

Do you see the possibility of maintaining separate financial accounts as a positive or a negative?

___ Positive   ___ Negative   ___ Uncertain

The Main Obstacle to Marital Unity

While most married couples readily admit that unity with their spouse is an admirable goal, few couples claim to have achieved it. The main reason why unity in marriage is so difficult to achieve (notice I said difficult, not impossible!) is because men and women are so *different*!

"Well, wow! There's a profound statement," you might be saying. "Men and women are different . . . and I paid good money for this book to find that out?"

Hold on. We all recognize that men and women are anatomically different; but in recent years, in one study after another, much to the disdain of those who would rather blur the distinctions between the sexes, science has confirmed that men and women function differently in a wide variety of ways—physically, emotionally, and yes, financially! Remember the old adage that "opposites attract." It's absolutely true . . . until those two opposite people get married to each other. Then the same characteristics that caused you to be attracted to your mate can become major irritations. See if this sounds familiar: One of you is on time for everything, while the other is almost constantly late. When one of you is too hot, the other is still cold. One is organized; the other is creative and messy. When it comes to money, one of you is a "spender," and one of you is a "saver." One is the "administrative planner" and the other is the "free spirit."

While you were dating, these contrary qualities fascinated, excited, and intrigued you about your potential mate. Now they just bug you. Perhaps you've wondered, *Why in the world did I ever marry this person in the first place?*

Whoa! Before you take another step down that path, let me remind you that opposites do attract. Most individuals marry their deficits; in other words, we marry a person who has the qualities that we don't. And that can work for you rather than against you, in marriage. The differences you and your mate exhibit can be turned into strengths if you will accept them as good points rather than as irritations. After all, as Larry Burkett of Christian Financial Concepts is fond of saying, "If two people just alike get married, one of you is unnecessary!"

One key to achieving unity in your marriage is that you must learn the language of your partner. Oh, sure, you think you heard what he or she said, but do you really know what your spouse meant? Someone sent me a tongue-in-cheek E-mail that might help explain this:

When a guy says, "Can I help with dinner?" what he really means is, "Why isn't dinner already on the table?"

When a woman says, "Honey, how was your day?" what she really means is: "Tell me every detail that happened, what color outfit the person wore, how he or she looked, what it sounded like, tasted like, how many people showed up, not simply expecting an answer such as, "Oh, fine."

When a guy says, "Take a break, honey. You are working too hard," the proper translation is: "I can't hear the game over the vacuum cleaner."

When a woman says, "Of course I want your input about the color of the dining room curtains," what she really means is, "Feel free to agree with me; otherwise hold your tongue!"

When a man says, "You look terrific in that dress," his thought is, "Please don't try on another outfit; I am starving!"

When a woman says, "Do you really want to wear that outfit?" what she really means is, "Please, go change your clothes!"

And if you hear the male in your life mutter, "I'm not lost. I know exactly where we are," what he really means is, "No one will ever see us alive again!"

Someone else told me some other ways in which men and women differ:

Women love to shop and find bargains. Men want to identify the target, kill it, and bring it home.

Men go on a seven-day trip and pack five days' worth of clothes; women pack twenty-one outfits because they never know what they will "feel like" on any given day.

The average number of items in a woman's bathroom is 123, and the average guy is hard-pressed to identify half of them.

Men think that leaving their dirty socks on the bathroom floor is the same as putting them in the hamper.

Women never have anything to wear.

The above stereotypes are humorous and sometimes even true, but we must remember that the foibles and idiosyncrasies of our marriage partners can be overcome with love, acceptance, commitment, and a desire to work toward unity in the marriage. Trying to change your marriage partner will be futile; it will simply create more stress for both of you. We must learn how to accommodate each other, to respect one another—especially in the areas in which we differ—and work together to create unity in the marriage.

Why is this important? Because unity in a marriage is one of the keys to building financial peace and maintaining a **More Than Enough** lifestyle.

Money Highlights the Differences

More than anything else in marriage, your attitude toward and use of money will exacerbate the differences between you and your spouse. For example, I teach audiences all across America that a major step toward their financial peace is to have a special "emergency fund," an account in which you keep enough money to cover at least three to six months' worth of your expenses. When I say this, I can see the lights turning on in the eyes of the women in the audience. They are not seeing dollar signs; they are seeing security signs. Men, on the other hand, who tend always to look for a bigger and better deal, want to protest, "Why would I want to leave ten thousand dollars in a low-interest account when I could invest that same money in pork rinds and make an extra gazillion dollars on it?"

Trust me on this one, guys. You will get a much better return on your money by creating the emergency fund and then leaving it alone—and the return will not just be measurable in dollars and cents. Every aspect of your marriage will improve when you and your wife work in unity to establish and maintain an emergency fund.

Your financial picture will improve because you won't be tempted to use credit when something breaks down around the house or in the car. Your physical health will improve because you'll sleep better knowing you are not broke. And believe it or not, even your sex life will improve because your wife—who is probably more relationship-oriented, feels safer and more secure knowing that you have enough money on hand to cover life's little emergencies—will be more comfortable and relaxed and . . . well, you get the idea.

> *The best investment you will ever make is*
> *an investment in your marriage.*

Think back to some of the "bigger and better deals" into which you have sunk money in the past. How did you and your spouse differ in approaching these deals?

_____

_____

_____

Money is at the top of the list of what most couples fight about, but "dollars and cents" need not be fighting words in your home. Money can be either the greatest bridge to communication in your marriage or the worst; it is up to the two of you. When it comes to money matters, you really cannot communicate too much—the more the better! But in your conversations, be sure to listen to your partner; listen not just with your ears but with your heart. Listen to one another's needs, wishes, desires, and dreams, and be willing to put some of your own desires on hold so you can help your spouse achieve some of

---

Talk Before You Buy

❖ Many couples have found it helpful to agree together that they will not buy anything more than a certain amount of money—say $300—without talking it over between the two of them first. If they cannot agree, the purchase is not made.

---

theirs. In every financial matter, ask yourself the question "What is best for the two of us together?" Beyond that, ask, "How will this affect our children?" Learn to look beyond yourself and you will begin to build unity into your marriage by your attitudes toward money.

The Dreaded "B" Word

Part of your conversations about money must include setting both short-term and long-term financial goals. This means you must establish and stick to a family budget, or a "cash-flow plan," as I like to call it. Don't let the idea of a budget scare you. Simply put, a budget is a written plan for how you want to spend your money. A budget doesn't tell you *how* to spend your money; you can spend it anywhere you want. It is, after all, *your* money. A budget simply helps you to spend it on purpose rather than by default. Let's start with some basic information to see how much you know about your family's financial picture right now.

Without looking at any financial records such as your tax forms, bank statements, or check ledgers, answer the following questions:

1. What is your total monthly income? (Include your monthly take-home pay, plus your spouse's, plus income from any other source.)

2. Approximately how much does your family spend each month on items such as food, gasoline, and clothing?

Food: _____

Gasoline: _____

Clothing: _____

3. Do you have a savings account or money invested anywhere? Where and how much?

Where: _____

Amount: _____

If you have no savings or investments, write NONE in this space: _____

4. On a scale of one to ten, how stressful is paying the monthly bills to you? (Circle one.)

1   2   3   4   5   6   7   8   9   10
Not stressful at all   Extremely stressful

5. How stressful would you say paying the monthly bills is to your spouse? (Circle one.)

1   2   3   4   5   6   7   8   9   10
Not stressful at all   Extremely stressful

6. What general conclusions are you drawing already concerning your need for a workable budget to handle your family's finances?

_____

_____

_____

Where's All That Money Coming From?

The first step in creating your budget is to determine what money you have coming in this month. You can use the "Income Source" page below to track the money you anticipate receiving this month. Income sources include your take-home pay, your spouse's take-home pay, and any other income from part-time jobs. You may have numerous other sources of income as well, so be sure to list all money you anticipate bringing in from bonuses, rental properties, royalties, freelance work, investment interest or dividends, alimony and child support, unemployment, Social Security, annuities, disability, trust funds, and even gifts of money that you might receive. If your budget is going to work, you must be accurate in reporting all your income.

Your Income Sources

Source	Amount	Period/Describe
Salary 1		
Salary 2		
Salary 3		
Bonus		
Self-employment		
Interest Income		
Dividend Income		
Royalty Income		
Rents		
Notes		
Alimony		
Child Support		
AFDC		
Unemployment		
Social Security		
Pension		

Source	Amount	Period/Describe
Annuity	_____	_____
Disability Income	_____	_____
Cash Gifts	_____	_____
Trust Fund	_____	_____
Other	_____	_____
Other	_____	_____
Other	_____	_____
TOTAL	_____	_____

Spend It All!

Now that you have determined how much money is coming in this month, let's decide how you want to spend it. We're going to design your cash-flow plan so you get to spend every penny you bring in—at least you can spend it all *on paper*, that is. In other words, you can assign a designation to all the money you have so you know what you plan to do with it in advance of getting it. You may plan to give some money away, pay some bills, save for a college education, or blow the money on a new set of golf clubs, but whatever you plan to do with your money, you will be doing it on purpose, not by accident.

Your Monthly Cash-Flow Plan

Category	Budgeted $	Subtotal	% Take-Home Pay
Charitable Gifts	_____		
		_____	_____
SAVINGS			
Emergency Fund	_____		
Retirement Fund	_____		
College Fund	_____		
		_____	_____

Category	Budgeted $	Subtotal	% Take-Home Pay
HOUSING			
First Mortgage	_____		
Second Mortgage	_____		
Real Estate Taxes	_____		
Homeowners Insurance	_____		
Home Repairs	_____		
Replace Furniture	_____		
Other _____	_____		
		_____	_____
UTILITIES			
Electricity	_____		
Water	_____		
Gas	_____		
Phone	_____		
Trash	_____		
Cable	_____		
Computer On-line	_____		
		_____	_____
FOOD			
Grocery	_____		
Restaurants	_____		
		_____	_____
TRANSPORTATION			
Car Payment	_____		
Car Payment	_____		
Gas and Oil	_____		
Repairs and Tires	_____		
Car Insurance	_____		
License and Taxes	_____		
Car Replacement	_____		
		_____	_____

Category	Budgeted $	Subtotal	% Take-Home Pay
CLOTHING			
Children	_____		
Adults	_____		
Cleaning/Laundry	_____		
		_____	_____
MEDICAL/HEALTH			
Disability Insurance	_____		
Health Insurance	_____		
Doctor Bills	_____		
Dentist	_____		
Optometrist	_____		
Drugs	_____		
Other _____	_____		
		_____	_____
PERSONAL			
Life Insurance	_____		
Child Care	_____		
Baby-sitter	_____		
Toiletries	_____		
Cosmetics	_____		
Hair Care	_____		
Education (Adult)	_____		
School Tuition	_____		
School Supplies	_____		
Child Support	_____		
Alimony	_____		
Subscriptions	_____		
Organization Dues	_____		
Gifts (Christmas)	_____		
Miscellaneous	_____		
		_____	_____

Category	Budgeted $	Subtotal	% Take-Home Pay
BLOW $$	_____	_____	_____
RECREATION			
Entertainment	_____		
Vacation	_____	_____	_____
DEBTS ($0, you hope)			
Visa 1	_____		
Visa 2	_____		
MasterCard 1	_____		
MasterCard 2	_____		
American Express	_____		
Discover Card	_____		
Gas Card 1	_____		
Gas Card 2	_____		
Dept. Store Card 1	_____		
Dept. Store Card 2	_____		
Finance Company 1	_____		
Finance Company 2	_____		
Credit Line	_____		
Student Loan 1	_____		
Student Loan 2	_____		
Other _____	_____		
Other _____	_____	_____	_____
GRAND TOTAL		_____	
—TOTAL INCOME		_____	
		_____	

Notice, included in your cash-flow plan are goals for savings, both short-term and long-term. Your immediate emergency fund of $1,000 is a short-term savings plan, and your fully funded emergency fund of six months' worth of expenses is a long-term savings plan. So, too, are your retirement and college funds. Even though some of these long-term goals seem far off and hard to get excited about, you must begin to contribute to them now if you want to see them grow more quickly.

By the same token, categories such as *replace furniture, car replacement,* and *vacation* are shorter-term goals. You should add money to these categories each month until you have enough to pay for the item, whether or not you plan to purchase a new car or furniture or take a vacation this year. Similarly, you will have other categories in your budget that you may not need each month, such as appointments with your physician or dentist. It makes sense to contribute to those categories each month so that when you do have a need, the money is already there and the medical or dental work does not bust your budget. (For a more thorough, step-by-step program to help you learn to budget and to stick with it, see my book *The Financial Peace Planner*, published by Penguin Books and available at bookstores everywhere.)

All this emphasis on budgeting may seem unnecessary, or an odd way to build unity in your marriage. Most assuredly, it is not. Creating a budget you and your family can live with contentedly is one of the main ingredients in a **More Than Enough** lifestyle. Beyond that, you will discover that when you communicate with each other about your money plans, and agree on your cash-flow plan in advance, you are agreeing to much more than a mere budget. You are agreeing on your priorities, your passions, your fears, your hopes and dreams, and yes, the power flow in your home. As you and your spouse take time each month to work together on your cash-flow plan, you will be communicating on a deep emotional and spiritual level, which will in turn strengthen your bonds to each other and increase the unity in your relationship in a powerful way.

Which of the following statements best reflects your attitude toward creating a workable cash-flow plan with your spouse? (Check one.)

____ I don't really want to know how much we are spending.

____ It will be easy once we get the basic information together.

_____ I don't have time to work on a budget. I'm too busy working!

_____ I've wanted us to take better control of our expenses for a long time.

_____ What good is it?

_____ Knowing what we are spending our money on will draw us closer together as a family.

_____ Who cares how much we have coming in or going out, as long as everything gets paid?

_____ A budget would cramp my style too much.

_____ I'm afraid of what we might find.

Unite Your Dreams

Before Jane and Ken married, they lived in separate, one-bedroom apartments in New York City. Jane's apartment was larger, but it cost nearly twice as much as Ken's. They both dreamed of owning their own home, so as they discussed what they wanted in their future and the best way to go about getting it, they decided that they would rather start their marriage in Ken's smaller apartment. That way they would be able to save more money toward their first house.

Throughout the first few years of their marriage, Jane and Ken worked hard, lived closely to their budget, and saved every penny they could to put toward their home. At times the inconvenience and stress of living in the cramped quarters of the small apartment almost tempted them to go out and foolishly rent or buy the first larger place they could find, but they encouraged each other, and together resisted the urge to splurge. When at last they were able to purchase the house of their choice rather than one of convenience, they knew that their temporary sacrifice had been well worth it. Furthermore, having achieved their dream together added a richness, depth, and stronger trust to their marriage relationship.

Jane and Ken handled their money responsibly. Unfortunately, many other couples don't fare so well. The number one cause of divorce in America today is money. Fights between marriage partners, anger and stress over debts, and the perpetual battles spawned by selfishness cause many potentially strong marriages to spiral downward to destruction.

Perhaps the saddest part of all is that, in most cases, the relationship could have been saved had the couple worked together in unity and gotten a handle on their finances. Proverbs 31:10 says, "Who can find a virtuous wife? For her worth is far above rubies. The heart of her husband safely trusts her: So he will have no lack of gain."

When you have unity in your marriage, you will have no lack of gain. That doesn't mean you will be unconscionably rich. But it does mean that you will be truly rich; rich in the things that matter—love, peace, security, and the ability to bless others. You will have **More Than Enough**.

Unity is an essential element in planning your future. It is essential in every area of your life, but especially in your workplace and in your home. As the Scripture (Matthew 12:25) says, "A house divided against itself cannot stand." But when you can combine your efforts with those of like mind and like heart, it will lead to better productivity, better attitudes, and better results. Unity, whether with your friends, family, neighbors, colleagues, or others in the community, will enhance your relationships, and position you to discover **More Than Enough**.

Aisle Three—Unity

1. Business Section

TAKING INVENTORY

On a scale of one to ten, how well does your company or business promote unity among your coworkers? (Circle one.)

1	2	3	4	5	6	7	8	9	10
Not very well				Okay				Extremely well	

What pet ego issue keeps you and your coworkers from enjoying unity in your business?

_____

Who or what might be able to change that situation?

_____

How might you offer assistance that will lead to unity at work?

_____

How frequently is the habit of handing negative matters up the chain of command and positive matters down the line incorporated in your business?

___ Hardly ever ___ Occasionally ___ Usually ___ Almost always

Your "To Do" List

List three things you can begin to do this week to help foster unity in your workplace.

1. _____

2. _____

3. _____

How do you plan to handle the situation when someone tries to pull you into negative or disloyal discussions in your workplace?

_____

Schedule a meeting with your manager to discuss how your company can better handle negative comments and information, sending it up the chain of command rather than down through the ranks.

List three areas in your workplace where you often find yourself tempted to be selfish rather than working with a "team" mentality.

1. _____
2. _____
3. _____

❖   ❖   ❖

2. Marriage Section

TAKING INVENTORY

What do you see as the largest obstacle to unity within your marriage?

_____

_____

List several areas of self-interest that are the toughest for you to keep from taking priority over the quality of your marriage relationship.

_____

_____

_____

What goals do you have that your spouse does not share?

_____

_____

_____

How are you presently handling the frustration that may exist as a result of those unshared goals?

____ I ignore those goals to work on goals we can agree on.
____ I tend to allow resentment to build because of my spouse's lack of interest in those goals.

_____ We have enough mutual goals that I am willing to allow my personal goals to wait for a while.

_____ I get angry when I realize that I am not fulfilling my dreams partially because of my spouse's attitude.

_____ I bring the subject up often and my spouse and I talk through our mutual and personal goals.

How faithful are you to doing a monthly budget together with your spouse? (Circle one.)

Extremely faithful   Occasionally   Once in a while   Rarely   Hardly ever

Your "To Do" List

When you are not too tired, hungry, or stressed out, you and your spouse should list several of the obstacles to unity in your marriage. Then swap papers and discuss your findings and your feelings. (Be sure to use phrases such as "I feel . . ." and "It hurts me when . . ." rather than making accusatory remarks about your spouse such as, "You always do . . ." or "Why can't you just . . .".) Remember, the goal is better communication and more unity, not firing verbal shots at each other.

List three things you can do as a couple that will increase communication and unity in your marriage. (For instance, "We can work out a monthly budget that we agree on." Or, "As a matter of trust and respect, we can agree to never spend more than $_____ without first discussing it.")

1. _____
2. _____
3. _____

As individuals, think of three things that your marriage partner has done for you recently that have genuinely touched you because of the unselfish nature of your spouse's actions. Share them with each other.

3. Parenting Section

TAKING INVENTORY

As a parent, which of your past behaviors have most disrupted your unity with your children?

_____

_____

_____

What steps have you taken to avoid such family divisiveness?

_____

_____

_____

What methods of discipline have you found to be most effective with your children, while maintaining love, respect, and unity in the family?

_____

_____

_____

If you have more than one child, how are you attempting to teach your children about the values of teamwork and working together toward common family goals?

_____

_____

_____

What steps have you taken to make sure that your children cannot divide your spouse's and your unity by trying to "play one parent against the other" to get what they want?

_____

_____

_____

Parents' "To Do" List

Discuss with your children the power of unity. Share with them examples from this chapter (for instance, the story of the geese, or the knots) that might help them see the value of teamwork.

Discuss with your children the destructive power of gossip and how it impairs unity. Let them give you examples of how they or their friends have been hurt by gossip.

Make it a rule in your family that the children must always speak positively about their siblings in the presence of the other children and their friends. They should bring any negative comments and concerns directly to you or to your spouse.

Discuss with your children what "team" activities they would like to participate in (after you and your spouse have discussed it between the two of you!). For instance, they could become involved with a church youth missions trip, a local group such as Habitat for Humanities that helps to build houses for low-income families, school sports, or other team recreational activities.

4. Singles' Section

TAKING INVENTORY

As a single person, it is easy to develop a selfish attitude since so much of your life revolves around you. What are you doing to avoid selfishness and to foster unity with others in your life?

_____

_____

_____

List several people with whom you feel you are currently working in unity.

_____

_____

_____

_____

List some ground rules that are important to you as you seek to establish unity in your workplace and in your personal relationships.

In the workplace: _____

_____

_____

In your personal relationships: _____

_____

_____

What are some other areas in which you would like to develop more unity?

_____

_____

_____

Singles' "To Do" List

List three steps that you feel you can take to increase the unity in the above areas in which you indicated that you would like to develop greater unity.

1. _____
2. _____
3. _____

Although it may be painful to recall, list two incidents in which you put "things" above people whom you love.

1. _____
2. _____

How will you change your priorities (if you have not done so already) when this sort of matter arises again?

Write out a short plan that will help you respond the next time someone attempts to pull you into a negative or disloyal discussion.

5. Financial Section

TAKING INVENTORY

Why is unity in your workplace such a powerful benefit to your "bottom line"?

_____

_____

List some ways that financial unity with your spouse will actually save you money.

_____

_____

_____

Since money problems are known to be among the leading causes of divorce, what steps are you currently taking to bring unity rather than division into your relationship with your spouse and your children?

_____

_____

_____

On an average day, how frequently would you estimate that you think about financial matters? (Check one.)

____ 0 to 10 times a day
____ 11 to 25 times a day
____ 26 to 50 times a day
____ 50 to 100 times a day
____ More than 100 times a day

How frequently would you estimate that your spouse thinks about financial matters?

____ 0 to 10 times a day
____ 11 to 25 times a day
____ 26 to 50 times a day
____ 50 to 100 times a day
____ More than 100 times a day

On a scale of zero to ten, how much does accumulating a large amount of money really matter to you?

0	1	2	3	4	5	6	7	8	9	10

Hardly at all   It's a major part of my life   It matters immensely

Your Financial "To Do" List

Describe the best financial investment you ever made in your marriage or family.

_____

_____

_____

List three ways that a fresh approach to budgeting will impact the unity you hope to have with your family members.

1. _____
2. _____
3. _____

Write out your "dream budget," basing it on your vision and goals and the amount of money you feel is sufficient to live a **More Than Enough** lifestyle.

FIVE

Hope—Fuel for the Explosion!

When we walk to the edge of all the light we have
and take that step into the darkness of the unknown,
we must believe that one of two things will happen:
there will be something solid for us to stand on or
God will teach us how to fly.

—*Patrick Overton*

HOPE IS THE FUEL in your life and in your finances. Hope sets you afire. It lights up your life and gives you the energy to achieve your vision and your goals. Hope is a motivator; it moves you to action. Hope is the power within you that drives you to reach for your dreams. Hope is absolutely essential in developing a **More Than Enough** lifestyle.

Without hope, paralysis sets in, productive forward motion stops, and the law of entropy—which basically says that everything is slowly but surely disintegrating—takes over. Without hope, negative attitudes abound. People without hope develop "can't-sir."

"I can't, sir. I can't do it. I can't make it. I can't take any more. It can't be done." And like the disease, this "can't-sir" can be a killer.

"I can't" is related to "I don't want to" and "I'm not going to." Instead of saying "if," we need to start saying, "I will." Instead of saying, "This is an impossible situation," we need to remember that all things are possible to those who will believe.

People who have lost their hope are prime candidates for depression. Their energy evaporates. They don't want to get out of bed, or if they do get out of bed, they just mope around, pace back and forth, walk in circles, or slouch through the day long enough that they can rationalize going back to bed.

"What's the use in trying?" they cry.

Not surprisingly, people who have lost their hope are often their own worst enemies. They are down and tend to bring everyone else around them down. They walk slowly, eyes down on the pavement; they rarely smile; they talk slowly, and when they do speak all they can tell you about are their problems. They have stopped searching for solutions. Their creativity has long since gone out the window. They may be trying to bring about change, but they have given up doing something different that might bring about new results. After a while, even people who might be able to help get so put off by them that they no longer want to be around the whiners. Nobody wants to hang out for long with a person who has no hope.

People without hope often begin blaming anyone or anything else for their problems. It's the government's fault. It's my spouse's fault. If only I had more of this or less of that. Mediocrity is my lot in life. It hurts too much to try anymore. My problems are just too overwhelming and can't be fixed.

One of the most dangerous things that happens to people who have lost their hope is that they start feeling sorry for themselves. Whether they say so or not, their attitude is, "Poor, poor, pitiful me. I think I'll go eat some dirt." And they do!

If the above description sounds like you or someone close to you, I have good news for you. There's *hope*! Most likely you have been placing your hope in the wrong places, and once that is corrected your hope can be rekindled, and the resulting fire will definitely stimulate you to move!

> Hope is one of the greatest gifts one human being
> can ever give to another.
> —*Ashleigh Bryce Clayton*

Scouting Fluid

❖ Going camping was a special part of my childhood. One of the best parts of camping out under the stars was the campfire that we made each evening. The campfire was more than light and warmth. It was community. It was the gathering place at the end of the day. It was the focal point around which we gathered to spin yarns or tell spooky stories until our sleep-heavy eyelids just wouldn't stay open any longer. Beyond all that, the campfire was just plain fun.

Building the fire, however, was not always so much fun. Sometimes the wood was wet, or too green, so it was difficult to light. Despite what you may have heard or seen in old Western movies, you can rub two green sticks together for a long time before you get a spark!

Consequently, my friends and I often resorted to what we called "scouting fluid." We doused the wood with gasoline, stood *way* back, and someone flipped a match toward the stack of sticks.

Whooooosh! A ball of fire erupted and suddenly, we had a campfire, a fire that gave off wonderful light, around which we could cook our meals, warm our bodies, and tell our stories. Looking back on it now, it's a wonder we also didn't have a forest fire or worse!

Okay, okay, so my friends and I were extremely foolish for doing something so dangerous, but I have never forgotten the ball of fire that came from that tiny spark.

Hope is much like that. The embers of your life may be dying, or barely even smoldering, but just a little bit of hope can cause those embers to reignite with incredible fire.

Since hope is essential to financial and family success, we must find ways to build it and protect it. In the pages to follow, you will discover four secrets of successful people that will help you stir up hope within yourself.

1. You Must Learn to See Failure as Temporary

Failure is only permanent if you allow it to be. Instead, if you see failure as simply a temporary setback, you are already getting prepared for a comeback! The only people who never fail are people who never try, so don't allow your failures to get you down. Stack them up and use them as building blocks to your future.

What is your usual reaction when you have poured all you have into something, whether a job, a business, or a personal relationship, and it doesn't work out? (Check all that apply.)

____ I get angry.
____ I get even.
____ I get depressed.
____ I get down on myself.
____ I blame God.
____ My sense of self-worth drops through the floor.
____ I view my failure as a stepping-stone.
____ I try to learn from what went wrong.

How would you like to respond differently to these kinds of setbacks in the future?

_____

_____

> Success is going from failure to failure without loss of enthusiasm.
>
> —*Winston Churchill*

Let's face it. Failure happens. It happens to all of us. How we respond to failure, however, will make the difference in our success. What do you do when you truly gave your best effort, only to fail again? When you worked as hard as you could, were as creative as you could be, and still fell on your face? What do you do? You get back up again and start over, that's what! Automaker Henry Ford said: "Failure is the opportunity to begin again more intelligently." And that is true. When you try something and it doesn't work, you are that much further along to finding the key that will work.

Thomas Edison, the indefatigable inventor who patented close to eleven hundred of his experiments, failed ten thousand times in his attempt to create a lightbulb. Was he wasting his time during those early endeavors? No way! He could say, "I now know nine thousand nine-hundred and ninety-nine ways how *not* to make a lightbulb." Thomas Edison refused to allow himself to become depressed over the failures he experienced as he expanded his knowledge. His motto was: "When things get you down, remember Jonah; he came out all right!"

You're not the first person to make a mistake; millions of people do it every day. The big difference between the failures and the fighters is that when a good fighter gets knocked down, he gets back on his feet and gets back into the ring.

So you've failed a time or two. Woody Allen, the famous film producer, *flunked* a class in motion picture production at the City College of New York. Leon Uris failed English three times in high school. He went on to write one of the most popular novels in history, *Exodus*.

Talk About a Failure!

See if you recognize this fellow: He was the tenth of eighteen children. His father was a heavy drinker; his mother deserted the family when the boy was only five years old. Consequently, this young man grew up in a series of foster homes—well, let's say he lived in them occasionally. He ran away eight times before he was seven years of age.

He failed two years of school and eventually was put into a reform school to straighten up his life. He did, and he became one of the best-known comedians of the 1970s. You can still catch reruns of his television programs today. When Flip Wilson flaunts his famous line "What you see is what you get!" he may be more psychologically accurate than he knows. Because how we view ourselves—as a failure, or as a success in progress—will make all the difference in whether we discover **More Than Enough**.

How have you handled failure in your relationships with your spouse or with your children?

_____

_____

What do you normally do when you make a career or business blunder that costs you big bucks, or possibly even your business, job, or career?

_____

_____

Don't Measure Your Future by Your Past

Some of us tend to brood over and analyze every detail of every mistake we make, sometimes dissecting each section of our failure for months, years, and possibly even a lifetime. What a waste of time! The only thing such intense introspection accomplishes is to dim your hope. Worse yet, by continually re-playing the mistakes of the past, you superimpose the image of failure on your subconscious mind, robbing yourself of hope in the future.

Your success in the future cannot be measured by the degree of failure in your past. Quite the contrary, truly successful people take the "baby-learning-to-walk" approach to failures. They recognize that before you get anywhere in life, you are bound to slip, stumble, and fall down numerous times; but that is all part of the process of learning to walk.

Imagine if that child learning to walk fell down and thought, *Well, that's it! I tried this walking thing and it didn't work. I'll just lie here for the rest of my life and somebody can take care of all my needs. I see that some people can walk. My brother and sister can walk, but not me. Somebody will have to carry me from now on. I just don't have what it takes to get up and walk.*

Would that be ludicrous, or what!

Furthermore, would you allow your child to quit trying after one fall? What about after ten attempts at walking, which resulted in ten failures? Would you say, "Well, I guess that poor baby is never going to make it. That child is never going to amount to anything."

Of course not! Why? Because you know that with every stumble, every tumble, and every fall, your baby is getting that much closer to standing up and saying, "Watch out, folks! Here I come!" With every defeat, the child gets closer to victory. You realize that the child's past failures are no indication of his or her future success.

And neither is yours!

Look at it this way: Failure is a necessary ingredient to success. No one wins at business, wealth-building, sports, love, or any other area of life without experiencing a few failures. Even golf's "six-million-dollar man," Tiger Woods, had to lose a few tournaments before he truly appreciated his success.

Success is not a tropical island where the sun is always shining but you never get sunburned, where the trade winds are always blowing but you never get a tropical storm, or where the water is always turquoise or blue but there is no chance of drowning in the waves. Success is usually steeped in smelly, wrenching, wearisome experience.

"What a minute!" you might be saying. "That sounds a lot like failure."

You're right. In fact it is failure, and lots of it; because most great success stories are built on mounds of failure. That's the true view from the top—the successful person standing atop a large pile of failures.

Great marriages are not built and solidified by everything working like a fairy tale. They are strengthened through the tough times, the pressure points, the stressful times that stretch you like a guitar string until you think you are about to snap. But you don't snap; instead, you become an instrument that is capable of beautiful music.

Similarly, great wealth is not usually acquired by winning the lottery, or inheriting a windfall. Great wealth comes from hard work, from sweat and sacrifice—not from leisure and laziness. Great success comes after trying a zillion times and falling flat on your face.

But through it all, those who want **More Than Enough** persevere and discover that our failures will lead us to success if we simply do not give up.

List several successes you have enjoyed in your life. What would you estimate your failure to success ratio to be for each success? (For instance, ten failures for one success.)

I succeeded at: _____
My failure to success ratio was: _____

I succeeded at: _____
My failure to success ratio was: _____

I succeeded at: _____
My failure to success ratio was: _____

List some lessons that you have learned through some of your failures.

_____

_____

_____

What provided you with hope through those failures and kept you going, giving you the strength to continue moving toward your goals?

_____

_____

_____

Let your past successes and the hope that helped achieve them motivate you to greater things today. Think of several of your past achievements that give you hope for tomorrow, and then write a statement indicating your reason for hope. (For instance, Because I succeeded in saving enough money to get out of debt, I have hope that I can save for a new house. Or, Because I lost twenty pounds, I have hope that I can lose ten more over the next five months.)

Because I succeeded _____

_____, I have hope that I can _____

Because I succeeded _____

_____, I have hope that I can _____

There are no elevators that will whisk you to the top in life; only staircases that you must climb inch by inch, step by step. When you stumble and fall, you simply get up, brush yourself off, and start back up the stairs again. Sure, it hurts sometimes when we fail. Yes, of course, it is embarrassing to take a tumble down the stairs, especially when a crowd is watching our progress. But don't dread failure. Use it to correct your course, learn from your mistakes, build on them, and stand tall and take another step up toward the top of the pile.

Someone once asked famous radio commentator Paul Harvey to reveal the secret to his success. Harvey responded, "I get up every time I fall down."

Similarly, each time you get back up after a fall, it will build hope in you, and that hope will spur you on to success.

2. Keep Perspective!

Another way to build and protect hope is to keep a proper perspective on the daily ups and downs of life. Life is a long-term investment, not a short-term cash cow. It is a marathon race, not a one-hundred-yard dash.

Interestingly, the ancient Chinese words for
"crisis" and "opportunity" are exactly the same.
It all depends how you look at it.

Someone once asked the great theologian J. Sidlow Baxter, "What is the difference between an obstacle and an opportunity?"

"Our attitude toward it," Baxter replied. "For every opportunity has a difficulty, and every difficulty has an opportunity."

Life can become overwhelming if we do not learn to measure current events and the immediate crises against the backdrop of time. Every day presents us with tremendous opportunities. But let's be honest, every day also presents plenty of worries, problems, and troubles that can steal our hope if we allow them to. Stan Mitchell, a pastor in Nashville, contends that most people spend much of every day struggling in some manner, dealing with frustrations, and that it is only as we look back over time that we are able better to see the victories that have been won.

Molehills can quickly become mountains when we lose perspective. Slight irritations become irreconcilable differences when we lose perspective. That's why we need to be careful when we become discouraged, or when we are not progressing as rapidly as we had planned. Give yourself a bit of time and maybe you will see things differently.

Time certainly has a way of providing us with perspective. For instance, on November 13, the *Boston Globe* headline read, ENERGY CRISIS LOOMS. The question in the subhead was even more ominous: "World to Go Dark?"

The year? 1857! The article painted a bleak picture because whale blubber was scarce, and thus the writer feared that the lanterns in Boston would soon be going out. Looking back from the perspective of time, we see how silly such doomsday predictions were. That gives us hope to face the future with a new strength and a knowing smile on our faces.

Births, Weddings, and Funerals

Those special occasions in all of our lives also help us to put things into perspective. Watching a newborn baby, for instance, reminds us that God is pro-life, that there is a future generation, the human race will go on, and the problems we face today, as serious as they might be, are simply that—problems to be solved, and obstacles to be overcome. And that gives us hope.

Weddings provide another excellent opportunity for us to put life in perspective. Have you ever attended a wedding and the entire time you were sitting in the congregation, all you could think about was your own wedding? As the music played, and as the bride swished down the aisle, didn't something well inside you, something in your heart that said, "Yes, we've had our struggles, and we'll have some more, but I am so glad for my spouse!" Something about that wedding made you want to squeeze the hand of your marriage partner just a little more tightly. Something about that wedding announced to the world, *There's hope*!

Perhaps the most sobering experience of life is when we are confronted face-to-face with death. Attending a funeral of a loved one or a close friend also puts life into perspective. It causes us to see more clearly those things that really matter, and it helps us to sort out the trivial things that are not going to stand the test of time.

Recently, a good friend of mine died in an auto accident. He was only fifty-one years old, and left behind a loving wife and three children, two of whom are still living at home. My friend was as good a man as I have ever known, a humble man who lived a simple lifestyle, and taught the Bible every day of his life . . . and lived by the book, too! He taught me much of what I know about the Bible. More than one thousand people attended his funeral, and every person there could have told a special story of how our friend had touched our lives.

Walking away from a grave site will cause us to reflect on our own lives like few other experiences. At times such as those, we need to ask ourselves the tough questions: Am I living for things that are going to outlast the grave? Have I contributed to the world what I ought? Am I taking the steps to make sure that my life matters? Have I touched other people in a positive way, a way that engenders faith and hope in their hearts?

What would you like people to say about your life when they attend your funeral? (Try to do this seriously! In other words, don't say, "He told us he was sick"!)

_____

_____

What things are you doing now that would inspire people to describe you in this way?

_____

_____

What things do you need to do in order to realize your vision of yourself?

_____

_____

3. Place Your Hope in Things That Last

Many people find themselves running shy of hope because they have placed their confidence in a person or a thing that has let them down. Sound familiar? In a way, we are set up for such disillusionment beginning in childhood. We trust and believe in our parents, and then one day we make a horrible discovery—our parents are human! They don't know everything; they don't have all the answers, and sometimes they do some things that are just downright wrong!

When we go to school, we expect our teachers to be bastions of all wisdom, but after a few years, we realize that they are even more imperfect than our parents!

Sometimes we place our hope in friends, or on our scholastic or business achievements, popularity, nice clothes, or nice cars. We place our hopes in our appearance or our material possessions or our financial accounts. Of course, when we get married, we hope that our spouse will be able to meet all our needs, and no human being can possibly do that. Sometimes we place hope in our pastors, or the church itself, and are let down. The truth is, none of these things can satisfy, so when we place our hope in people or things, it is only a short time before our hopes are dashed again.

What have been some of the "hope bashers" in your life? (Check all that apply.)

____ death of a spouse
____ destruction or robbery of my irreplaceable possessions (such as heirlooms or photos)
____ bankruptcy or potential bankruptcy
____ stress due to compulsive behavior, such as food, drugs, or alcohol addictions
____ divorce
____ death of a child or a parent
____ divorce of parents
____ exclusion from school, church, or other organization
____ chronic medical conditions
____ loss of job
____ missed opportunities
____ an unhappy marriage relationship

How have you backed off certain relationships because of disappointment with other people in your life?

_____
_____
_____

Most of us have thought at one time or another, *I'll be happy when* . . . What are some of the things that you have mistakenly thought would bring true happiness in your life? (Check all that apply.)

____ my education
____ my spouse

____ having children

____ reaching my financial goals

____ living in the "right" neighborhood

____ being able to buy whatever I want

____ my church

____ a new car

____ more money

Like the little boy's unfair expectations of his teacher, we, too, often impose our unfair expectations on other people. If we place our hopes in people or things, they are sure to be dashed. Parents are human; teachers and coaches are not gods; material things rust, break, and wear out. If your hope is in your house, car, jewelry, or some other material possession, somebody else will come along with more or better one day soon.

Debt, a Result of Misplaced Hope

When we worship at the altar of "stuff," we are engaging in short-term thinking that inevitably leads to increased debt and dwindling hope. We foolishly believe that if we can just acquire enough stuff, we will have happiness, health, popularity, acceptance, and prosperity. Instead, what most people discover is that they are in debt up to their eyeballs with tens of thousands of dollars on credit

---

"That Man!"

❖ One day, a first grader who had a "crush" on his teacher saw the teacher in the grocery store. The little boy was shocked when he discovered that his teacher was accompanied by a man! That man was the teacher's husband. The schoolboy's crush was crushed, as was the illusion that his teacher was at the school for his benefit.

cards, car loans, and other foolish purchases. We pay more than 20 percent interest to purchase things we really don't need with money we really don't have, to impress people we really don't like!

Moreover, when we suffer from "stuffitis," we are more likely to make other unwise financial decisions as well. We buy—or worse yet, we *lease*—an automobile that we cannot afford, the value of which decreases the moment it is driven off the sales lot. Nowadays, the average new-car payment costs $378 per month and takes fifty-five months to pay off. That same car loses a whopping 60 percent of its value during the first forty-eight months you are paying for it!

People who are desperate look at the monthly payment to determine whether they should purchase the vehicle, but people with hope will save their money and purchase an automobile that they can pay for with *cash*. If that is a $1,500 car, drive it with joy. If it is $10,000 vehicle, pay for it without financing it, and enjoy driving that car without having to worry about making any monthly payments.

If you learn to delay gratification and save for what you want, rather than going into debt to get what you think you deserve, you will discover the secrets of compound interest working in your favor, instead of against you. It's tough to catch up on your bills when you have interest rates of 18–22 percent added to your bills every year. On the other hand, if you are earning 10–12 percent interest on money you have invested, the amount of money you can amass in a lifetime is absolutely amazing!

Take that car payment of $378 a month that we mentioned above. If you invest $378 per month in a good growth stock mutual fund at age twenty, by the time you are seventy years old, that money will have grown to more than $14 million! You won't have to worry about buying a car—you can buy a company!

Savings Evoke Hope

Certainly our hope is not in money, but there is something about having some money laid aside for a rainy day that causes hope to well in your heart. When you have a significant amount of money in savings, you tend not to sweat the small stuff . . . or even much of the big stuff, because you know that you have enough money in the account to handle it. Can you imagine how much better people sleep at night when they don't have to worry about having enough money to replace the tires on the car that are wearing out, or having enough money to get the kids some new school clothes? Can you imagine how peacefully you can sleep when you know that you are not relying on a Social Security check to pay for your food?

Whatever stage in life you are currently enjoying, you must develop a savings and investing plan. The first step in your plan is to prepare for the unexpected—the child that gets sick and needs immediate medical attention that your insurance doesn't cover, the water heater that gives out on you, or the spouse who is suddenly laid off from work, significantly reducing your anticipated income. These unexpected calamities of life, although not usually life-threatening, are often the storms that can sink a financial ship that is barely limping along.

The best way to prepare for the unexpected is to *expect* it! Anticipate it, plan for it. It is not negative thinking to be wise, to see potential problems in advance and take steps to avoid them. That is simply wise economic planning.

The first step in your plan is to establish an "emergency fund," a savings account or a money market account at your local bank or credit union. Don't worry about trying to get a high rate of interest on this account. Instead look for liquidity—open an account in which your money is readily available to you and into which you can easily make deposits and withdrawals that won't penalize you for using your own money. Your first goal, what I like to call the first "baby step," is to save $1,000 in this account. This is the beginning of your emergency fund. When things break or must be replaced, this is the account from which you draw the money, not a credit card or a loan. As soon as possible, after paying for the flat tire, or the broken window, or whatever the emergency might be, you replenish this fund and keep at least $1,000 in it at all times.

Once you have the $1,000 cushion, begin adding to your emergency fund until you reach your goal of having enough money in that account to pay six months' worth of your basic living expenses. This is your "fully funded emergency fund." It is the account that you maintain and from which you draw money to deal with life's little emergencies. This is not a vacation account or a new-car account (unless you must suddenly purchase a very inexpensive used vehicle in an emergency). This account is to help you sleep better, knowing that you don't have to go into debt to handle the day-to-day financial "surprises" that hit you.

How would it affect your life if you knew that should you or your spouse lose your job tomorrow, you have six months' worth of living expenses set aside?

_____

_____

How would that knowledge affect your stress level?

_____

Investing, Hope for the Future

If your savings account gives you a bit of security, learning to invest money will absolutely announce to your heart and mind that you are believing in a great future! As with your savings account, it is not how much money you start with, it is simply important that you *start*! Sure, you will most likely start small. That's fine. You don't have to be in the same income brackets as Donald Trump or Bill Gates before you begin investing. You can start by putting a few hundred dollars in a mutual fund or some other strong-performing investment vehicle that will grow your money at a healthy rate of at least 10–12 percent. For more specific information concerning how to decide what you should invest in, see my books *Financial Peace* and *The Financial Peace Planner*.

As a general rule, you should seek to invest at least 10 percent of your income. If you can invest more in college funds, IRAs, 401(k) plans, or whatever, that is better yet!

Don't keep your investments a secret from your loved ones. Let your family know that you are investing together in the future. By informing them that you are working together to build a strong financial base for their future, you will diffuse their worries and engender hope in your family members. Your family will recognize that you are looking out for their long-term interests, that you are seeking to help them fulfill their dreams (not just saving to acquire your latest whim or new toy), and that will help create more hope, the financial fuel that your family can use to reach even further in order to achieve more of their dreams.

Have you started investing in your future?

_____ Yes _____ No

If not, why have you not begun to set aside *something*, even if it is even a small amount of money, as an investment?

_____

If you can't afford to start investing now, when *will* you be able to afford it? (Hint: This is a trick question!)

_____

List three "expense" items in your monthly cash-flow plan that you might be able to reduce and thus find some money that you could invest.

1. _____
2. _____
3. _____

4. Hope from Above

In you want to have **More Than Enough**, you must realize that the only safe place you can put your hope is in God. He is the only one who is truly worthy of your hope and he is the one who will never ultimately disappoint you. One of the ways you can better track God's work in your life is by keeping a journal. A daily written account of the problems you are experiencing as well as the opportunities and successes that you achieve will be an invaluable aid in raising your level of hope. Write down your fears and concerns, your joys and your triumphs, your disappointments and your goals. Look for the little things—the beauty of a flower or the joy that the smile of your child brings to your heart. Don't worry about writing a masterpiece or trying to impress anyone with your literary ability. Just write from your heart.

Months or years from now, when you read through the pages of your journal, you will see how God has never let you down, how he has continued to provide for you, and how your faith in him was validated. Your faith will expand and your hope will increase as you realize how good and faithful God has been to you.

Another way to increase your hope is by serving others. When you are tempted to feel down about your circumstances, look around you and find someone else who is hurting and needs a hand. Sometimes the best thing you can do is to volunteer at your church or at your local city mission and help serve those who are less fortunate than you.

In the midst of a divorce and a bankruptcy, one fellow I know volunteered to serve and clean up at the Sunday meals at his local Salvation Army. He later said, "I had been feeling sorry for myself and wallowing in self-pity, but when I walked in those doors and saw so many other men whose lives had been decimated by their circumstances, I realized that my problems were minuscule. I had a home, a car, food in my refrigerator, and people around me who loved me and were willing to help me get back on my feet. Most of the guys for whom I was passing out food and cleaning tables had none of those things that I was taking for granted. First I apologized to God, and then I thanked God for the many blessings he had poured into my life. I went there to help and to be a blessing. But I came away being the one who was blessed by being there. Serving at that Salvation Army was the first step in my own recovery."

Finally, to increase your hope, establish some symbols in your life that remind you of what God has done for you. The lighthouse has become this kind of symbol for my coworkers and me. Around our office we collect and display lighthouses everywhere—in paintings, books, and ceramic representations. If it looks like a lighthouse, we'll put it where somebody can see it. Why? Because to us, the lighthouse symbolizes what our company does. Just as a lighthouse along the seashore gives hope and direction to a ship lost out in the fog, our company provides hope and direction to people who are financially lost, or possibly getting ready to smash against the rocks of life. For those who are doing well, we point them to safe harbors where they can rest, relax, restock, and prepare for the next exciting leg of the trip. To us, the imagery of the lighthouse is a potent reminder that we are not just coming to work each day, we are providing help and hope to people.

What are some symbols or stories that have impacted your life in a positive way, providing comfort, peace, and hope?

_____

_____

_____

What symbol of hope can you display around you that will remind you of your blessings? (For instance, you may display family pictures in your office, or a particular motivational quotation, or some trophy that inspires you and those around you.)

_____

As you practice the **More Than Enough** lifestyle, you will discover each day that hope is essential to creating abundance and wealth. Hope is the "scouting fluid" that will help ignite your creativity. Fan the flames of your hope today by reviewing these reminders:

1. Hope is an act of your will; it is a decision.
2. Failure is normal; it will happen. Don't allow failure to steal your hope.
3. Hope allows you to act, rather than being stuck in the mud.
4. If you and your spouse are in the midst of a crisis, help each other to find the hope that will guide you through it.
5. Hope will not be found in things, institutions, people, or material goods.
6. Do not use credit cards or shopping sprees to make yourself feel better; these are not generators of hope, but rather robbers of it.
7. Use a symbol of hope—be it a lighthouse or something else—as a way to raise your chin toward heaven when you lose direction.
8. Give to others, because in giving you will find perspective and subsequently hope.
9. Remember your visions and goals because the road toward making them a reality offers hope.

Aisle Four—Hope

1. Business Section

TAKING INVENTORY

In what ways has your company's past failures and current "crisis-of-the-moment" impacted the growth of your business?

_____

_____

_____

On a scale of one to ten, how much of your personal hope for your future has been linked to your company's success? (Circle one.)

1	2	3	4	5	6	7	8	9	10
None	Very little		A moderate amount			A great deal		All of it	

Do you feel that you have placed too much hope in this area?

___ Yes ___ No ___ Uncertain

Other than money, what other significance do you derive from your career or employment? (For instance, I find meaning in helping other people achieve their dreams):

_____

_____

_____

Your "To Do" List

List three failures in your life that have later led to success.

1. _____
2. _____
3. _____

What are some practical things you can do to help keep your business and career in perspective?

_____

_____

_____

Briefly describe three times when you have misplaced your hope in relationship to your business dealings, and what you learned from each experience.

1. _____
2. _____
3. _____

If success is "standing on a pile of failures," what does that mean for your company or business?

_____
_____

2. Marriage Section

TAKING INVENTORY

How have your unrealistic expectations let you down in your marriage, while poking holes in your hope?

_____
_____

In your opinion, what percentage of your marital spats and disagreements with your spouse are caused because *you* are not looking at the long-term picture?

____ 10 percent
____ 25 percent
____ 50 percent
____ 75 percent
____ 100 percent

What percentage of your marital disagreements are caused because your spouse is not looking at the long-term picture? ____

List several small failures in your marriage that have actually served to draw you and your spouse closer together.

1. _____
2. _____
3. _____

Are you currently holding on to any resentments toward your spouse or hurt feelings from failures in your past?

_____ Yes   _____ No

Who would you be willing to talk to concerning such matters if they existed in your marriage? (Check all with whom you feel you could confide.)

_____ my spouse
_____ my pastor
_____ a professional counselor
_____ a close friend
_____ my parents
_____ my spouse's parents
_____ nobody

Your "To Do" List

List three things that you believed about your spouse before you were married that turned out to be false or misleading. Discuss with your spouse how these things have impacted your relationship.

1. _____
2. _____
3. _____

Develop a written "Marriage Peace Treaty" concerning what steps the two of you will take to prevent small irritations from exploding into "World War III."

Discuss with your spouse how sharing your visions and goals has increased hope in your relationship.

Discuss specific ways in which you have unfairly placed your hope in each other. (Caution: Keep your comments positive and personal. Remember to use terms such as "I feel . . ." and "It hurts me when . . .")

3. Parenting Section

TAKING INVENTORY

What are some of the things your children have taught you about the positive power of failure?

_____

_____

What impact has raising children had on your perspective? On your understanding of what is important against the backdrop of time?

_____

_____

In what ways are you attempting to teach your children to place their hopes accurately?

_____

_____

In what ways are you teaching your children to handle failure? (For instance, when Danielle missed the ball during a soccer game, allowing the opposition to win the game, I tried to point out to her the many other fine defensive plays she made.)

_____

_____

_____

Parents' "To Do" List

Use the example of learning to walk to initiate a discussion with your children about failure and its relationship to achieving their goals and getting where they want to go in life.

If your children are mature enough, have them list several things or people in whom their peers are placing their hopes, things that will only lead to disappointment and disillusionment.

Teach your children about the power of hope by reminding them of some symbols like the lighthouse, which provides hope and direction to people who need it. Encourage your children to establish their own symbols of hope.

4. Singles' Section

TAKING INVENTORY

List several areas of your life in which you are currently struggling with a lack of hope. (For instance, "my social life—I am so lonely," or "my finances—I just can't seem to get ahead.")

_____

_____

_____

List two instances in which you placed your hope in the wrong things.

1. _____

2. _____

What is the most important lesson you learned as a result of those experiences?

_____

Is there some past failure in your life that you feel is still holding you back?

___ Yes ___ No ___ Uncertain

If yes, how can you turn that failure into a step that you can use to move up the ladder of success?

_____

_____

In what ways have you been able to regain your perspective after having lost it briefly?

Your "To Do" List

Think back to the areas in which you designated a current lack of hope. What do you believe has caused that lack? What truth in this chapter encourages you that you will soon see your hope increased in these areas?

Recall three times in your life that failure has proved to be nothing more than a stepping-stone to success.

Purchase a book or check one out of the library that will inspire you (for example, the Bible, *Barlett's Quotations*, or others). Make reading portions from these books a part of your daily regimen.

Establish some symbols of hope in your life.

5. *Financial Section*

TAKING INVENTORY

List three of the worst failures in your financial history, whether they were your fault or not.

1. _____

2. _____

3. _____

What lessons did you learn from those failures that have kept you from making the same financial mistakes again?

_____

_____

_____

List three of your greatest financial successes.

1. _____

2. _____

3. _____

What repeatable lessons did you learn from those successes that will help you when facing new financial challenges?

_____

_____

_____

Your Financial "To Do" List

List several ways that having money in savings has inspired hope in you.

_____

_____

_____

How has this hope affected your attitude?

_____

_____

How has this hope affected your health and physical appearance?

_____

_____

How has this hope affected your ability to earn money for your visions and goals?

_____

_____

Plan to attend your house of worship this week. Either when you enter or before leaving, take a few moments to express to God that you are placing your hope in him. Thank God that you can safely and securely trust him with your hope.

Create or purchase a "symbol of hope" that you can keep in a visible spot in your workplace. Each time you see the symbol over the next six weeks, remind yourself of what that symbol means in your life.

SIX

People Who Need People—Support and Accountability

You must fly with eagles, not scratch with turkeys.
How can the synergy of turkeys create anything but
getting your goose cooked?

—*More Than Enough*

WE ALL NEED other people in our lives—people from whom we can learn and draw support and strength; and people who will love us enough to tell us the truth about ourselves. When we clam up and withdraw from the people who love and support us, choosing to live in self-imposed isolation, we seal our own tombs. As much of a pain as other people can be sometimes, we really do need each other!

William Thayer, a wise biblical scholar, said: "The best companion is one who is wiser and better than ourselves, for we are inspired by his wisdom and virtue to nobler deeds." That's what *accountability* is all about—not somebody looking over your shoulder waiting for you to make a mistake, but someone who knows you at your worst and your best, and who chooses to inspire you to nobler living.

The truth is, we tend to become very much like the people with whom we spend the majority of our quality time. Have you ever heard born-and-bred northerners who have lived in the Deep South for ten or fifteen years? Why, you'd think they took speech lessons from Scarlett O'Hara! Or, have you ever noticed the evolution of a married couple? After a decade or so together, they actually tend to look a little alike! (Now that's a scary thought for my wife!)

It's true. We take on the mannerisms, the verbal expressions—and more importantly—the *attitudes* of the people with whom we spend the majority of our time. That's why if you want to succeed, it is important for you to associate with people who have succeeded and are succeeding. Find someone who is doing what you want to do, who is the kind of person you want to be, and invest your time there. Keep your mouth shut more often, and your eyes and ears open, and you will soon discover the secrets of the people who have **More Than Enough**.

If your goal is to be a party animal, hang out with the party animals. If your goal is to be a football fan who knows the intricate details of the game, hang out with people who really know football. If your goal is to have a better marriage, spend time with other couples who take their marriage commitment seriously, who enjoy working on their relationships to make them better, and who are constantly striving to improve. Of course, in this regard, it also helps if you hang out with your spouse!

If your goal is to prosper financially, to have **More Than Enough**, you will want to be around people who will help you learn more, be more, and have more. Ironically, other *people* are almost always key ingredients in whether you will succeed or fail in having **More Than Enough**. The only question is: With what sort of people will you surround yourself? People can help lift you up, or people can pull you down.

At this point in your life, who are the individuals that are having the most impact on you, whether positively or negatively? List at least three names, and then check a P (positive), an N (negative), or an I (indifferent) next to each name to describe the type of influence that person is having on you.

Person	**Type of Influence on Me**
1. _____	___ P ___ N ___ I
2. _____	___ P ___ N ___ I
3. _____	___ P ___ N ___ I

Relationships That Matter

Nothing will have more long-term influence on you than your personal relationships. Television, as pervasive as it is, will not; nor will the internet, with all its opportunities and drawbacks; no college course or book will touch your life as profoundly as the people with whom you associate. Relationships are what really matter in this life. But relationships take *time*! Relationships require the commitment of effort and communication, two things that are rapidly disappearing from our culture. Unfortunately, in our "gerbil-in-a-wheel" world, where we are running around more and enjoying it less, we are also losing touch with the art of mentoring, teaching and learning how not only to do something, but to be somebody.

A mentor is not some ethereal sage from East Asia or some ghostly figure wrapped in a shroud who appears in the middle of the night with words of wisdom for us while we sleep. No, a mentor is simply a wise and trusted person who is willing to invest time and energy in you, and to whom you are willing to grant permission to examine your life, to point out areas in which you can improve, and to encourage you in the areas in which you are doing well.

We need mentors whose lives we can emulate. We need mentors who have "been there and done that" and can show us the way. These mentors cannot do the work for us, but they can serve as guides, pointing us in the right direction. They can be positive influences in our lives, people who will hold us accountable to keep reaching for our visions and goals, and who will insist that we make a habit of doing what is right and what is good for us.

For these mentors to be credible in our lives, we must believe in them; we must know that they have achieved the goals we are trying to achieve, that they have succeeded in the areas in which we are looking to them for advice and wisdom. To put it bluntly, I don't go to my divorced friends for advice on how to improve my marriage (even though some of them have learned some valuable lessons from which I can gain insight), and I don't go to people who are broke for advice on how to handle my money! For accountability to really work, we must find mentors and "fellow travelers" whose advice we can respect.

What does accountability have to do with discovering how to have **More Than Enough**? Simply this: When you surround yourself with wise people to whom you are accountable, you will build more wealth in your life. These people will help you avoid making the same financial mistakes over and over, and they will also help you to keep your priorities straight as you are trying to maintain the delicate balance between work and family. Moreover, if you do slip and stumble, your "accountability partners" will be there to help you get back on your feet again.

We may have a wide variety of accountability partners over the course of our lives. Your parents, your spouse, a coach, a mentor, or a small group designed to deal with a particular behavior pattern can be good accountability relationships. The most important accountability partners we usually find in our lives are our parents, prior to our marriage; and our spouse after we marry.

Think back to your childhood for a few moments. In which ways did your parents make you accountable for your attitudes and actions? (For instance, "Mom always made sure that I had my school projects in on time." Or, "I had to be in by midnight or I lost my driving privileges for a month.")

_____

_____

_____

Some areas of accountability that most parents remind their children about are:

1. schoolwork
2. chores
3. being prepared and on time for after-school activities
4. potential conflicts

In looking back, some adults think, *Oh, yes, I remember Mom and Dad nagging me about those things*. Others rub their chins or bald heads in amazement as they realize, *Now I see what Mom and Dad were doing!* They were:

1. helping me to excel in school
2. teaching me to be responsible
3. ensuring that I would receive a well-rounded education
4. showing me appropriate ways of dealing with conflict

All too often, accountability is not fully appreciated until you can look back on it and see its benefits.

List some individuals other than your parents who have helped you to learn accountability as a young person. Next to their name, describe what they taught you and say thank you. (For example, Uncle Ronnie. Thank you, Uncle Ronnie, for teaching me what to look for in buying a used car.)

_____

_____

_____

Accountability Partners for Life

If you are married, your primary accountability partner will be your spouse. That is not to say you cannot have other accountability partners, but your spouse and you should have a relationship in which you are each other's best checks and balance system. This can certainly create friction—especially regarding the topic of money. Who spent what and why are not always fun issues with which to deal in marriage. Many couples slip into a habit of telling subtle (and sometimes not so subtle!) lies about how their money is being spent. "Oh, that new car is just a few dollars more per month than what we're paying now." Or, "Well, if you think that I'm spending too much on groceries, why don't you do the shopping this weekend and I'll stay home and watch the game on television!" That's just one more reason why we need a cash-flow plan. It will help us to be honest about what we are really spending, rather than what we are pretending.

Furthermore, every couple should have a spending cap, a dollar figure that each of you will not exceed as individuals, no matter how great the deal, without your spouse agreeing to the purchase. Notice I said *agreeing to*, not simply being informed about the purchase. My wife, Sharon, and I have a hard-and-fast rule that we will make no major financial decisions without both of us agreeing to them. For us, "major" translates to "any purchase over $300." But it also means that we do not keep any dirty little financial secrets from one another. Nor do we make major money decisions on impulse. Knowing that we are both accountable to each other in this regard builds trust into our relationship, and probably also saves us big bucks each year.

As main accountability partners, you and your spouse must be aware that sometimes your motives may become blurred by your own self-interest. That is natural in marriage, but it can also be counterproductive. For instance, if your spouse wants you to do better in your career simply so he or she will have more money available, that is not always the best motive. Similarly, if one of you is trying to encourage new habits in your marriage partner, be careful that you are not a "control freak" just trying to get your spouse to do what *you* really want done, rather than acting out of love and concern for your partner.

True accountability in marriage is centered on unconditional love—that you love your partner not for what he or she can do, but for who that person is. You love your spouse not for how much money your mate can earn, but who you can be together. In this case, one plus one should equal more than two. Together as one, you are better than the sum total of the two of you as individuals. If your spouse messes up, you are not there to nag or criticize, but to help him or her see more clearly a better way of handling the situation. Even when corrections must be made, your love should not be rescinded or quenched in any way. To have that kind of accountability in your marriage, you must spend a great deal of time together, making sizable deposits in each other's emotional love bank.

You must also view nagging as a serious overdraft, a bounced check in your account, sucking out everything you have invested in that relationship and sometimes more! Don't do it! Speak positive words of encouragement to each other. Encourage the actions and attitudes you want in your spouse (and in yourself), rather than emphasizing what you don't have or what you don't want.

Money Talk

❖ Try to incorporate statements such as the following when you are talking to your spouse about money matters:

WIFE TO HUSBAND:

"Honey, I need *your help*."

"Would you *invest* some time in our marriage by helping me with this?"

"Sweetheart, it would be such *a help to me* if you could sit down with me so we can figure this out together."

HUSBAND TO WIFE:

"Honey, I'd really like to have *your advice* on our budget."

"We need to think about how we are going to save money, but I can't do this *without you*."

"Our future is important, and *both* of us need to plan it *together*."

When talking with your spouse about money matters, be sure to use "I feel" statements rather than accusatory comments. When you say, "I feel abandoned when you won't help me with the bills," it is gentler than saying, "You abandoned me and your children because you won't help with the bills."

Singles Need Not Be Alone

Some amount of accountability accompanies a wedding ring whether a married person wants it or not. There are legal and moral obligations implicit in a marriage that are not always in place for the single. Moreover, just the fact that a married person must face his or her spouse provides some measure of accountability as to how he or she has used time, money, food, beverages, or other resources.

However, if you are unmarried, please do not ignore the matter of accountability, thinking, *Aw, that's only for those married folks!* On the contrary—a single person needs accountability in his or her life as much or more than do married couples. Many singles have nobody but God to whom they must answer for what they are doing with what they have. That's probably one of the positive points about being single, but it is also one of the most dangerous!

If you are single, you should seek out a friend or a trusted adviser or a group of people with whom you meet regularly in some type of accountability relationship. This should not be somebody you are dating unless you are engaged, and very close to your wedding day. Prior to then, you should have an "outside" adviser whom you can trust for wise, objective insights concerning your life, possibly your pastor, your boss, or a group of people with whom you have some common interests. When you are about to do something foolish or harmful to your relationships or your finances, you need someone who is willing to throw some cold water in your face (figuratively, of course) to get your attention.

A Few Is Better

Let's face it. Whether single or married, you are probably not going to find a large number of people to whom you want to grant permission to enter the inner chambers of your life. And frankly, many people nowadays simply do not want to be bothered with a mentoring or accountable relationship with another person. Not everyone can commit the time and energy necessary for such a relationship. That's okay. You will benefit more by meeting regularly with a smaller group of people in a more open, vulnerable environment—in other words, where you can speak freely with each other without fear of condemnation, reprisal, or rejection.

Where do you find such a group?

Close friends are often better candidates than family members, because our family members are sometimes as much a part of our problems as they are the solutions. People at your church may possibly enter into such a relationship with you; your pastors (although most pastors need accountability groups of their peers); teachers, coworkers, or those in similar professions as yours might provide the foundations for a good accountability group. Many large churches nowadays encourage "cell" groups—smaller meetings in the homes of members of the larger congregation. Like any support group, we usually do best with people with whom we have common interests. You may choose to be part of several groups, each with a different focus.

Over the years, I have watched our Financial Peace University attendees become support groups to each other in the areas of money and relationships. About twenty people per class in various cities around the country meet together for thirteen weeks to view our Financial Peace video series, to discuss the "homework" assignments associated with each class, and to hold each other accountable for doing the work of getting out of debt and moving into financial abundance. It is thrilling to watch these groups of people—most of whom have never met prior to becoming part of the class—meld into a small platoon of crusaders, determined to help each other find financial peace and then move on to having **More Than Enough**. Some members of the groups choose to stay in contact long after our course is completed, keeping each other accountable to do the things that will help them prosper financially.

If you can find a small group of people that you trust, with whom you will be honest, and a group that will be straightforward enough with you to look you in the eyes and tell you the truth, that group will be one of the most valuable assets of your life. It will be a buoy when you are sinking; it will be a ladder to help you out of the pits; it will be a supercharged booster rocket that will help you reach for the stars.

It can also be an "in-your-face," "smack-you-upside-your-head," "get-back-on-track-or-else" sort of group if you want it to be. That corrective aspect of accountability is a bit disconcerting to some people and may actually keep the more timid among us from becoming involved in a small group accountability relationship. But we all need some people around us who care enough to shoot straight with us, to look us in the eyes and say, "I don't think that is a wise thing to do," or "I wish you would get more information about that investment before you sink your life savings into it." Most important of all, we need somebody to tell us, "I think you are wrong."

> The trouble with most of us is that we would rather
> be ruined by praise than saved by criticism.
> —*Norman Vincent Peale*

List several people whom you would trust and who you think may be willing to be involved in a supporting, teaching, or mentoring type relationship with you.

1. _____

2. _____

3. _____

4. _____

Note: Your most pressing need for accountability may change over time. For example, at present, you may need guidance and accountability in the area of your personal relationships; in the days ahead, you may need more wisdom in the area of your finances. In what areas of your life do you currently feel the greatest need for accountability? (Check all that apply.)

____ marriage and family

____ getting out of debt

____ making wise financial plans for my future

____ learning how to live prosperously and contentedly

____ academic and educational guidance

____ establishing positive, productive social relationships

____ career guidance

____ mutual understanding of my colleagues and professional peers

____ using my creativity

____ other (be specific):_____

Which of the potential supporters, teachers, or mentors that you listed above would be most effective in helping you in regard to your current priorities?

1. _____

2. _____

Which of these individuals will you contact to discuss their possible interest in an accountability relationship and when will you make that contact?

"I will contact _____ by (date) _____ to determine his/her level of interest in establishing an accountability relationship with me."

Four areas in which we require ongoing accountability are:

1. our finances
2. our career goals
3. personal goals
4. our spiritual life

These areas may be addressed by one person or by several in your life. However you choose to address these issues, your financial accountability partner should help you stick to your budget, and, just as importantly, make sure that you are investing in your future by saving and investing wisely. With an accountability partner checking with you on how you use your money, you will not be so prone to spend your "food money" on a new toy. Nor will you omit your deposits to your savings and investment accounts, because you know that your accountability partner is going to say, "Show me the money!"

In the area of your career goals, you should feel free to let your accountability partner serve as a sounding board, someone you bounce ideas off without fear of sounding silly or selfish. Your accountability partner may have specific ideas how you can achieve your goals and how you can deal with setbacks and negative circumstances. Ideally, a good accountability partner is encouraging and supportive, yet strong enough to push you, to prod you toward greatness.

A good accountability partner will not allow you to be too soft on yourself; he or she will not condemn you for failures, but will expect better of you.

Concerning your personal goals, your accountability partner can be both a cheerleader and a gentle taskmaster. Regardless of whether your goal is to run a marathon or to read every book James Joyce wrote—including *Ulysses*—the role of your accountability partner is to make sure that you stay on the path, that you do not veer too far toward anything that will distract you for long from achieving your vision.

In the area of your spiritual life, you probably already enjoy the encouragement, teaching, and role models provided by your pastors or a class teacher. That's admirable, and you should continue to drink deeply from those wells of inspiration. But an accountability partner should probe much more deeply into your spiritual life than the average pastor can do in a thirty-minute sermon. You should encourage your accountability partner to ask you frequently about your attendance at church services, the amount of time you spend studying the Scriptures (some people like to set goals for reading the Bible through in one year, for instance). "How is your prayer life?" is another question you should give your partner permission to ask you.

Moreover, many people in spiritual accountability relationships encourage each other to deal with issues of community service and constructive use of free time. Some people in this sort of relationship have found that making daily entries in a spiritual journal is quite useful. When they get together with their accountability partners, they review the notations in the journal together. However you choose to allow someone to encourage you in your spiritual life, keep in mind that it will be of little value unless you put some "teeth" into the disciplines you require of each other.

Choose your accountability partners very carefully and very deliberately. This is not a casual relationship, so you should treat it with prayer and serious consideration. If you cannot connect with an individual, you may find better success in joining a group centered around a common goal. These kinds of small groups are especially effective at helping you to change your behavior in one particular area. For instance, if you desire to lose weight, you may want to join Weight Watchers or a Weigh Down Diet group. If your goal is to handle your finances more effectively, a group such as Financial Peace University may be most helpful to you.

These groups provide both support and accountability that focus on a particular aspect of your life. At Weight Watchers, part of the accountability relationship will require you to weigh yourself every week, and either explain the increase or celebrate the decrease in your weight. At Financial Peace University, you will have to disclose how well you have stuck to your budget since your last meeting. If you have blown your budget out the window, you will feel the heat from the other members of the group—kindly but firmly demanding that you do better next time. These small groups work when the people involved take them seriously. What makes them so powerfully effective is the fact that everyone is in the same boat, working through the same process, aiming at a similar goal. You won't find too many self-righteous prigs in these support groups. Everyone there knows how badly it hurts to fail and everyone there is rooting for each other to succeed.

Have you ever thought of becoming involved in a support group?

—— Yes —— No

List three obstacles you must overcome if you are to join an accountability group focused around a theme such as weight loss or financial improvement.

1. _____

2. _____

3. _____

Accountability Is a Two-Way Street

Certainly, there are times when you are the person in need of counsel, encouragement, and support from your mentor or accountability group. But to be fair, you should also be a support and encouragement to the others involved in your accountability relationship. Accountability should go both ways: you should not always receive and never give. Besides, you have learned a few things in life that might be of help to others. It is your responsibility to contribute to the group.

List some of the skills, special areas of knowledge, or expertise that you possess that might be of value to others. Don't be bashful or excessively modest. Try honestly to assess your strengths, not to be boastful but to be helpful.

1. _____
2. _____
3. _____
4. _____
5. _____

What life challenges have you experienced that might be of value to others? (For instance, "I was a member of a championship sports team, through which I learned discipline, sacrifice, and teamwork." Or, "I lost everything I ever held dear through unwise financial investments, and have had to rebuild from scratch.")

_____
_____
_____
_____

Choose three of your best skills or areas of influence. On a scale of zero to ten, circle a number that represents how well you have been sharing your gifts and talents with friends, family members, or colleagues.

1. Area of expertise: _____
   Level of sharing:
   0   1   2   3   4   5   6   7   8   9   10

2. Area of expertise:_____
Level of sharing:
  0   1   2   3   4   5   6   7   8   9   10

3. Area of expertise:_____
Level of sharing:
  0   1   2   3   4   5   6   7   8   9   10

List three specific ways in which you can help mentor someone else over the next two weeks.

  1. _____
  2. _____
  3. _____

As you are formulating your action plan, keep in mind that support can be given in many ways. Sometimes it is simply a kind, listening ear. At other times your encouragement may need to be corrective in nature, helping someone see the better path to choose. Loving correction is not telling someone what he or she must do; it is not nagging your spouse; nor is it bossing your coworker. Loving correction is offering the knowledge, skills, and wisdom you have in a helpful and respectful manner. Remember, you cannot make anyone do anything—except perhaps your young children! Your role as an accountability partner, or simply as an encourager, is to point the way. As in any meaningful communication, you must earn the right to be heard.

Best-selling author and marriage counselor Gary Smalley likens this situation to making deposits in a bank. In a relationship, you must make deposits *before* you need the resources, so that when it becomes necessary to make a withdrawal, the emotional "money" is in the account. Those people who want **More Than Enough** will learn the value of making regular emotional deposits into our relationships, not just our bank accounts.

Undoubtedly, the most valuable currency in strong relationships is *time*. We all know that, but how many of us really and truly believe it? And if we really believed it, what would we do differently?

For instance, at the risk of putting us all on a guilt trip, let's answer a few specific questions concerning time and our primary relationships:

When was the last time you spent an hour just swinging in a hammock or sitting on the back porch with your spouse? _____

How many of your son's or daughter's soccer, Little League, or other games did you attend this past season? _____ How many did you miss? _____

How much time have you spent talking to your best friend in the past week? _____

Did you send a birthday card to your niece or nephew this year?

____ Yes   ____No   ____ I can't remember

How much time have you taken to explain the new computer system (or some other technical matter) to your colleague(s) this month?_____

How many brief notes of encouragement have you written this month to friends or family members, just "I was thinking of you" notes, not business letters or notes with any other strings attached? _____

How much time have you spent in personal recreation this month? _____

How much time have you spent in intimate moments (not necessarily sexual) with your spouse this week? _____

An old adage reminds us that "we usually do what we think is important." Clearly, how we invest our time in our primary relationships makes a statement about how important we think those relationships are. The good news is that we can improve almost any relationship by spending even a few minutes thinking about and doing something special for the other people in our lives.

❖   ❖   ❖

Before we enter the **More Than Enough** Store again, think for a moment about the differences between support and accountability. Most of us know many people who we may consider to be our supporters: friends and family members who will lift us up when we fall, put salve on our wounds, and help us find healing and health. When you are down in the dumps, your supporters will help pull you up out of the pits. They will help you learn from your mistakes so you won't repeat them so readily. They will cheer you on and lend you a helping hand when you need it. But as valuable as supporters are, and as much as you appreciate their kind words and actions, you also need some people to whom you can be accountable.

Accountability partners are people who are slightly ahead of you in the journey, or who are making the same journey as you. They are people who have earned the right, and to whom you have granted permission, to offer suggestions for course corrections in your life. You may not always agree with their assessments; you may not always do what your accountability partners suggest, but you must always consider and respect their views, and value and appreciate their willingness to invest their time and energy in the details of your life. These are the people you are counting on to warn you of any blind spots in your life, to caution you if they see you veering off course, and to encourage you to go after your goals with gusto and confidence.

Okay, it's time for a stop at the **More Than Enough** Store, to peruse the support and accountability aisle. Of course, you could just skip on to the next chapter; after all, you are a busy person (aren't we all). But in this fast-paced world, taking the time to pause long enough to consider afresh your goals and relationships in the context of support and accountability will result in far greater rewards than the time you "lost" could have netted. Happy shopping!

Aisle Five—Support and Accountability

1. Business Section

TAKING INVENTORY

In the context of your company, business, or career, list three people who currently constitute an "inner circle" of support for you.

1. _____
2. _____
3. _____

Who else in your business would you like to have as a contributing member of your support team, and what sort of insight might this person provide that you do not already have access to?

1. _____
2. _____

How often do you ask your loved ones for input concerning your business or career? (Check one.)

___ Frequently ___ Occasionally ___ Rarely ___ Almost never

If the human being who loves you most were able to express candidly what he or she thought of the way you do business, what might that person say?

_____

Other than your boss or immediate superiors, who would you be most likely to accept correction from concerning your business matters? Note why you would respect this person's insight.

_____
_____

Your "To Do" List

List three business leaders whose business acumen you admire and briefly describe why you want to emulate them.

1. _____
   _____
2. _____
   _____
3. _____
   _____

Choose one of these successful leaders and write a letter to him or her, asking for insight concerning how he or she achieved success. (You may be surprised to discover how delighted successful people are to share their success secrets with others who truly desire to learn.) If the person you plan to contact is located in or near your community, you may want to invite him or her to lunch to discuss their career milestones. (Note: Be sure that you are prepared to pay for lunch!)

When facing a career or business crisis, who would you call to form an emergency advisory board?

_____
_____
_____
_____

On a scale of zero to ten, how well have you been nurturing the above relationships? To put it another way, how often do you make any "deposits" in the bank of these relationships?

0	1	2	3	4	5	6	7	8	9	10
Not at all		Occasionally		When it is convenient			Frequently			Constantly

2. Marriage Section

TAKING INVENTORY

List several ways in which you are making yourself accountable to your spouse. (For instance, I make myself accountable to my spouse by always calling home if I am going to be more than half an hour late.)

1. _____
2. _____
3. _____
4. _____

On a scale of zero to ten, how well are you making "emotional deposits" in your spouse's love bank?

0	1	2	3	4	5	6	7	8	9	10
None		Hardly at all			Moderately well			Very well		Fantastic

In your spouse's opinion, what would it take to raise the above number up a few notches?

_____

_____

How would you describe your level of commitment to accountability with your spouse? (Check all that apply.)

____ I am committed to maintaining accountability regardless of the cost.

____ I could take it or leave it.

____ I really don't care to have to answer to my spouse, but I do so to avoid hassles.

____ I refuse to let anyone else run my life.

____ What accountability?

Describe a time within the past year that your spouse's support made a difference for you. (For instance, "When I had to have the project done on time, my spouse postponed our anniversary celebration for a week so I could devote myself to getting the job done.")

_____

_____

Your "To Do" List

Discuss with your marriage partner the ways in which you would like each other to hold one another accountable in the relationship.

Discuss with your spouse the ways he or she would prefer that you make "emotional deposits" in your marriage relationship.

Discuss with your spouse the benefits of increasing your accountability to each other and describe how you might be able to do that.

3. Parenting Section

TAKING INVENTORY
List several ways in which you are teaching your children to be accountable.

1. _____

2. _____

3. _____

What are some ways in which you made "emotional deposits" into the lives of your children last month?

_____

_____

In what specific ways does peer pressure work against your child's accountability to you or to the school or church?

_____

_____

How do you propose to counteract negative peer pressure in your child's life with positive peer pressure?

_____

_____

Parents' "To Do" List

Think about the ways in which your child's accountability to you must change as he or she matures. Discuss with your spouse: How comfortable are we in relinquishing the reins as our child takes on more adult responsibilities?

Discuss how you can help your child shift total accountability from you to other mentors; for instance, a professor, guidance counselor, or a support group of some sort.

What sort of residual accountability issues still exist between your parents and you? Discuss with your children how these issues affect your expectations of them.

Have a family discussion with your children and ask them what they would consider to be a good way of increasing the "emotional deposits" in their love banks. Let the kids do the talking and listen carefully to which words or actions they are seeking from you.

Plan a "date night" with your child, in which you as the parent do something that your child would consider special.

4. Singles' Section

TAKING INVENTORY

To whom are you accountable?

_____

_____

_____

If you are not in an accountability relationship, why have you avoided such an involvement? (Check all that apply.)

____ I don't want anyone to know that much about me.
____ I haven't been able to connect with a group in my area.
____ I have many acquaintances but few close friends, so accountability has been difficult.
____ I've been burned before and I now have trouble trusting anyone with the details of my life.
____ It's my life. Why should I tell anyone else anything?
____ I have not found anyone who cares that much to get involved with me.
____ I am uncomfortable with the idea of attending a support group.
____ I consider myself to be self-sufficient.
____ I'm too lazy.
____ I don't have time.

List three people to whom you can turn for support and encouragement.

1. _____
2. _____
3. _____

Have you offered to be an accountability and support partner to anyone?

____ Yes   ____ No

Who do you know that might benefit from the wisdom you have to impart as an accountability partner?

_____

In a time of personal crisis or temptation, to whom can you be vulnerable enough to admit your needs, fears, failures, and struggles?

_____

Your "To Do" List

List three individuals from whom you would be willing to receive correction, as long as it was suggested out of love and without condemnation.

1. _____

2. _____

3. _____

Consider writing a note to these individuals to express your willingness to learn from them. If the person is married, be sure to express a willingness to include his or her spouse so your motives cannot be misinterpreted.

Create a plan by which you can purposefully make three "emotional deposits" within the next three weeks in the lives of three people you care about.

If you were to form a personal board of advisers, who would you invite to participate?

1. _____

2. _____

3. _____

4. _____

Write a thank-you note this week to at least one person who has been an inspiration to you.

5. Financial Section

TAKING INVENTORY

Why do you think most people resist being accountable in the matter of finances?

_____

On a scale of zero to ten, how open do you allow yourself to be when discussing financial matters with your primary accountability partners?

0	1	2	3	4	5	6	7	8	9	10

Very secretive   Slightly open   Open but cautious   Transparent

How have your accountability partners helped you to avoid unwise financial decisions while building wealth?

_____

_____

Your Financial "To Do" List

Arrange a "financial date" with your spouse or accountablility partner to go over your financial records in detail, including your budget, recent check registers, bank statements, investment reports, insurance policies, and your will.

Pretend you are being audited by the Internal Revenue Service. Take all necessary steps to explain your financial matters and substantiate your records to a make-believe auditor. (Make the auditor tough!)

SEVEN

Intensity—
Move the Rock

*If you want something you've never had, you'll have
to do something you've never done.*
—More Than Enough

INTENSITY IS A key ingredient in the lives of people who win. It is also a common characteristic of people who have **More Than Enough**. Whether it is getting out of debt or acquiring an abundance of wealth, people with intensity will find a way to get the job done! Productivity will be increased, expenses will be cut, and prosperity will follow your hard work as surely as the sunrise follows the night.

Other people may play key roles in your endeavors, but when all is said and done, the effort that *you* apply to a given project, goal, or vision will determine whether you succeed or fail. To succeed, you must apply the values and principles we have already discussed, and you must do so with an intensity which will cause you to focus, which will create momentum, which eventually will lead to success!

But don't fool yourself. Success does not come easily, and usually, it does not come quickly. Most anything worth having takes prolonged, intense effort. Major obstacles must be overcome or moved as you make your way toward your dreams.

List some of the obstacles that stand in your way, blocking the path you want to travel.

_____

_____

_____

The Rock That Wouldn't Roll

❖ Once upon a time, a king received numerous complaints about the way he was running the kingdom. The king noticed that the people who griped the loudest and the longest usually contributed the least. They seldom offered any solutions. They simply liked to complain.

The king decided to search his kingdom for someone who was willing to take responsibility for his or her own success. He held numerous interviews, to no avail. He sent messengers throughout the land, looking for a person who best displayed the traits of intensity, determination, and perseverance, but sadly, none could be found. Not even the messengers returned.

Finally, the king decided to set up a test. He instructed his remaining servants to place a large boulder in the road to block the way. Then the king sat in a grove of trees, out of sight, to watch what his subjects might do about the obstacle in their way.

First, a man dressed in expensive finery approached the boulder. This man, apparently a rich merchant, was accompanied by several servants. He studied the boulder, then announced loudly to all who would hear, "This boulder is clearly a result of the king's lack of management skills." The rich man made no attempt to remove the boulder from the road. He simply led his followers around the boulder, and went on his way . . . feeling quite smug, at that.

Next, a philosopher came up the road. A highly educated and thoughtful man, the philosopher studied the obstacle and pondered whether it truly existed. After a long while, he concluded that the boulder did indeed exist. But why? What was its meaning? Why was it there? "This problem," the philosopher pontificated, "is a symbol of our king's lack of leadership." With that, the philosopher went on his way.

The next man who came to the boulder in the way was a simple peasant. He was a hardworking man whose main goal in life was to feed his family and enjoy a peaceful and happy existence. When the peasant saw the rock, he studied the problem from every angle. Then without a word, he crouched low, put his shoulder to the boulder, and began to push. He grunted, groaned, and bellowed, but the boulder wouldn't budge. The peasant perspired profusely as he continued to push with all his might.

Several more travelers came along, and when they saw the peasant working so hard with so little to show for his efforts, they mocked him and chided, "Why are you doing the king's work and not your own?"

The peasant refused to respond, but simply continued to push.

Wait! What was that?

The boulder rocked back and forth ever so slightly. The peasant gave a mighty thrust and the rock rolled forward a few inches. Seeing an opportunity, the man pushed even harder, and the huge boulder turned over completely. The man kept up the pressure. Suddenly, the momentum of the rolling rock multiplied the man's efforts and the rock began to roll. Faster and faster, it rolled until it rolled off the road, down a hill, and into the brush.

When the man walked back up to the road to retrieve his belongings to continue his journey, he spied a large bag where the boulder had been. The man picked up the sack, and to his amazement, he discovered a sum of gold, making him fabulously rich.

The king and his servants emerged from the grove where they had been secretly watching the proceedings. "Congratulations, my man," the king gushed. "And welcome to my royal court. Finally, a man who not only recognizes the problem, but is willing to do something about it!"

The peasant became one of the king's most trusted advisers, and taught the lesson of the rock to rest of the kingdom . . . and, of course, he and his family lived a life of **More Than Enough**, happily ever after.

How can you best overcome those obstacles, beginning today?

_____

_____

_____

Which of the above obstacles is the first one to which you will apply your might with real intensity?

_____

Just Do It!

Talk is cheap, and education, while valuable, is useless if you don't do something with it. Almost every day, people call me on our radio talk show looking for easy answers. I do my best to be kind and patient—we strive to be gentle with our callers—but sometimes I just want to scream into the microphone, "There aren't any easy answers!" Sooner or later, if you want to improve your lot in life, you are going to have to leave the cave, go out and kill something, and drag it home! And that takes some intensity. If you want to get anything out of this life, you've gotta go for it!

One evening after a seminar, I was autographing books for members of my audience, as is my usual practice. A handsome young man who looked to be in his early thirties handed me a copy of one of my books, and as I began to sign it, he said, "Boy, Dave, I'd give anything if I could be as successful at what I do as you are at what you do."

That piqued my imagination, so I asked, "Oh, really? What do you do?"

"Well, I used to be in the real estate business."

"So was I," I replied as I scribbled a personal note of encouragement in his book. "What do you mean, you *used* to be?"

"I quit."

"Why? Didn't you like it?"

"Oh, no. I loved it. I took a class at our local community college, and I did fairly well. But once I got out there with an agency, I just couldn't get the hang of it—all those interest rates, and amortization schedules, and closing costs . . ."

"How long were you in real estate?" I asked.

"Mmm . . . about six weeks, I guess."

"Six weeks! That's hardly even getting started. You quit after six weeks? I thought you said you'd give *anything* to be successful."

"Well, not exactly *anything*," he replied with a sheepish grin. "I figured I'd give it a try and if I caught on, great! If I didn't pick it up quickly, I'd cash in my chips. I guess I just didn't want it badly enough."

In our "instant society," we have grown accustomed to immediate success stories. Guess what? It just doesn't happen that way. Most "overnight" success stories actually take years of hard work and determination to develop. Whether you are aspiring to be a real estate agent, a college professor, an astronaut, or the world's greatest mom, the one characteristic that will put you on the path to where you want to be is intensity. You've got to *want* it! You must have a burning desire within, if you are ever going to set lofty goals and achieve them.

Intensity is a developed habit. It's not something that you will just wake up with one morning. You were not born with an innate intensity or lack of it. Certainly, your temperament, personality traits, and emotional makeup may play a part, but you must *learn* to be motivated in the right direction for the right reasons. Read books, listen to tapes, attend seminars, talk with other people who are doing what you want to do, ask questions, and then develop a plan and work it. Develop an attitude similar to the champion high jumper, who, when asked how he could jump to such record-setting heights, answered, "I just throw my heart over the bar, and my body follows!" Throw your heart into your plan and the intensity will follow.

Intensity is not something that can be driven into you by someone else. Pep rallies are encouraging, sales quotas and quarterly reports are stimulating (and sometimes costly if you miss them), sermons are inspiring, and motivational seminars are challenging, but none of these things will bring about lasting results unless the intensity begins to build from within you.

Incentives are helpful, and as Tom Peters and Bob Waterman, authors of *In Search of Excellence,* have taught us, hoopla and recognition awards can be used effectively to spur people on toward greatness. The only problem with external incentives is that the law of diminishing returns soon sets in, and the incentive must continually be increased to get the same type of results.

That's what has happened to a lot of lazy, spoiled-brat kids. Mom and Dad started them out on "Come here, little Dumpling. Clean up your room, and you can have a scoop of ice cream!"

Then what does it take? Two scoops!

Then what? A pizza!

Yo, Adrian!

❖ Sylvester Stallone was turned down by nearly every major producer in Hollywood when he attempted to peddle his script. That script eventually became the megablockbuster *Rocky*.

What next? A Porsche!

Then what? A condo on the beach in Hawaii!

We must get to the place where we have a passion within us, where we are willing to pour ourselves into something worth living for simply because the goal is worth it. And the goal of living a **More Than Enough** life is worth it!

Is there some project that you believe in, but nobody else does? Is there something that you want to do, or to be, that others simply cannot see? Briefly describe your dream below:

_____

_____

Applying intensity as you never have before, how can you best sell what you want to do?

_____

What are the first three steps in your plan to proceed intensely with this goal?

1. _____
2. _____
3. _____

> The greatest mistake we make is living in constant
> fear that we will make one.
> —*John Maxwell*

Negative Motivation Won't Cut It

Intensity will rarely thrive when we are motivated more by fear than we are by love, honor, or integrity. When we are afraid that the boss will get angry if we don't get the job done correctly and on time; or we are afraid that our bottom line might suffer; or worse yet, that we might get fired—we may become tense, or intense, but the energy we produce will be negative rather than positive.

Similarly, we fear that if we don't live in the "right" part of town, our kids will attend substandard schools and get a poor education. We fear that if we are not the perfect parents, our children will grow up to be computer-virus-spreading hackers.

Certainly, some fear motivation is valid and even necessary. Where would we be if years ago Mom and Dad hadn't warned us: "Don't play in the streets. You might get hit by a car!" or, "If you don't keep your hands away from the stove, I'm going to smack them!"

As a rule, though, fear motivation fosters a negative lifestyle rather than a **More Than Enough** lifestyle. Fear becomes the great compeller; it forces you to do something. We frequently hear people who are motivated by fear using phrases such as: "I have to" or "I'm afraid I must," rather than "I want to," or "I get to," or "I can."

"Hey, Bob, are you going to the big game this weekend?"

"No, I have to work."

No, he doesn't. Bob doesn't *have* to work. He may *choose* to work this weekend. He may *get* to work this weekend, but he doesn't have to! He can decide not to work. Of course, in doing so, he may also be deciding to seek a new place of employment. Nevertheless, you'd be amazed at the difference in Bob's attitude and performance if he developed a habit of answering questions like this:

"Hey, Bob, are you going to the big game this weekend?"

"No, it sounds like fun, and I'm sure it will be a great game, but I want to earn a few extra dollars toward that new set of golf clubs I've been saving up to buy. One more weekend and I'll have enough for a complete set of Callaways."

Sounds crazy? Try it. You will be pleasantly surprised at the results as you redesign your thoughts and language to begin intensely pursuing the goals you have set for yourself.

List several "I have tos" in your life. On the line below, change your "I have tos" to "I want tos" or "I get tos." For example: Change "I have to take another class before I can be promoted" to "I want to further my education so I can increase my options."

I have to: _____

I _____

I have to: _____

I _____

> The average person puts only 25 percent of his
> energy and ability into his work. The world takes off
> its hat to those who put in more than 50 percent of
> their capacity, and will stand on its head for those
> few and far between souls who devote 100 percent.
> —*Andrew Carnegie*

Perhaps all this emphasis on intensity brings to your mind an image of some wild-eyed maniac crashing his or her way through life, running on raw energy and bowling over everything and anyone who dares to get in its path. That's not intensity—that's stupidity. On the contrary, intensity is energy focused on a specific task for a prolonged period of time. Notice those two factors: focus and time.

Michael Knows More Than Basketball

❖ Former Chicago Bulls all-star and living legend Michael Jordan says, "Heart is what separates the good from the great." Notice that Michael did not say that the key ingredient is skill; nor did he say that in order to be successful, one must have a degree from a prestigious university. He didn't say anything about growing up in the "right" neighborhood or under the "right" circumstances. Nor did he mention anything about skin color or sex. No, Michael Jordan realized that the "good" are easily found, but only those with *heart*—those who are willing to pursue their goals with intensity— become great.

Focused Energy

The ability to focus your energy on one area at a time is part of what makes intensity work for you. When your best efforts are scattered all across the board, you spread yourself too thin to have much of an impact. Think of the difference between an incandescent lightbulb and a laser beam. The lightbulb will serve a purpose; it will provide light and some degree of warmth to the room in which it is used. But when a beam of light, under the correct power, can be finely focused, it can become a laser that will literally cut through steel.

Have you ever seen a professional golfer walking the fairways at a golf tournament? Thousands of people may be lined along the way, many calling out encouragement or other comments as the pro walks by. But it seems he doesn't even hear the crowd; he is in a "zone"—the eyes are straight ahead; the gait is quick; the head is up, already scanning the landscape ahead of him, planning the next shot. He is focused on what he wants to do. That is a picture of intensity.

When asked about the first requirement of success, inventor Thomas Edison said that it is "the ability to apply your physical and mental energies to one problem incessantly without growing weary. If you get up at seven A.M. and go to bed at eleven P.M., you have put in sixteen good hours, and it is certain with most men that they have been doing something all the time. The only trouble is that they do it about a great many things, and I do it about one. If they took the time in question and applied it in one direction, to one object, they would succeed."

Which of the following have you experienced within the past six weeks as a consequence of a lack of focus? (Check all that apply.)

_____ boredom
_____ unusual amounts of stress
_____ financial pressure
_____ a sense of drudgery
_____ a lack of enthusiasm for my work
_____ lashing out at my loved ones as a result of my frustration
_____ lack of sleep
_____ unusual or inordinate compulsive behaviors

What goals have you been neglecting because of a lack of focus?

_____

_____

List, in order of importance (one being most important), which of the following might help you to refine your focus and motivate you to develop more intensity about what you do.

_____ my family
_____ my faith
_____ my finances
_____ my work

Many people struggle through life with little joy or enthusiasm because they have never discovered true intensity in their lives. They are laid-back, easygoing, and comfortable. While that sounds good, a fine line separates the comfortable from the complacent. The reason why many people have never lived with zest and zeal is because they have never considered anything so worthwhile that they would die for it.

Who or what in your life would you die for?

A Prolonged Span of Time

It is not enough to find something that inspires your passion for an hour. All too often people get great ideas that they believe will make them millions of dollars. They set out to explore the possibilities, but before long they give up. Or they fail to follow up on their ideas. Why? Because they think that success is going to happen overnight. They are not willing to hang in there and to keep pitching over the long haul.

We see it all the time in the town in which I live and work—Nashville, Tennessee. Every year, thousands of aspiring songwriters and potential music artists stream into town by plane, bus, car, or bicycle. Many of them are extremely talented and have tremendous earning potential. But after a few rejections by entry-level music company employees, the aspiring artists often pack up and go home. Their dreams have been dashed. Their visions of superstardom have evaporated. It's over, they think. What's the use?

Many of the waiters and waitresses in our town are musicians who haven't quit. They are waiting on tables while they hone their craft, knowing that if they produce excellent material long enough, sooner or later somebody in the music business will give them a break.

The more mature you are, and the more important your goal is to you, the more likely you are to develop and maintain intensity. Most of us can muster a short burst of intensity. But the larger prizes in life are reserved for those individuals who maintain a higher level of intensity over longer periods of time. In most cases, the longer the time span, the greater the reward. Sometimes the reward comes in the form of lessons learned; other times the reward is reflected in relationships that are grown, and quite frequently the reward is measurable in dollars and cents. Regardless of the reward, however, people who have learned how to focus their intensity for long periods of time usually lead extremely rich and full lives.

Most successful entrepreneurs know that the first few years of operating a new business are almost all work and no pay. Then after about ten years of building the business, one failure upon another leads you to one success after another and you reach a modicum level of security and prosperity. About that time, somebody will finally notice that you exist and call you an "overnight success." Overnight? How about ten years' worth of early mornings, long days, and short nights, working until you could not keep your eyes open any longer, and then sleeping just long enough that you'd have enough energy to hold your head up straight? Ah, yes, an overnight success. In actuality, what you know that outside observers don't is that you are just now being paid for the work that you did five years ago. And your focused intensity will continue to pay dividends in the future, as long as you don't quit.

Focus on Your Finances

Focused and prolonged intensity is essential for you to reach your financial goals. Many people make the mistake of trying to cover all the financial bases at one time. They want to get out of debt quickly, save for the future, establish a college savings account for the kids by investing in long-term mutual funds, fully fund their 401(k) retirement plan, and even give thousands of dollars away in philanthropic ventures. All of these are noble and worthwhile goals, but if you try to do them all at the same time you will become extremely frustrated (unless you are fabulously wealthy already). It is more than likely you will throw up your hands in despair and say, "I just can't do it all." And you will be right . . . and wrong. You can do it all, but you must take one step at a time.

Step number one is: *Stop*. Stop doing everything! Stop trying to pay off credit card debts, stop trying to double up on your mortgage payments, stop contributing to your 401(k) plan at work, stop everything . . . for a while. Take a breath, regroup, and lay out a workable, reasonable financial plan before you do anything else.

Then, with focused and prolonged intensity, start saving money to establish an extra $1,000 in a readily available savings account. Pay nothing extra—no extra house payments, and contribute nothing additional to your savings—nothing, until you get that $1,000 in savings.

Next, plan an attack on your bills by using the Debt Snowball method. Under this plan, you will make minimum payments on all your bills *except* the smallest one. The smallest bill will be the object of your focused and prolonged intensity until you have paid it off. Every extra penny that you can squeeze out of your budget, every cent of unexpected income—including gifts from Mom and Dad—is to be directed with laserlike precision on that least of all debts.

Scramble every way you can to make as much extra income as you can as quickly as you can. One of the best ways to do this is to sell stuff. Most of us have way more stuff than we need. In fact, most of us have stuff crammed into closets, attics, basements, and storage facilities that we haven't used in ages. Pull it out of those nooks and crannies, slap a price tag or a FOR SALE sign on it, put an advertisement in the paper, and have yourself a grand garage sale. Sell so much stuff that your kids think they will be next if they stand still for too long!

Then use the extra money you make to pay the smallest debt you owe. Focus on that smallest debt until it is totally eliminated. When it is paid off, you simply raise the laser's sights a bit. Don't have a party and spend more money. Focus on that next debt, which is now the smallest one remaining. Take the same amount of money that you *were* paying previously, add to it the amount that you had been paying on the debt you have already eliminated, and put that new amount toward paying off the debt that is currently the smallest. Each time you pay off a debt, you have more money to pay off your remaining debts. The snowball is beginning to roll and it is picking up power and energy as you stay intensely focused for a prolonged period of time. At any point, if you back off, you will have to start over again to get the snowball rolling, so it is much better to keep up your intensity level until every debt is gone.

Here's how to get started:

List your two smallest debts here (for example, Discover Card, $250; MasterCard, $500).

My two smallest debts are (the larger amount): $___ of which I make monthly payments of $___ to _____, and (the smaller amount): $___ of which I make monthly payments of $___ to _____. I will intensely focus my financial energy on paying off: _____. I plan to get extra income by (for example, working extra hours, having a yard sale): _____
_____.

When I have paid off _____, I will take that former monthly payment of $___ and add it to the amount I am currently paying to _____, which is $___, for a total of $___. I will now apply this amount each month toward paying off _____ until the debt is gone.

You can use this process all the way up your list of debts. As you pay off one debt after another, no matter how small, you will discover an amazing phenomenon: you are getting excited about getting out of debt. Your focused, prolonged intensity is creating an intangible but very real factor in your success: momentum!

Momentum—The Mother of More!

Momentum is almost magical in its power to create movement. Do you remember the story of the peasant and the boulder? Once he got the obstacle to

The "Magic" of Compounding Interest

❖ It takes twenty years of saving $325 per month at 12 percent to get the first $300,000, but the second $300,000 will be added to your account in just the following five years. Then almost another $300,000 will be there in just over three more years.

Number of Years It Took	Amount Saved
Twenty	$321,000
Twenty-five	$610,000
Twenty-eight	$887,000

budge an inch, the momentum took over, and by keeping up the pressure he was able to roll that huge, seemingly insurmountable stone out of the way. Something similar will happen to you when your focused financial intensity begins to push that Debt Snowball out of your way.

Now it really gets exciting!

Once your debts have been eliminated, you are in a position to begin accumulating wealth! Now you can put more money into your savings accounts, creating a fully funded emergency fund equal to six months of your normal monthly expenses. Then you can start adding money to your retirement accounts. And to college savings plans, and on and on, accumulating more all the way along. You will have more money to live on, more to give, **More Than Enough**!

As you get the momentum moving in your saving and investing, the money begins to roll in exponentially. But again, it takes focused intensity over a prolonged period of time to reap such results. Let me show you:

Are those numbers too overwhelming for you? Okay, let's start from scratch. As you save and invest, you will discover the wonderful joy of having compound interest rates work *for* you as a saver, rather than *against* you as a debtor. For instance, as a very basic illustration, imagine that you have $100 in an account that earns 10 percent each year. At the end of the year, if you have made no further deposits, you will have $110.

In contrast, if you owe $100 to a credit card company that is charging you 20 percent interest each year, and you make no other payments, at the end of the year you will owe $120. The compounding of the interest rate is working against you, stealing your money and your motivation because the momentum is not in your favor.

Have you ever seen a fine football team that has lost its momentum? It seems they can do nothing right. Every play they try ends in failure. Maneuvers they have meticulously executed in practice dozens of times before fall apart on the field when the momentum is against them.

On the other hand, it is a delight to watch a team's momentum change. They are going through the motions in a lackluster manner, when suddenly something happens. It may be a big thing—a turnover, a fumble, or an interception—or it may be some seemingly insignificant play that turns out to be pivotal—a stretched-out catch, a grunted-out first down, or a goal-line defensive stand. But when it happens, the people in the stadium, as well as the spectators watching on television, can sense it. The momentum has changed.

You can feel something similar with a winning company. The sales may be down, the stock reports sagging, morale around the office is morbid. But then something happens—a fresh ray of sunshine seems to pervade the place, and suddenly the momentum changes. It's a new start.

The same thing occurs often in a marriage that has grown cold or dull. One or both partners are bored, tired, frustrated, or frazzled. Nothing seems to be working right. Everything seems headed toward the pits. But then a miracle takes place. The momentum changes, and the marriage is not only saved; it is revived, refreshed, and goes on to be even better than ever before.

Granted that it is sometimes difficult to quantify just what makes the momentum change. Usually a variety of factors are involved. But inevitably, if you look closely enough, you will discover someone has placed a goal out in front of him or her and are pursuing it with relentless, persevering, "I-won't-take-no-for-an-answer" intensity.

Napoleon Hill, author of the motivational classic *Think and Grow Rich*, studied the lives of many successful people, including the tremendously successful inventor Thomas Edison and auto magnate Henry Ford. Hill concluded, "I had the happy privilege of analyzing both Mr. Edison and Mr. Ford, year by year, over a long period of years, and therefore the opportunity to study them at close range, so I speak from actual knowledge when I say that I found no quality save persistence, in either of them, that even remotely suggested the major source of their stupendous achievements."

The writer was not taking anything away from the two great men. Hill was simply saying that the same persistent intensity can also reap similar achievements in our lives.

Aisle Six—Intensity, Focus, and Momentum

1. Business Section

TAKING INVENTORY

On a scale of zero to ten, how would you rate the current intensity level of your company or business?

0	1	2	3	4	5	6	7	8	9	10
Extremely poor		Lackluster		Average		Energetic		Tremendous intensity		

Whom do you see as primarily responsible for fostering intensity in your workplace? (Check all that apply.)

____ my boss

____ the company owners

____ my coworkers and me

____ me

____ stockholders or other outside interests

What might be some benefits of greater intensity in your business or company? (Check all that apply.)

___ increased profits
___ better team spirit
___ better relationships among coworkers
___ fewer distractions
___ better focus on the primary goals of the business
___ acquisition of new customers or clients

What might be some of the drawbacks of fostering greater intensity in your business?

_____

_____

_____

What immediate steps can you take to improve the focus and prolonged time span required to enhance your intensity on the job? (For instance, "I can clear my desk of everything but the project on which I am currently working.")

_____

_____

_____

On a scale of zero to ten, which way is the momentum of your business moving?

0	1	2	3	4	5	6	7	8	9	10
Negatively					Static					Positive

What can you do within the next six weeks to help raise that number a notch?

_____

Your "To Do" List

Write out a plan of action that you believe will enhance your company's intensity level.

If you are in management, assign a small group of team members to research how your business might benefit by intensely focusing on one area rather than spreading your resources over a broad base.

Find somebody at work (or one of your clients) who is having a difficult month, and attempt to encourage that person regularly until you see the momentum begin to change in a more positive direction.

2. Marriage Section

TAKING INVENTORY

If your marriage is currently experiencing an obstacle in its path, why do you think you have not yet been able to get the boulder out of the way? (Check all that apply.)

____ My obstinate spouse won't help me.
____ Our children are disrespectful.
____ My boss's demands are creating too much stress at home.
____ Lack of money.
____ Lack of spiritual power.
____ I'm a loser.
____ I haven't been pushing hard enough or long enough.
____ It is an impossible task.
____ I'm too tired when I get home from work to worry about marriage problems.
____ We haven't addressed the matter directly as a couple.
____ Other: _____

What area of your marriage could most use some intense focus and prolonged attention?

_____

In which direction is the momentum in your marriage currently moving?

____ positively
____ negatively
____ uncertain

What can you do this week that might create some positive momentum in your relationship with your spouse?

_____

Your "To Do" List

Plan a weekend where you and your spouse can intensely focus on each other. Perhaps you can go away and leave the children with Grandma and Grandpa, or maybe you can simply take a stroll around the neighborhood or park each evening. Regardless of the activity, attempt to minimize all distractions so you can give each other your undivided attention.

Discuss with an accountability partner some of the changes you feel that you need to make in your relationship with your spouse. (I need to be more considerate of my spouse's need for _____.) Ask your accountability partner to check up on you to see how you are doing in this area each week.

If you are not yet debt-free, discuss with your spouse how the two of you can "get mad" and take the necessary steps to start toward financial peace and freedom.

Intensity often spawns initiative and initiative often enhances creativity. What are some ways that you and your spouse can improve the creativity in your relationship?

3. Parenting Section

TAKING INVENTORY

On a scale of one to ten, how well do you think you are teaching the value of intensity to your children?

| 1 | 2 | 3 | 4 | 5 | 6 | 7 | 8 | 9 | 10 |

Not well at all   Very well indeed

Our culture craves more information, but more knowledge without action will bring about little change. Which do you need to provide more of for your children? (Check one.)

____ More opportunities to gain knowledge

____ More opportunities to use the knowledge they are learning

In which ways are you modeling focused intensity for your children?

_____

_____

_____

Do your children see your intensity level as a positive or a negative in the family?

____ Positive   ____ Negative

Why do you think they have this opinion?

_____

List some ways you are attempting to motivate your children to use the gifts, talents, and potential they have.

_____

_____

_____

Parents' "To Do" Section

During a casual family discussion, ask your children in which ways they would like to see you focus more on your family, your faith, and your finances.

What are some ways you and your spouse can encourage your children to keep up their intensity levels even when the going gets tough?

Think of some short, reachable goals for your younger children to aim for. Ideally the goals should be their own (saving for a new doll or a new baseball glove). Help your children see the value and the fun of saving their own money for what they want, and the joy of buying it debt-free.

Evaluate with your spouse your child's momentum in each of the following areas:

academically
socially
physically
spiritually

What are some ways you might be able to help your child take it up a notch?

4. Singles' Section

TAKING INVENTORY

Which of the following "boulders" have you had to push out of the way or otherwise overcome within the past year? (Check all that apply.)

___ disrespect
___ unwarranted critical comments
___ temper outburst aimed in your direction
___ financial setbacks
___ a negative relationship with a person of the opposite sex
___ personal moral compromise and the accompanying guilt
___ work-related issues

On which area of your life are you currently focusing most intensely?

_____

Does this require long-term, prolonged intensity, or will you be able to accomplish your goal in a relatively short period of time?

_____ A long-term commitment of time and energy will be necessary.
_____ A short, concentrated effort is necessary.

List two future goals that you feel are within your grasp if you focus your intensity on them.

_____

_____

When will you begin to actively pursue these goals?

_____

Singles' "To Do" List

Discuss with your accountability partner ways in which you can increase your intensity.

Examine your checkbook to see where your spending habits and priorities may need to be adjusted. What is the relationship between your expenses and your income?

If the effort you put into something is indicative of the joy you will get out of it, is there someone around you who needs help, into whom you can pour your energy? Perhaps you can strike up a friendship with a senior citizen who has no family members nearby to visit him or her. Or volunteer to help in a "big brother" or "big sister" program. Surely you have some things you have learned the hard way that would be of value to a younger generation. Focus on them rather than on yourself.

Do you have a strong desire to be married? If so, begin to prepare yourself now for that relationship. Read books on marriage, attend marriage classes, and watch married couples with whom you interact regularly. Make a list of the kinds of characteristics you want in your marriage (not simply in your marriage partner), as well as those you do not.

5. Financial Section

TAKING INVENTORY

Intensity is a key to financial peace—most people do not get out of debt until they get mad enough to attack the problem. List three obstacles that must be overcome as you pursue financial peace. (No fair saying, "My boss, my boss, my boss!")

1. _____
2. _____
3. _____

Intensity is equally important in your quest for **More Than Enough**. Most people do not begin vigorously saving, investing, and making other wise financial moves until the goal is big enough to excite them. What event, circumstance, or need has prompted you to see the importance of initiating drastic, prolonged, intense actions toward achieving your goals?

_____

_____

On which two of your financial goals are you currently focusing the most energy in an effort to see them accomplished in the best way possible?

1. _____
2. _____

Have you accurately counted the costs concerning the amount of time it will take to achieve these goals?

___ Yes   ___ No   ___ I'm not certain, but I hope so

Your Financial "To Do" List

Write a brief paragraph that summarizes in a nutshell your financial plan for the next three years. Hint: To do this, you must truly focus on your priorities, and pursue a *workable* plan.

_____

_____

_____

List several ways you intend to make momentum work for you rather than against you in regard to your financial goals.

_____

_____

_____

Make arrangements to move all of your savings out of low-interest accounts, except for your emergency fund or other cash-on-hand types of accounts. Invest the money instead in high-interest, long-term mutual funds or other financial instruments with a proven track record of at least five years of strongly profitable returns.

EIGHT

Diligence—That Dirty Little Secret

Work is doing it. Discipline is doing it every day.
Diligence is doing it *well* every day.
—*More Than Enough*

A PARABLE is told of a farmer who owned an old mule. One day the mule fell into the farmer's well and couldn't get out. The farmer sympathized with the mule's dilemma, but there was little he could do. Finally he decided that neither the mule nor the well was worth saving, so he hauled in a load of dirt to load into the well and bury the poor mule, thus putting him out of his misery.

When the farmer started shoveling the dirt into the well, the mule became hysterical. As each shovelful of dirt hit his back and fell to the bottom of the well, the mule heed and hawed and whined and squealed. The sounds reverberating off the cold stone walls created an awful bedlam, which caused the mule to howl even more. Then suddenly a thought struck the old mule. He realized that every time a pile of dirt hit him, he could shake it off and then step up on top of it. Shake it off, step up; shake it off, and step up.

This he did, blow after blow, shovelful upon shovelful of dirt. The mule thought the farmer would never stop throwing dirt down the well. "Shake it off and step up; shake it off and step up," the mule repeated to himself. No matter how trapped he seemed, or how painful the blows, or how dirty he felt, the old mule fought off the feelings of panic that threatened to do him in, or

---

Plan for the Dirt

❖ When dirt happens in your life—and it will, unfortunately—you will handle it better if you decide now that you will shake it off and step up. Too often, we tend to adopt a "wait and see" attitude in times of stress. While we wait to see what is going to happen next, we get steamrollered. You will be much better off if you develop a plan of action. Even a poor plan is better than no plan at all.

---

which might cause him to give up. Instead, he just kept shaking off the dirt and stepping up.

By the time the farmer finished shoveling, the dirt was nearly to the top of the well. The old mule—battered and exhausted but still very much alive—stepped up one more time, and stepped over the wall of the well to freedom. What looked as though it might bury him had actually brought him inch by inch closer to victory because of the way the mule chose to react to the dirt—shake it off and step up.

That's life. Dirt happens. And if we just sit back and accept it and do nothing, it will bury us. Look around you. You'll see the walking dead everywhere. Some are buried by an overwhelming load of debt. Others are buried in baggage from their pasts. Still others are buried by a pile of unresolved bitterness and anger in their marriage and family relationships. Some people are buried in mediocrity.

Those who are determined to have **More Than Enough** refuse to be buried alive! They shake off the dirt and use it to make good things happen. As Steven Covey, author of the bestselling book *Seven Habits of Highly Effective People*, says, "The number one habit of highly effective people is that they are proactive." Similarly, those who live a **More Than Enough** lifestyle "happen" to things; they do not sit back waiting for things to happen to them. Usually the way they make things happen involves work.

Life's Dirtiest Word

For many people, *w-o-r-k* is one of life's nastiest four-letter words! Some people hate it. Others get nauseated at the mere thought of it. Many avoid it with alacrity. Yet work is one of the key elements in a **More Than Enough** lifestyle. It is not drudgery; it is an honorable activity. Evangelist Billy Graham has often stated that he believes work will be a central activity in the next life, as well, that we will do some sort of work even in heaven!

Work does wonders for your self-image. It is not how much you get paid, or even getting paid at all, that matters. Doing housework or yard work can be just as meaningful (although not as profitable, perhaps) as doing legal work or work in some other profession. The most important aspect of work is what it does for you on the inside. Work satisfies. You feel better about yourself when you know you are accomplishing something. It gives your life a sense of meaning, some reason to get out of bed each morning and to charge into the day. Work energizes you.

Nowadays it seems that many people feel they are exempt from work. Some people actually believe that the world, or the government, or *somebody* actually owes them a living! Nothing could be further from the truth. Almost two thousand years ago, some people got so "heavenly minded that they were no earthly good," and felt that they didn't need to work up a sweat. Concerning that crowd of sluggardly saints, the Apostle Paul said, "If anyone will not work, neither let him eat."

Interestingly, the apostle didn't say anything about being overqualified or underqualified for a position; neither did he mention sagging economic conditions or a depressed job market (both of which existed at that time). He simply said, "Get to work. Get up and do it!" Stop being lazy and undisciplined; quit being a busybody and get your body busy! The early Christian welfare system took excellent care of widows, orphans, and others who were in need. But the standard was this: If you are physically able, then you'd better be working at something.

> Work keeps us from three evils: boredom, vice, and poverty.
>
> —*Voltaire*

Mama Knows

My mom taught me from an early age that there is a place to go when you are broke—it's called "to *work*!" Yet as an adult, when I first started hosting a financial talk radio program where I answered callers' questions about money matters, I was amazed at how many intelligent people with whom I talked could easily have solved their financial problems by working a few extra hours each week. But for some reason, that thought had never occurred to them! "Me? Work more? You've got to be kidding," seemed to be the prevailing attitude.

Merely putting more time in on a job, however, will not necessarily lead to having **More Than Enough**. You must work *well*. You must do your job with excellence, whether anyone else sees your work or not. Work is doing it. Discipline is doing it every day. Diligence is doing it well every day. But it all starts with work. Work is a surefire moneymaking scheme!

How would you describe your attitude toward work, not necessarily your present job, but work in general? (Check all that apply.)

____ It is repugnant to me.

____ I love to work. Even if I were unemployed, I'd be working at something.

____ Work cranks my motor.

____ I hate it and try my best to avoid doing any more work than necessary.

____ I look forward to retirement, when I no longer need to work.

____ I sleep better after a hard day's work.

____ I'd rather sleep than work.

____ Work is for poor people.

___ Work is a means to an end. I work to make money to buy things.

___ I live to work.

___ I'm a workaholic.

___ I dread work.

Think back over this past week. How much time did you spend on the job?

_____

How much time did you spend actually *working*?

_____

What can you do this week to increase your productivity at work? (For instance, "I can get to work fifteen minutes earlier than usual to get settled and prepared for the day," or, "I can spend less time at the coffee machine or water cooler, engaged in idle conversation with my coworkers.")

_____

Hard Work Pays

A young farm boy from northern Illinois traveled to Chicago to find a job and start a career. He held several jobs as a drugstore clerk, but nothing looked promising. Eventually, he went to work for a druggist on Chicago's South Side, but the boss was a real taskmaster with an overbearing attitude and the young man was about to quit. Instead, he decided to give it his best shot, to do the best job he could in a tough situation. He figured that he'd work there until he could find something better.

The store owner noticed the boy's hard work and gave him a raise. The young clerk took it as a challenge. He worked even harder and received another raise. With his earnings, he was soon able to begin studying pharmacy at night.

He earned a degree in pharmacy and in 1901 he purchased his own drugstore—just a quaint neighborhood shop on Chicago's South Side, not much different from the many other drugstores in the city. But by now, the young proprietor had learned the secret of doing his best and putting service first. His work became fun for him. Customers noticed; they enjoyed doing business with him because he made them feel wanted and important.

One of his favorite ways of serving his customers was by delivering their prescriptions to their homes. Often when a customer phoned in an order, the pharmacist repeated the order loudly so his helper could package the prescription while the pharmacist engaged the caller in conversation. Meanwhile the helper hustled out the door to deliver the order by bicycle.

Sometimes a caller interrupted the conversation, saying, "Oh, excuse me, there's someone at my door." Upon answering the door, the customer was surprised to find the pharmacist's helper standing there with the order.

The young pharmacist's enthusiasm and hard work were contagious. Soon his employees began to emulate him, and before long he opened a second drugstore; then a third. The young man's name was Charles R. Walgreen Sr.—and today, Walgreens is one of the largest drugstore chains in America. Hard work pays!

Have you been tempted to give up on your job lately?

—— Yes —— No

What is the most meaningful and most personally fulfilling aspect of what you do for a living?

_____

_____

In what area would you like to improve your job skills? (For instance, I'd like to learn how to use certain computer programs required in my workplace.)

_____

_____

What is one thing you could do to help better serve your customers, clients, or your company?

Write down one thing that you do, or perhaps do differently, that might make your service more valuable to your customers or to your employer? (For instance, "I can work toward my college degree by taking correspondence courses or night classes at the local university.")

> I'm a great believer in luck, and the harder
> I work the more I have of it.
> —*Thomas Jefferson*

Hard Luck Versus Hard Work

A woman named June called my radio show in distress. Her dentist had sued her over a $500 unpaid balance she owed him. She had been making payments and was furious that the dentist had the audacity to sue for his money. "What are my rights?" she wanted to know.

"How long have you owed the money?" I asked.

"About eighteen months."

"And how much have you been paying each month?"

"Ten or fifteen dollars per month," she replied hotly.

"Do you have a job?"

"No."

"Are you a stay-at-home mom?" I probed, trying to get a better understanding of her situation.

"No, we don't have children."

"Well, how much does your husband make a year?" I asked.

"About twenty-four thousand dollars a year," she answered.

We talked a bit further and she admitted to me that she was physically able to work; she just didn't like to. My answer probably ran her off as a listener and may have ruffled other people's feathers as well, but I told her the truth.

"You need to quit being so lazy and go get yourself a job!" I said. "It's a wonder the dentist didn't sue you a long time ago. Get off your butt, go to work, and get that debt paid within the next four weeks." I guess it never occurred to her that she could avoid a lawsuit by just going to work for a few weeks.

Like June, some people seem to have an aversion to hard work. Sometimes they are just plain lazy. Others may have been brought up that way, but many people have simply gotten overwhelmed by a financial mess and they have lost their hope.

James, a listener in Kansas City, called my show one day worried about a "huge debt." He couldn't see how he could possibly make it, and was wondering if he should file bankruptcy.

"How much is this huge debt?" I asked.

"Six thousand dollars," he responded bleakly.

Obviously, James's definition of "huge" was much different from mine, but the pressure he felt from this debt was very real indeed. "How much do you make a year, James?"

"Ten thousand dollars."

"And how many hours a week do you work?"

"About twenty."

"Are you disabled?" I asked.

"No."

"James, you don't need to file bankruptcy. You need to get a job! Maybe two jobs or even three if you have to!" I explained to James that by working about eighty hours a week—not for the rest of his life, but for a few months or less—he could completely eliminate that $6,000 debt and be well on his way to financial peace. His voice lit up as we talked and our listeners could hear hope building within him. I could tell that unlike many people who want advice only if it is what they want to hear, James was actually going to do it.

James was not lazy or incapacitated; it had just never seemed possible to him that he could *work* his way out of a financial mess.

Maybe you've had some hard luck; hard work will go a long way toward curing that. You can worry or you can work; the choice is yours. Worry will kill you, but hard work will open doors of opportunity for you. The truth is, if you want to have **More Than Enough**, you must work for it. There are no shortcuts; the only lazy people who are wealthy are folks who inherited their money or people who won the lottery, neither of which is likely to happen to you.

Teaching Your Children to Work

As parents, we get the privilege of teaching our children many valuable lessons in the few short years that children are entrusted to us. John Croyle, president of Big Oak Ranch, a foster home for children whose parents were not interested in teaching them about life, puts it this way: "You have eighteen years to pack their suitcases. The question is: What are you going to put in their suitcase, what will you teach your kids that will prepare them for life once they leave your home and get out on their own?"

Of all the important things we can teach our children, teaching them to work ranks high on the priority list. Work is a life skill that must be taught; it doesn't come naturally to kids. You have to work at teaching your kids to work. It won't happen by accident.

Start early to teach your children the value of hard work. Establish some chores that even the youngest can do and which the older kids are expected to do.

"Oh, but that's child abuse!" some misguided mom or dad might say.

No, child abuse is crippling your son or daughter by allowing him or her to grow up without learning responsibility. Child abuse is a little fat boy with his butt in front of the Nintendo for hours on end eating yet another whole bag of Doritos!

Even your youngest children can learn to put their toys away when they are done playing with them; with a little help from Mom or Dad, a three-year-old can make a bed. Older kids can help with housework or yard work. As your child completes a chore, give him or her lots of praise, and then watch your baby stand up straight, throw his or her shoulders back because of a job well done, and say, "I did good!"

Nowadays, our schools are scrambling for new and improved methods of teaching kids self-esteem. Yet despite society's best efforts, millions of kids have a sense of meaninglessness. Is it any wonder that life itself has been so devalued? When you are taught that you come from a mass of goo and you are going to return to a puff of dust, what difference does it really make whether you live or die? And why shouldn't I just use other people to get what I want in the meantime—or worse yet, attempt to destroy anyone with whom I disagree or who gets in my way?

Could it be that if we taught our kids the value of hard work, their self-esteem might rise? Would they have greater respect for themselves and each other? Would they understand the price that must be paid for those things that really matter?

Mmmm. This work stuff is powerful.

No Allowances

Do not pay your children *allowances*. Do give your kids *commissions* for work they do around the house. Allowances give the false impression that your child should be allowed to have money merely because he or she exists. (You've probably met a few adults who are laboring under this misconception, as well.) But people who have **More Than Enough** know that in the real world nobody gives you much of anything just because you are breathing and taking up space. (The only people who will do that are the ones trying to hook you on their high-interest credit cards.)

Commissions, on the other hand, are paid for work completed. Do the job, get the pay. Blow off the job, and you've blown your money for this pay period.

Real-world stuff, right? Tell your kids, "If the room isn't cleaned, or the grass isn't cut, or the garbage is not taken out on time, don't expect any commissions."

A simple, workable plan is to have three levels of chores around the house. The first level consists of the mandatory chores. These are the ones that must be done just because your child is part of the family. For younger kids, making their bed or cleaning up their messes might fall into this category.

Next, have some weekly chores that the kids can do for which they will be paid. These are not optional. The only difference is that you will pay the child when the chore is done, and not until then.

The third level should be bonus work. These chores are totally optional, things your kids don't necessarily have to do, but if they do them, you will reward their extra effort. In no case should you pay the child a commission on work that is not done.

How much you pay your children for doing these chores depends on your budget. If you can afford it, you may want to start the younger ones out at half the child's age; in other words, your six-year-old will get $3 per week (total) if she does all her mandatory chores, plus the weekly chore of dusting the furniture. Your ten-year-old gets $5 per week (total) if he feeds and takes the dog out for a walk each afternoon, cleans up any dog messes, and gives the dog a bath each week.

When the kids are younger, keep the chores and commissions schedule simple so your children (and you!) can easily determine the amount of money earned for the amount of work completed. A going rate of $1 per bonus chore is acceptable.

Older kids can be paid for baby-sitting, cutting the grass, washing the car, or other things that are age-appropriate. Older children should also be encouraged to make money outside the home, by getting a job at a fast-food restaurant (have you seen what those guys are paying these days?), working as a ticket taker at a local movie theater, working in a grocery store, or some other part-time employment. (Don't forget waiting on or busing tables.)

Children's Chore Chart

❖ Your children's chore chart will look something like this, with your own list of age-appropriate duties and bonus chores. Doing homework is not really a chore, but you may want to include it on your child's list as well. Post the chore chart either on your children's bulletin board, on the refrigerator, or someplace where the family will be able to see it regularly. Your children should check off each chore as it is completed, and then once each week, as a family, the commissions and bonuses should be passed out.

BOBBY (AGE SIX)

Daily chores	Sun.	Mon.	Tues.	Wed.	Thurs.	Fri.	Sat.
Make my bed	—	—	—	—	—	—	—
Pick up my toys	—	—	—	—	—	—	—
Help clear the table after dinner	—	—	—	—	—	—	—

Weekly chores ($3 weekly commission)
Bring all the bedclothes to the laundry room   Done ___
Sweep the basement floor   Done ___
Take the trash to the garage   Done ___

Bonus chores (worth $1 each!)
Dust the furniture $1 ___
Give the dog a bath $1 ___

SUSIE (AGE TWELVE)

Daily chores	Sun.	Mon.	Tues.	Wed.	Thurs.	Fri.	Sat.
Make my bed	—	—	—	—	—	—	—
Keep my room clean	—	—	—	—	—	—	—
Put dishes in dishwasher	—	—	—	—	—	—	—

Weekly chores ($6 weekly commission)

Vacuum my room and the upstairs hallway   Done ____

Fold the clean towels   Done ____

Clean bathtubs and sinks   Done ____

Clean cat litterbox   Done ____

Polish shoes or clean sneakers   Done ____

Bonus chores (worth $1 each!)

Weed the flower garden $1 ____

Polish the silverware $1 ____

Dust keepsakes in curio cabinet $1 ____

Whose Money Is It, Anyhow?

What do the kids get to do with the money? Blow it? No way! Not only should you teach your children the value of work, you must also teach them the value of saving, investing, and giving. It is not their money to do with it whatever they please. Sure, they should be allowed to spend some, but they should also save at least 10 percent and give at least 10 percent. Concerning their use of the other 80 percent: You have a responsibility to help your child set reasonable financial goals. For example, your seven-year-old can do an extra chore each week so he can save some money for that special toy he saw at the store. Divide the cost of the toy by the number of weeks or months it will take to reach that goal so your child knows how much he must save each week (or how many extra chores he must do) if he wants to buy that toy by that date. Do the same with your fourteen-year-old who *just has to have* a new stereo system. Few things will bring more sheer delight and do more for your child's self-esteem than when he or she takes his or her own money—money that he or she has worked hard to earn—and makes a purchase for which he or she pays out of his or her own savings.

Speaking of savings, use a clear jar for younger kids' savings so they can see the money stacking up. Older kids should be taught how to manage a savings account at a bank, including the deposits and withdrawals. By the time they are ready to graduate high school, they should be handling their own money in their own checking accounts, with your oversight, of course. Your job as a parent is to gradually remove the reins and expand the boundaries, but as long as your children are living under your roof, you should have input as to how their money is used.

Older children should also be encouraged to save for their first car purchase. If you can afford the incentive, you may want to match them dollar for dollar in their savings, but whatever approach you decide to use, *do not* buy your child a car. Make him or her earn the money to make the purchase, and pay cash. Do not finance your child's vehicle. Not only will they take better care of the car, they will drive much more carefully, knowing just how much it took to pay for that vehicle. Insurance and tire replacement all go along with car ownership as well, so be sure to include those costs in your teenager's financial goals.

Other big-ticket items such as school trips, class rings, and at least part of their clothing budget should be your children's responsibilities as they mature.

Throughout your children's lifetimes, you must also teach them to give of their financial resources. A good guideline is to give 10 percent (the tithe) to your local house of worship. Again, this should start even (especially) when your children are very young. If your four-year-old earns $2 by doing his chores, teach him to give at least 20 cents to his Sunday school class, or the Salvation Army Angel Tree project, or some other worthy cause. Certainly, it is a wonderful thing to see your children develop a giving spirit.

Remember, you are not just teaching your kids about money; you are teaching them about character. If you give them money and they fail to learn how to work and develop character, they will never have enough money. If your children develop character, however, they will always have money.

What steps will you take, starting next week, to improve your child's appreciation for work and its rewards?

_____

_____

_____

What do you need to do to better teach your children about the value of saving money?

_____

_____

Discipline—Work's Big Brother

If work is doing it, discipline is doing it consistently, every day. Having discipline regarding your financial dealings means you understand that getting rich quick is a myth. The way most rich people have acquired their wealth is surprisingly similar: one step at a time, they get out of debt, then start to save a little bit, then a little more, then make wise investments over a long period of time. Discipline is a key to building wealth and having **More Than Enough**.

But let's not kid ourselves. Discipline is tough to maintain. You may need to trick yourself into being disciplined when it comes to your money. For instance, if your employer offers an automatic deposit system for your paycheck, use it. You can also have many of your monthly bills autodrafted from your checking account. Personally, I love automatic drafts. Not only do I save gas by not having to drive to the bank and post office so frequently, but I never miss getting a discount for paying my electric, water, insurance, and other bills early each month.

Automatic savings plans can be extremely helpful as well. Sure, we want to touch our money; we want to hold it in our sweaty palms, dreaming of what we could do with it. But it is much easier to save money if you never see it— if it goes directly from your paycheck to a savings plan before you get a chance to put your grubby paws on it.

Self-control is not my strongest suit, and I know it, so I also have arranged automatic deposits for my mutual funds, IRAs, and our children's college funds.

Sure, it hurts sometimes. But if you save just $166.67 per month, that is $2,000 a year. If you put that money in an IRA, invested in a good growth stock mutual fund that averages 12 percent interest per year, and if you do that from the time you are twenty years of age until you celebrate your seventi-eth birthday, you will have $6,509,853! Six and a half million bucks!

Of course, you must be disciplined. You must consistently deposit $166.67 every month for fifty years. That's six hundred months. Some of those months, you may have a few financial emergencies. The car may break down. The kids might need braces. Your company just got downsized. (Incidentally, that's why your emergency fund is so vital, if you want to have **More Than Enough**.)

Regardless of what other pressing needs you have, you must maintain your discipline and deposit your savings every month. If you fudge even a little, you'll lose a lot.

In my book **More Than Enough**, I recounted the story of two brothers, Ben and Dan, both of whom planned to save $100 each month from age twenty-two to seventy-two. For the price of a few pizzas and cable TV each month, they will retire with $3,905,833. Ben faithfully made his deposits with-out making any withdrawals, but at age twenty-seven, Dan decided to use $5,000 as part of a down payment on a home. Dan continues to make his monthly deposits, but that down payment will cause his retirement fund to drop to $2,828,099, still a handsome sum, but a loss of more than $1 million!

Does discipline matter when it comes to your savings? I can give you a million reasons why it does!

What are some ways you can "trick" yourself into being disciplined in the area of your finances?

_____

_____

Does your company or business have an automatic deposit method for your paycheck?

_____ Yes _____ No _____ I don't know

If so, what might be the advantage of using such a plan?

_____

Why might you be reluctant to use a direct-deposit program for your paycheck?

_____

Why would you be reluctant to participate in a "direct" savings plan?

_____

"Twelve percent over fifty years. That's great," you may be saying, "but I didn't start saving when I was twenty-two and I'm much older than that now. I don't have fifty years to save, even if I could muster the discipline to do it." If you don't have fifty years to save, it is even more important that you start today. David Chilton, author of *The Wealthy Barber*, reminds us, "The best time to plant an oak tree is twenty years ago, the next best time is now." Perhaps you can double up on some savings deposits, or maybe the truth is you are just going to have less money to live on at your retirement. But if you don't get started today, you will have even less!

Discipline Doesn't Come Naturally

Recently, my company renovated the offices where we do our financial counseling, conduct our thirteen-week course Financial Peace University, and broadcast our daily radio program around the country. During the construction, one of the young men who was doing some of the dirtiest and most difficult work on the project took a keen interest in what we do at our company. One day, he stopped me in the hallway and asked several questions about some investments he was considering.

"What do you think about commodity investing?" he asked.

"Investing in commodities is extremely high risk and an easy way to lose your money," I told him. "No way would I advise you to put your money there."

"Well, can't you get rich easily in real estate?"

It was obvious that this guy had been watching too many late-night infomercials, and had been duped into believing the "get rich quick" fallacy. So I stopped what I was doing for a few minutes, sat down with him, and explained that the best way to get rich quickly is to get rich slowly, by making steady, solid investments in mutual funds over a long period of time. The entire time I was talking to the young man, an older, wiser workman was standing on a ladder, smiling, and nodding his head. He knew that what I was telling the impetuous young man was what he needed to hear.

The truth is, Ed McMahon and Dick Clark are probably not going to show up on your doorstep with a check and a camera crew. You are probably not going to win the big powerball lottery. State lotteries and other forms of legal gambling are simply government gobbledygook—another way to tax people who either can't or won't do the math, who refuse to recognize that they have as much chance of winning the lottery as they do of getting hit by a meteor.

The way you get rich is by getting up, going to work, living on less than you make, disciplining yourself to save money and make wise investments, and keeping at it for an extended period of time!

The Scripture says, "A faithful man will abound with blessings, but he who hastens to be rich will not go unpunished." It's not easy, but if you work, save, and invest, you will become wealthy—you will be rich in much more than mere money. You will have **More Than Enough**.

Diligence: Vision with a Guarantee

What does it take to have **More Than Enough**? In a word, it takes *diligence*. Remember the formula?

"Work is doing it. Discipline is doing it every day. Diligence is doing it *well* every day."

Or you could think of it this way: "Work is good, discipline is better, and diligence is best."

Diligence means that you are not simply working hard or often, but that you are working with a consistent level of excellence. Diligence in your work, as well as in your personal relationships, will cause you to prosper and flourish even when others around you are faltering and floundering.

Working toward your vision with this sort of attitude comes with a guarantee—not just from my publisher or from me, but from a much higher authority.

Proverbs 10:4 says, "He who deals with a slack hand becomes poor but the hand of the diligent makes one rich." How about that for a warranty! God says that if you are diligent about things that matter over a long period of time, you are guaranteed to be rich. Let's see, who should we trust? Merrill Lynch, Tony Robbins, Morgan Stanley, E. F. Hutton, or God? Any idea about who might have the inside information here?

> Diligence has an element of vision to it that tells you
> a real comfortable place to live is just inside your
> income.
>
> —*More Than Enough*

Diligence is a true sign of maturity. Children, whether they are four years old or fifty-four years old, are always in a hurry, looking for the shortcuts. But people who want **More Than Enough** have learned that there are no real shortcuts, and they have developed a long-term plan and outlook. They are committed to doing what they do with a consistent excellence. Granted that consistent excellence is a rare thing to observe, but then so is true wealth.

Diligence has an eye on the future. You do your work well now, while knowing that it will pay dividends in the future. Diligence knows that there is always a price. There are no free lunches, and you are not somebody else's project. You will either pay a price now by making large deposits into your savings, investments, and personal relationships, or you will pay a much higher price later. Those who deal with a slack hand, the Scripture says, will reap nothing but poverty; they will retire broke and lonely. Please understand, you *will* pay a price; the only question is whether it will be relatively small and slightly inconvenient now, or large and perpetually destructive later in your life. As John Maxwell says, "Pay now, play later . . . Play now, pay later." The choice is yours. Keep in mind, however, that the price goes up the longer you wait. The longer you put off working with discipline and diligence, the more difficult it will be to achieve your goals. The great opera singer Beverly Sills said it succinctly: "There is no shortcut to any place that is worth going."

Diligence means that you are doing those things that matter and dealing with the details. How well are you doing due diligence in each of the following areas? Rate each area by circling the response that best reflects how well you are doing.

In my spiritual life, I am:
excellent   great   good   okay   not so hot   needing to do some work
In my marriage, I am:
excellent   great   good   okay   not so hot   needing to do some work
With my kids, I am:
excellent   great   good   okay   not so hot   needing to do some work
In my career, I am:
excellent   great   good   okay   not so hot   needing to do some work
In financial matters, I am:
excellent   great   good   okay   not so hot   needing to do some work
In my physical health and well-being, I am:
excellent   great   good   okay   not so hot   needing to do some work
In my investments, I am:
excellent   great   good   okay   not so hot   needing to do some work
In my preparation for the future, I am:
excellent   great   good   okay   not so hot   needing to do some work

I have prepared and updated a will designating how my estate should be divided upon my death:

____ Yes ____ No

I have a term life insurance policy in the amount of ten times my average annual income to provide for my family upon my death:

____ Yes ____ No

I have long-term insurance in place to cover nursing home expenses if necessary for me or for my parents:

___ Yes   ___ No

If you answered no to any of these questions, the time is *now* to do something about it.

It's Too Hard for Me!

I never cease to be amazed over how many people think that hard work, maintaining discipline, and doing things with diligence are just too much to ask of them. It's as though they think that excellence just "happens," that God gave certain people special, super genes that produce megadoses of success. It doesn't work that way.

The United States armed forces know that soldiers are not born; they are trained. That's why every soldier's first stop is "boot camp." There, the military takes a ragtag bunch of young people and teaches them to work, to be disciplined, and to be diligent about their duties. Often, a different person emerges from boot camp than the young man or woman who entered. The person is changed, challenged, and chomping at the bit to get on with the real-world experience.

Why is the boot camp experience so successful? It is mandatory. Every soldier must go through it. Nobody ever said that it was easy or that it was fun. But the end result is worth it—to the individual, to his or her branch of the service, to the country, and ultimately to the world.

Our **More Than Enough** "boot camp" is much gentler, and unfortunately it is not mandatory. You aren't required to do anything with the information you find in these pages. But aren't you mature enough to set some self-imposed requirements upon yourself, some things that you believe are worth doing, because life and death may well hang in the balance?

In 1968, in the part of the country in which I grew up, we weren't all that interested in special physical fitness programs. Nobody in our neighborhood hired a personal trainer because everyone worked hard. We didn't need any fancy, high-tech exercise equipment to work out on, because most of us had grown up on farms where we "worked out" quite literally. We figured that the only people who needed to work out were professional athletes. In our area, if you saw someone running down the street, we assumed that they were being chased!

But one morning just after dawn, my parents saw a neighbor running down the road, wearing an old gray sweat suit and tennis shoes. The next morning, my parents saw the jogger again. Morning after morning, the ritual continued. My family members were intrigued. Why was this guy running even though nobody was chasing him?

One morning my dad pretended to be going out for the newspaper just as the jogger approached on his daily jaunt. With our little noses pressed against the living room window, my siblings and I watched as the jogger interrupted his run long enough to talk with Dad. Oddly, the man never stopped lifting his feet up and down while he talked. After a few minutes, the jogger continued his journey and Dad returned to the house to reveal the secret.

It really was nothing mysterious. Apparently our neighbor had suffered a slight heart attack, and his doctor had told him, "If you want to live, you'd better lose some weight and get your body back in shape." The doc had recommended the morning runs. We kids figured out who was really chasing the jogger—it was the Grim Reaper! When the diagnosis is "jog or die," getting out of bed before dawn for a sunrise run gets a whole lot easier!

Similarly, when we realize what is really at stake, no price is too high to pay for our families, ourselves, and our God. You'll find the courage and the stamina to do what is necessary. The more that you have invested in reaching a goal, the more likely you are to stick with it. I like what the loquacious Green Bay Packers football coach Vince Lombardi said: "The harder you work, the harder it is to surrender."

Winners are built on purpose. Wealth is built on purpose; most current millionaires were not born rich. Of America's current millionaires, 80 percent are first-generation rich. They did not inherit their wealth. They have worked hard for their money.

Most people who read this book will have the potential to retire as a millionaire; all will have the capacity to retire with dignity. Anyone reading this book has the ability to improve the primary relationships in their lives. It will take work, discipline, and diligence, but you *can* do it.

And as you do, you will have **More Than Enough**.

Aisle Seven—Work, Discipline, Diligence

1. Business Section

TAKING INVENTORY
Approximately what percentage of your time on the job do you spend working diligently?

_____

How disciplined are you about making deadlines, meeting quotas, and hitting goals on schedule? (Check the statement that best describes you.)

____ I am extremely disciplined about such matters.
____ I do my best, but I'm not a fanatic.
____ I don't take such artificial lines too seriously.
____ I rarely worry about such things.
____ I am extremely undisciplined in those areas.
____ I have a reputation for doing good work, but missing schedules.
____ I have a reputation for doing mediocre work and missing schedules.
____ Other: _____

Think back on your job during the past month. How good have you been at shaking off failures or dirt thrown in your direction, and "stepping up"?

___ excellent
___ very good
___ okay, but not without feeling mighty dirty
___ not so good
___ awful

On a scale of one to ten, how disciplined are you concerning your time and work habits?

1	2	3	4	5	6	7	8	9	10
Very poor				Average				Very good	

How likely is it that your boss, coworkers, or customers would refer to you as "a diligent worker"?

Boss:
___ Quite likely ___ Possibly ___ Doubtful ___ Are you kidding?
Coworkers:
___ Quite likely ___ Possibly ___ Doubtful ___ Are you kidding?
Customers:
___ Quite likely ___ Possibly ___ Doubtful ___ Are you kidding?

What can you do to improve your value (or your reputation) in the workplace?

Your "To Do" List

Write out a morning schedule for yourself that includes time for exercise, breakfast, reading, and prayer.

While looking over your daily planner or schedule, go through each item currently on the calendar and "pad" it with enough extra time that you will not be rushed, nor will you risk missing or being late for an important date or meeting.

List three things that a disciplined work ethic involving the diligent pursuit of consistent excellence will mean in your business or career.

1. _____

2. _____

3. _____

2. Marriage Section

TAKING INVENTORY

When people say "marriage takes work," what does that mean to you?

_____

_____

On a scale of one to ten, how would you say your marriage is "working"?

1	2	3	4	5	6	7	8	9	10
Poorly				About average					Fabulously

What one thing can you do for the next six weeks that might raise that number by one notch?

_____

Steven Covey contends that one of the habits of effective people is being proactive. What does being "proactive" mean to you in regard to your marriage?

_____

_____

How diligently are you pursuing a better marriage? (Circle the phrase that best describes you.)

___ Very diligently.
___ When I feel like it.

___ When my spouse deserves it.
___ I'm not.

Your "To Do" List

List three tangible things that you are currently doing in an effort to demonstrate your love for your spouse.

1. _____
2. _____
3. _____

List three tangible things that you plan to do to within the next three months to demonstrate your love for your spouse.

1. _____
2. _____
3. _____

Discuss with your spouse how you can both better work together to be disciplined in the area of your money, in your relationship with each other, and in your relationship with your children.

3. Parenting Section

TAKING INVENTORY

What are the most important lessons you want your children to learn by observing you in your personal work ethic?

_____

_____

_____

How are you attempting to impart to your children a positive impression concerning work?

_____

_____

Keeping in mind the categories of work, discipline, and diligence, how pleased are you concerning your children's progress in each of the following areas?

Emotionally
Tremendously pleased ___ Average ___ We need to work on that ___
Physically
Tremendously pleased ___ Average ___ We need to work on that ___
Financially
Tremendously pleased ___ Average ___ We need to work on that ___
Spiritually
Tremendously pleased ___ Average ___ We need to work on that ___

List two ways in which you are teaching your child to be proactive.

1. _____
2. _____

Who taught you the most concerning diligence? (Check all that apply.)

___ My parents taught me.
___ My school taught me.
___ My church taught me.
___ I taught myself.
___ I have yet to learn.

Parents' "To Do" List

Write out three to five age-appropriate chores for each of your children. Discuss these with your spouse to make sure they are fair and achievable before presenting them to the kids.

Read the "shake it off and step up" story to your children. Ask them to tell you how it might apply to them.

This month, plan at least one weekend day when you and your children can do some work together around the house. (These may or may not include chores.)

If you have teenagers, discuss with them what it means to be disciplined and diligent in regard to a relationship with a person of the opposite sex.

4. Singles' Section

TAKING INVENTORY
How would you describe your attitude toward work?

_____

What does it mean to you to be disciplined in each of the following areas:

Spiritually: _____
Physically: _____
Financially: _____

Who do you see yourself emulating the most in your work habits?

____ my dad
____ my mom
____ my older sibling(s)
____ my boss
____ a coworker
____ other: _____

Sometimes it is easy to get "dirt" thrown on you as a single person. What does it mean to you to "shake it off and step up"?

_____

_____

Singles' "To Do" List

Write out a morning schedule for yourself that includes time for exercise, breakfast, reading, and prayer.

Establish deadlines for some practical, reachable goals in your life. (For instance, I will clean out the refrigerator this coming Saturday!")

Write a brief paragraph describing how a renewed emphasis on work, discipline, and diligence will make you a better potential marriage partner or a more content single person. Mail this paragraph to yourself.

In what specific area will you pour on some extra effort for ninety days to see a particular goal met?

_____

On what date will you begin? _____

By what date will you have accomplished the goal? _____

5. Financial Section

TAKING INVENTORY

How does the "shake it off and step up" story relate to some of the financial setbacks you have incurred?

_____

What has been your greatest aid in "shaking off the dirt" and stepping up to new financial opportunities?

_____

How do you usually feel after you have completed a hard day's work? (Check all that apply.)

____ Tired but contented
____ That I have earned my money

___ Disgusted that I have to go back to the job another day

___ Relaxed and ready to enjoy the time off

___ That I have done something meaningful

___ That another day out of my life has been shot

___ That I have accomplished something significant

How important a factor is the financial remuneration you receive for your work? (Check all that apply.)

___ I'd do my job for free if I had to.

___ If it weren't for the money, I'd be gone tomorrow.

___ I appreciate my paycheck, but I work hard because it makes me feel good about myself.

___ The money is all that matters to me. I could make or sell widgets if the money were right.

___ I work hard and well because I believe God blesses diligence.

Your Financial "To Do" List

List several reasons, other than money, why it is imperative that you teach your children the value of hard work.

_____

_____

_____

At the risk of sounding too nostalgic (or old-fashioned!), compare with your children the drastic differences in prices since your childhood and theirs. This can be an entertaining activity as you and your kids marvel at the prices of gasoline, a new car, household items, and other goods.

Describe the amount of work it took to earn the money to purchase these items and compare it to the time that will be required of your children to earn enough to buy similar items today.

· N I N E ·

Patience Is Power

*Patience is golden because patience will
increase your gold.*
                    —*More Than Enough*

AS I DROVE UP in front of the house, I could see its potential. It must have been a magnificent home in its day—the Georgian columns, the sitting area on a second-story patio, the fact that it was stately, and elegant—everything about the place just cried out, "Buy me!" This was the sort of house that a person could become emotionally attached to—which is dangerous if you're an investor negotiating to purchase the place, renovate it, and resell it for a profit.

But I also recognized that this house could easily be a money pit, sucking money out of my account like a powerful vacuum cleaner. The question was: Were its drawbacks outdistancing its sales potential? Since the house was built sometime around 1908, I was certain that the interior of the house contained ornate wood moldings and solid wood floors that would have to be redone before I could sell it. Wild trees and weeds had grown up through the sidewalk leading to the porch, numerous windows had been broken, and a fire on the first floor had done serious structural and smoke damage.

The owner, as I suspected, was so emotionally attached to the home that he couldn't see all the repairs that needed to be done. All he could picture were his wonderful memories associated with the home, and its tremendous future potential. All I could picture were dollar signs.

The seller wanted $100,000 for the place, not a bad price considering that once it was renovated, the home could easily sell for $200,000. But I knew that it would take at least $80,000 to make the place presentable, and with interest, insurance, realtor fees, and my time, anything over $60,000 for the house was a losing proposition for me.

No deal. As much as I loved the house, I had to walk away.

Six months passed and the bank foreclosed on the owner. I offered the bank $50,000 for the property, but banks are not in business to lose money—they wanted $90,000. Again, I had to walk away.

Another fellow bought the home and began the refurbishing process. He soon realized that he was in over his head and put the place back up for sale. He wanted $110,000 for it now! "No way," I said, and for the third time, I walked away from a house that I really wanted. Before long, the bank foreclosed on this owner, too. The bank put the house up for sale, and two and a half years from the time I had first "discovered" the bargain, I bought the place for $40,000. Patience is power.

But I didn't always have that sort of patience. I didn't always have the power to walk away from a tempting situation. Before I learned to have patience in my personal life and in my business, I made more than my share of mistakes, bad business deals, and foolish purchases. I paid "stupid tax"—the money we waste on unwise decisions—with multiple zeroes on the end of it.

Power to Prosper

Power comes from having options—I don't have to do this, buy this, or be that sort of person. I can dare to walk away and patiently wait for a better opportunity.

The most common mistake people make when they are shopping and negotiating for a product or property is that they catch "buying fever." They know they want to buy something, anything, and the money is burning a hole in their pockets. They can hardly wait to spend it!

Once the "fever" sets in, you are in big trouble. Few cures exist for "buying fever." It will dull your senses, blind your eyes, and rot your brain all in a matter of minutes if you don't get away from the "carrier." The only real antidote for buying fever is walkaway power, and the only source of walkaway power is patience.

Otherwise, when you catch the fever, you lose your sense of reality; you forget that there really are other options. You do not absolutely need that house, or that car, or that new dress. But if you continue to remain in close proximity to the carrier, you will weaken, your eyes will cloud over, and you will not be able to see things clearly. Consequently, even if it is a good buy, the fever will cause you to pay too much! You have become "married" to the purchase, galvanized to it by heat of the fever. Now you can't shake it. You're stuck. You feel your hand reaching for your wallet or checkbook; a pen pops into your hand and you are ready to sign on the line—any line! Everyone in the area can see it coming. The salesman or real estate agent smiles openly. You are doomed. You bought it.

Patience is power . . . and lack of patience will put you in the poorhouse!

People who have **More Than Enough** have learned to be patient. They have learned patience in their personal relationships, and they have learned patience in their financial dealings. They have discovered an incredible power to prosper as a direct result of having patience. As the seventeenth-century writer Dr. Maistre said, "To know how to wait is the great secret to success."

What purchases have you made recently in which, looking back, you now realize you were in a "fever" when you made that decision?

_____

_____

_____

What effect do you think it would have had on the outcome had you walked away from those purchases for a while?

_____

_____

_____

Most of us regard patience as a virtue. Consequently, we tend to think of ourselves as patient people. Actually, we're not. Our adage is more like, "I want patience . . . and I want it *NOW!*" Which of the following irritants are most likely to bring out your impatience? (Check all that apply.)

____ automated telephone answering systems
____ delayed flights, buses, or taxis
____ balancing my checkbook
____ computers
____ long-distance phone companies
____ people who are often late
____ cellular phones

____ traffic jams
____ long lines at the store
____ obnoxious people
____ "customer service" representatives
____ stuck zippers
____ in-laws
____ dead batteries

Okay, just how patient a person are you?

How to Develop Patience

If patience plays an important part in having **More Than Enough,** the logical question is: How can we develop the kind of patience that will bring fiscal and personal power to our lives? That's where things get sticky. I don't wish any hard times on anyone, but I would be less than truthful if I did not tell you straightforwardly that the two key elements in developing patience are *trials* and *time.* Put the two of them together and you get *endurance.* And endurance leads to patience.

We often speak of a person who has a patient spirit as someone with the "patience of Job." Job (pronounced "Jobe") was the biblical character who suffered through extremely difficult times, losing his property, his health, his family, and his fortune. However, the one thing he did not lose through his trials was his faith. Because of that, God rewarded him and gave him back even more than he had lost. Ever since, Job has been known as a paragon of patience. Interestingly, the word "patience" is not used one single time in Job's story. The New Testament draws attention to Job's *endurance*. Clearly, Job didn't wake up one morning and say, "Let's see, today I will attempt to develop patience." It didn't happen that way. Job's patience was the result of the trials he endured over a period of time.

Most likely, your patience will be developed through a similar process. You may not go through the trials that Job did, but you can be sure that developing patience will be a process. It takes time to grow. It takes time to develop patience, but your patience will help you to become a success.

Dr. Thomas Stanley, author of *The Millionaire Next Door,* discovered during his research for that book that the "typical" millionaire in America today has been working in his or her chosen field for fifteen to twenty years! Success takes time.

You can't microwave success. Success requires a Crock-Pot. Success has to cook for a while. That's because success and patience go hand in hand, and patience necessitates that we learn to delay present pleasure for future prosperity. Patience will help you to become rich, but it won't happen overnight. Theologian and philosopher William Thayer comments: "Thousands of youths and older persons have made a failure of life's work because they did not know how to wait. Their impatience to achieve caused them to overlook some of the conditions, especially that historic one—that time is an element of success."

The patience that leads to **More Than Enough** is not synonymous with slackness. It is similar to a loaded spring, ready to be released. In 1656, Christian Huygens, a Dutch mathematician, discovered that a coiled spring, called a mainspring, could be set to slowly and precisely release its power to drive a pendulum. His discovery made our first pendulum clocks possible.

That same sort of tension is involved when we are going through the trials that are producing patience in us. Time seems to stand still. *It's taking forever to get through this mess,* we think. But like the slow release of energy from the clock's mainspring, if we endure long enough, not only will we develop patience, but the time will come when our patience leads to greater creativity and productivity, which will also help us develop wealth.

What trial are you currently experiencing—something that you would not have chosen if given a choice?

_____

How is this trial making you stronger and teaching you patience?

_____

When you think of someone you know who is patient, what other positive qualities seem to accompany that trait?

_____

_____

_____

What correlation can you see between patience and these other positive traits?

_____

Patience Will Make You Wealthy

Patiently following your dream and working toward your vision will eventually lead you to success. One step at a time is still the way to get there. Don't worry if you are not moving ahead rapidly, just keep making progress. As the old Chinese proverb says, "Be not afraid of going slowly; be afraid of standing still."

In a world that is whirling by us as rapidly as our modern, sound bite society, this sort of patience will set you apart from the crowd. No matter how much of an adrenaline junkie you are, the first rule of wealth building remains: Invest slowly and consistently and you will prosper. The second rule of wealth building is: You are not the exception to the rule! Success that is truly lasting is built on character, not on luck.

Oh, sure, some people get lucky and win the big lottery checks. But an interesting statistic has emerged concerning those big money winners. Within the past twenty years, 53 percent of the big-money lottery winners have filed bankruptcy!

How could someone win millions of dollars and then squander it all away in such a short period of time? Over half of the big winners have lost it all. Why? Because their character was not built on values that would cause them to invest their winnings wisely. Instead, the same facet of their personalities—that get-something-for-nothing attitude—did not change just because they had a temporary bulge in their bank account. The same get-rich-quick schemes and scams that led them to play the lottery in the first place were often their undoing. Many of the lottery winners lost their money trying to make more "easy money."

On the other hand, patience will make you money because it turns you into an investor rather than a speculator. An investor is not a person who bought some stock in eight-track tape companies once in the past. An investor is someone who consistently puts his or her money into a growing concern, such as a mutual fund, looking only at the long-term results. You are not really an investor if you are trying to hit it big in the stock market just one time. You are a speculator.

It's okay to be a speculator if you have lots of money you can afford to lose. And sometimes speculators make megabucks practically overnight. It does happen. But it's also possible to lose big bucks overnight. "Day trading," or buying and selling stocks that look attractive at the moment, is close to legalized gambling. When you put your money into a stock on a short-term basis, you can only guess where it will go. It may go up, or it may go down. You can count your cards at a Las Vegas blackjack table and do just about as well.

A healthy skepticism is also wise when dealing with stockbrokers nowadays. One of the downsides to the prosperity of the 1980s and the 1990s is that we have had such a consistently "bull" market, with stocks doing well, almost any stockbroker who can read and do math has been relatively successful. Consequently, the market itself has made many a gambling fool look much smarter than he or she really is. With the long-running bull market in the 1990s, you could have fallen off a cabbage truck and landed in a good deal that made money. Unfortunately, many of these brokers have arrogantly labeled themselves "experts," when in fact a sign on the door that says LUCKY GAMBLER would be more accurate. As always, buyer beware.

My advice? Invest in mutual funds. Over the past seventy years, good growth stocks have averaged over 12 percent return each year. In my book *The Financial Peace Planner,* you will find simple, easy-to-follow instructions for how to create an investment strategy and how to choose the mutual funds in which you want to invest. Take the time to do the homework. Don't invest in anything you don't understand and look for investments that have been around and profitable for at least five years. Put your money in those kinds of accounts and then leave it alone!

You don't need to worry about day-to-day stock-price fluctuations, because you are looking at your investments from a long-term perspective. Opportunists and doomsday prophets abound in about equal numbers nowadays. You can become extremely agitated and confused if you give either group much attention. Sure, watch what the market does, but unless the whole American economy falls apart, plan to leave your investments in place over the long haul. Continue to save and invest month after month and make it a rule that you will not touch those investments that are earmarked for your retirement or your children's college funds. With a little patience, you will discover one day that you are incredibly wealthy!

> How much grows everywhere if we do but wait.
> —*Thomas Carlyle*

Debt—The Death of Patience

Most debt is caused by a lack of patience. It stems from an attitude of "I want what I want and I want it now!" And "I *deserve* it!"

Well, if you deserve it, fine—save your money and pay cash for it.

"Why should I save up and pay for stuff," one fellow asked me once with a straight face at one of my seminars, "when by signing this little credit card slip, I can take it home with me today?"

Besides the fact that the insatiable desire for such immediate gratification is a clear sign of childishness, it is also expensive. The interest on those credit card payments is like an acid eating away your income, destroying your ability to save money, and robbing you of your future. We really need to get this into our heads: *Debt is the opposite of wealth*! It doesn't matter how big a house you live in, or how fancy a car you drive, or how many designer names you have in your closet—if you owe money to somebody, you are not wealthy. You are debt-poor! And you are getting poorer every day that you are still in debt.

Conversely, something wonderful happens when you don't have any debt payments each month. You are able to save money and invest in your future! When you don't have any debt to service, it actually becomes fun to look at your checkbook.

It's a funny thing—patience with money matters seems to spill over into our personal relationships, as well. Why? Because patience is a character trait that is rooted in one's value system. People who are willing to put off making a purchase until they have the cash are often kinder, more appreciative, and more willing to help others. The opposite is true as well: People who are constantly agitated over money matters make lousy companions. They tend to be selfish, shortsighted, compulsive or impulsive types of people who want to have all honey and no bees. They are unwilling to wait. They do not see the value in delaying present pleasure for future prosperity, so they are often users, people who will do almost anything to get what they want, now. These people do not make good friends, nor are they good business partners. They rarely make faithful and committed marriage partners.

What is the one area of your life in which you most need to develop patience?

       ___ personal relationships
       ___ financial dealings
       ___ spiritual questions and unanswered prayers
       ___ academic pursuits
       ___ career goals

How hard is it for you to put off making a purchase until you actually can afford to pay for it with cash?

___ Not hard   ___ I sometimes have trouble   ___ It is extremely difficult

What reminders can you place in your life to help you avoid the tyranny of the urgent, while helping you keep the long-term goal in mind? (For instance, I will display pictures of my children in my work space.)

_____

_____

_____

Doing Right Has Its Rewards

In my company, our employees and I have a saying that epitomizes our values: "We do the right thing, no matter what it costs us, because in the end, that is the shortest path to success." This principle governs everything we do at the Lampo Group. Granted, it occasionally costs us money in the short run. Sometimes this concept causes us temporary financial setbacks because we refuse to do business with partners who do not share our values. At other times, we choose not to hire the least expensive vendor if we know the vendor lacks integrity. We may take a hit on this month's Profit and Loss Statement, but we know that by doing the right thing, we will make our company more stable, and ultimately more profitable. It takes a bit of patience, but that small amount of patience will return huge dividends to us someday. Patience always wins.

In what area are you allowing something other than patience to win? (For example, selfishness, pride, the promise of fast, easy money.)

_____

_____

Are the trade-offs you are currently making really worth it?

_____ Yes _____ No _____ Uncertain

What must you do to turn this situation around?

_____

_____

Time Will Tell

Patience means having the ability to wait. It also involves the perseverance to keep hoping for the best while you are working toward your goal. Gibbon took twenty years to write *The Decline and Fall of the Roman Empire*. Noah Webster spent thirty-six years preparing the first dictionary that bore his name. For over a century now, the name Webster has been inextricably linked to the term "dictionary." Patience presumes that type of endurance. Interestingly, Webster's own definition of "patience" is still in the dictionary that bears his name: "Demonstrating uncomplaining endurance under distress."

Patience does not come easily for many of us—especially those of us who are ambitious, task-oriented, Type-A sort of folks. Moreover, our entire generation is unaccustomed to waiting. We are the microwave generation. We want it done now. When a computer takes more than a few seconds to boot up, we balk, forgetting that just a decade or two ago, we marveled at the speed and efficiency of a mimeograph machine! (That was a precursor to the photocopy machine, in case you have never had the joyous experience of taking a test printed in smudged blue ink on paper that still smelled of formaldehyde.)

Many of us struggle to think long term, to invest with vision, to make integrity-based decisions when only a slight compromise would increase the bottom line significantly. We struggle to wait for the right time before making strategic business moves. We struggle against loneliness in our relationships, refusing to give ourselves to just anybody, waiting for just the *right* person, because we know that the only thing tougher than being single is being married to the wrong person!

Sure, patience stretches us at times. But those of us who want **More Than Enough** have chosen to live by a different set of values. We refuse to accept the prevailing attitude of our culture that says, "Get it now; get it while you can." We rebel against being *normal* by society's standards.

For most people, normal means broke. Not us! "Average" is a word to which we have an extreme aversion! Average is far below where you and I want to live. We want to win! And if it takes patience to run the race, then bring it on! We're in this for the long haul. We're in this for **More Than Enough**.

Aisle Eight— The Power of Patience

1. Business Section

TAKING INVENTORY

Describe a time when a lack of patience cost you money or position in your workplace.

_____

_____

The saying "timing is everything" may be an overstatement, but it certainly carries a lot of weight. What specific goals are you hoping to pursue in your business or company, but you are currently waiting until the timing is right?

_____

_____

How will you know when the timing is right for the above goals?

_____

_____

On a scale of zero to ten, how patient are you in regard to your business, career, or company?

0	1	2	3	4	5	6	7	8	9	10

Not patient at all   Relatively patient   Extremely patient

A fine line sometimes exists between being patient and being lazy. How do you tell the difference in your workplace and in your work ethic?

_____

_____

Your "To Do" List

List three ways in which patience has helped you in your career or workplace within the past six months.

1. _____
2. _____
3. _____

List three other areas in which you hope to develop more patience in your career or workplace within the next year.

1. _____
2. _____
3. _____

Think back to a time when impatience cost you money or position. What specific things could you have done differently in that situation, things which may have prevented or improved the circumstances that led to the loss?

_____

_____

_____

If options lead to patience and patience leads to power, what will you do within the next six months to improve your options in your workplace or career?

_____

_____

How will you know that you have achieved this goal?

_____

2. Marriage Section

TAKING INVENTORY

Briefly describe a time when a lack of patience cost you dearly in your relationship with your spouse. _____

_____

_____

Timing is an important factor in any relationship, but especially in marriage. How is timing influencing you and your spouse's long-term decisions concerning your future? (For example, in regard to having children, buying a house, making other major purchases, making investments.) _____

_____

_____

List three areas in which you would like to improve the "patience level" between your spouse and you.

1. _____
2. _____
3. _____

On a scale of zero to ten, how patient are you with your spouse?

0	1	2	3	4	5	6	7	8	9	10

Not patient at all   Relatively patient   Extremely patient

Your "To Do" List

List three ways in which patience has helped you in your marriage within the past six months.

1. _____
2. _____
3. _____

List three other areas in which you hope to develop more patience in your marriage within the next year.

1. _____
2. _____
3. _____

Think back to a time when impatience cost you dearly in your relationship with your spouse. What specific things could you have done differently in that situation, things which may have prevented or improved the circumstances?

_____

_____

List some specific ways in which your patience is a reflection of your marriage commitment and your love for your spouse.

_____

_____

On a scale of zero to ten, how patient will your spouse say that you are with him or her?

0	1	2	3	4	5	6	7	8	9	10

Not patient at all   Relatively patient   Extremely patient

Discuss with your spouse how you can raise that number a notch or two.

3. Parenting Section

TAKING INVENTORY

In what specific ways are you attempting to teach financial patience and power to your children?

_____

_____

_____

Briefly describe a time when a lack of patience cost you dearly in your relationship with your children. _____

_____

_____

List three areas in which you would like to improve the "patience level" between your children and you.

1. _____

2. _____

3. _____

On a scale of zero to ten, how patient are you with your children?

0	1	2	3	4	5	6	7	8	9	10

Not patient at all   Relatively patient   Extremely patient

Your "To Do" List

List three ways in which patience has helped you in your relationship with your children within the past six months.

1. _____
2. _____
3. _____

List three other areas in which you hope to develop more patience in your relationship with your children within the next year.

1. _____
2. _____
3. _____

Think back to a time when impatience cost you dearly in your relationship with your children. What specific things could you have done differently in that situation, things that may have prevented or improved the circumstances?

_____

_____

List some specific ways in which your patience is a reflection of your commitment to and your love for your children.

_____

_____

On a scale of zero to ten, how patient will your kids say that you are with them?

0   1   2   3   4   5   6   7   8   9   10
Not patient at all   Relatively patient   Extremely patient

Discuss with your children how you can raise that number a notch or two.

Discuss with your children why it is so important that we all learn to delay present gratification for future blessings and prosperity.

4. Singles' Section

TAKING INVENTORY

Briefly describe a time when a lack of patience cost you dearly in a relationship with a person of the opposite sex. _____

_____

How is timing influencing the decision-making process in regard to some of the key areas of your future? (For example, in regard to your career, getting married or remaining single, buying a house, making other major purchases, making investments.)

_____

_____

_____

List three areas in which you would like to improve your "patience level."

1. _____
2. _____
3. _____

On a scale of zero to ten, how patient are you with friends or relatives?

0	1	2	3	4	5	6	7	8	9	10

Not patient at all   Relatively patient   Extremely patient

Your "To Do" List

List three ways in which patience has helped keep you on track in the pursuit of your goals within the past six months.

1. _____
2. _____
3. _____

List three other areas in which you hope to develop more patience within the next year.

1. _____
2. _____
3. _____

Think back to a time when impatience cost you dearly in a relationship either with your parents, a close friend, or someone you were dating. What specific things could you have done differently in that situation, things that may have prevented or improved the circumstances?

_____
_____
_____

List some specific ways in which your patience is a reflection of your commitment to God.

_____
_____
_____

On a scale of zero to ten, how patient will your best friends say that you are?

0   1   2   3   4   5   6   7   8   9   10

Not patient at all   Relatively patient   Extremely patient

Discuss with your friends how you can raise that number a notch or two.

5. Financial Section

TAKING INVENTORY

List three ways "buying fever" has influenced some of your past financial desisions.

1. _____
2. _____
3. _____

How will the information in this chapter help you to avoid catching "the fever" in the future?

_____

_____

What major purchase or purchases are you patiently saving your money for right now, and how long will it take you to save the amount necessary at your current rate of savings?

Item: _____ Cost: _____ Time: _____

Item: _____ Cost: _____ Time: _____

If you *chose* to speed up the savings process for those purchases, what steps would you take?

_____

_____

How can you develop more "walk-away power" in your financial decisions?

_____

_____

One a scale of one to ten, how good are you at delaying present pleasure for future prosperity?

0	1	2	3	4	5	6	7	8	9	10
Lousy		Okay		Fairly good			Very good			Excellent

Your Financial "To Do" List

Discuss with your spouse or a friend why patience is such an important part of your financial investment strategy.

Which of the following statements best describes your attitude toward time and money? (Check one.)

___ Time is money.

___ Time waits for no man or woman.

___ Time is on my side.

___ Time stands still.

___ There's no time like the present.

Gather some information on mutual funds and other long-term investment instruments. This information can be obtained for free from a reputable brokerage or on the internet. Notice the patterns of growth or loss over the long term, rather than the short-term returns.

Write in a few lines how patience will make you money this coming year. Tuck this note in your journal or datebook, or file it someplace where you can review it this time next year.

Contentment

Thousands of people are brought into a state
of real poverty by their great anxiety not to be
thought poor.

> —*More Than Enough*

ONCE UPON A TIME there lived a king who enjoyed the study of human behavior. One day, out of cruelty, he sent the royal guard to a village where they arrested a hardworking family man while his wife and children looked on in terror. The subject, having no idea which law he had violated, screamed and pulled against the ropes until he bled, but there was nothing else he could do as the guards threw him into a horse-drawn cart and started over the hill. With a forlorn expression on his face, the man looked back to catch a last glimpse of his wife and precious children before the cart reached the pinnacle, then dipped down the slope toward the king's castle.

Upon arrival at the castle, the prisoner was stripped of his ragged peasant's clothing. But much to his surprise, rather than being tossed into the dungeon, the man was bathed in lilac water and then suited in fine garments. The royal guard led him to a courtyard and placed the man in a cage made of solid gold. They slammed the cage's door behind the prisoner and locked the door with a golden key.

Stunned and confused, the man looked around the cage. There he was in a golden cage, dressed immaculately, and he was surrounded by fine furnishings, fine foods, and the grandest bed a man could dream of. The only problem was that he was locked inside of the cage.

He missed his family, too, of course.

Three times each day, servants brought fine meals to the man in the cage. At first he refused to eat, despondent over his imprisonment and longing to see his family. After a while, however, the tempting food and his hunger pangs worked in collusion to cause him to taste the food. Once he had tasted the gourmet delicacies, he realized how famished he was and what a fool he had been to ignore the fine foods before him. And my, was the food ever delicious!

Days later, the king came to visit to see how his experiment was going.

The prisoner pleaded to be released. He begged the king to tell him what wrong he had done and how he could make it right, and when he could return to his family, but the king ignored the man's groveling. "All your needs will be met," the king said, "and your family will be taken care of, but you will never leave this golden cage."

Over the following months, the prisoner was inundated with fine foods, drinks, clothing, and gorgeous gold jewelry. He lived in the finest of furnishings—or at least as many fine furnishings as would fit inside the cage.

The king sent fine books for the man to read. Since he had nothing else to do, the prisoner studied for hours on end, rapidly educating himself in the finest arts, sciences, and literature of his day.

Each time the king visited, the prisoner begged again to be released so he could go home to be the husband and daddy he had always wanted to be. But as always, the king assured him that his family was being well cared for. And he refused to allow the man to go free.

Months faded into years and eventually the man in the golden cage stopped asking about his family. He quit begging to be released, but he continued to read and to contemplate the great issues of life. His reputation for being so well educated prompted members of the king's court to seek out his wisdom. Visitors often stopped by the cage to ask the man's advice. His intelligence was so highly regarded, the king's advisers often sought the former peasant's insights on matters of state.

Eventually, the man began to think, *Maybe this golden cage isn't so bad. After all, I have the best of everything; plus, I have security and prestige.*

When the king noticed the change in the prisoner's spirit, he decided it was time for the second phase of his experiment. One morning the king visited the man in the golden cage as he was eating his gourmet breakfast. The king announced to all that he was setting the man free, although the man was not required to leave the cage. If he so desired, he could continue to live in the cage with all the finery, books, and prestige he presently possessed. "But if you ever set one foot outside the cage," warned the king, "you will be returned to your former state of poverty." At that, the king took the golden key, unlocked the golden door, and swung it wide open.

Freedom! The prisoner lunged for the door, but just as he was about to step outside, he stopped cold. *Maybe I should reconsider*, he thought. He slowly retreated back inside the cage.

That night, the man in the golden cage paced back and forth, pondering what he should do. Surely his family had forgotten him by now. And the king had promised that they were being well cared for. To walk away from all this finery just for freedom—freedom to be poor again—what sense did that make? Morning light found him still undecided about his future. So he dressed in his exquisite clothing and ate his gourmet breakfast and thought some more.

Friends dropped by to see him and were amazed that the cage's door was wide open. "Come out, come out!" they called.

But he declined. He had made his choice. He would continue to live inside the cage.

Legend has it that the man spent the rest of his life in the golden cage—a cage with the door wide open—but he was trapped, trapped by the "good life."

Trapped in the Golden Cage

Dan Scott, a pastor in Phoenix and a friend of mine, told the above story to illustrate the power of affluence—the golden cage—in our lives. One of the great dangers in our quest to have **More Than Enough** is that we allow our affluence to trap us, to cage us, to imprison us to the point that we are willing to sacrifice our family, our home, our values, and even our freedom on the altar of "the good life."

The danger is that we get comfortable; we grow accustomed to having so much "stuff." We enjoy living in our nice homes. We like driving nice cars. We relish eating fine foods. And as long as our "needs" are being met, we couldn't care less about the true cost. The message is trumpeted loudly and clearly that character doesn't matter anymore as long as the economy is booming. We are willing to overlook almost anything, as long as nobody messes with our "stuff."

However, those of us who desire a **More Than Enough** lifestyle must understand that "stuff" will never satisfy. How much is enough? Always just a little bit more. If you are seeking fulfillment by acquiring more material things for a "collection," you are setting yourself up for disappointment . . . not to mention disillusionment and some sort of imprisonment, often self-imposed. There is a huge difference between obtaining more stuff and having **More Than Enough**!

"But I've got to work longer hours, because we need the money to pay for the *stuff*."

"I hate hardly seeing my kids all week, but the boss says if I don't stay out there on the road, this project isn't going to get done. And if it doesn't get done, I am. Then how will we survive if I lose my job?"

"I know my spouse and I don't get to spend much time together anymore. We seem like two cruise ships crossing paths in the night, waving to each other as we go by, but not really getting near enough to have a life together. But we both need to work to make ends meet. Someday, a few years from now, maybe, we'll be able to slow down and enjoy more than a yearly vacation together."

"How do you think we pay for all the beautiful things we have? Look at that furniture. That vase alone cost over two thousand dollars. And that big-screen television with the DVD player. It connects directly to our stereo equipment and we have theaterlike sound in every room in the house. Do you think those things come cheaply? No, sir. Look at that fine china. It really decks out our new china closet, doesn't it? No, we haven't really had much chance to use it. Been busy, you know.

"And look out there in the driveway. See our new luxury automobile? You should see all the neighbors' eyes when we drive by in that baby!

"The kids? Uh, I'm not sure where they are today. I had to leave for work before they got up, and I think they had a soccer game or something after school . . . but I'm sure we'll catch up with each other on the weekend . . . well, maybe not this weekend. I do have that golf match, and I think the kids are going to a party somewhere. . . ."

Sounds a lot like a golden cage, doesn't it?

What is your idea of the "good life"?

_____

What are some cages in which society has been attempting to entrap you?

_____

_____

What material enticements are tempting you to stay in the golden cage? (Check all that apply.)

____ fine clothes
____ fine homes
____ prestige among my peers
____ money
____ a promotion at work
____ academic pursuits
____ fear of losing a lifestyle that I have grown accustomed to

Contentment Is the Key

The key to having **More Than Enough** is not making more money, getting out of debt, making better and wise investments, putting your kids through college debt-free, or having nicer or more comfortable living facilities. The key to having **More Than Enough** is *contentment*, that elusive ability to be happy regardless of your circumstances, whether you have a lot or a little, whether you are living in a gargantuan home or an over-the-garage one-bedroom apartment, whether everybody knows your name or nobody knows who you are.

Contentment is knowing that your life has significance and that you can be comfortable and secure with who you are, regardless of what you have or don't have. How liberating it is when you no longer worry about reaching the top, or keeping up with the Joneses (whoever they are!), when you no longer are obsessed with trying to be better than somebody else, when you don't need to possess more, do more, be seen more, or prove more to anyone. That is when you will truly discover the joys of not just *having* **More Than Enough**, but *being* **More Than Enough**!

Oh, What a Relief It Is!

❖ What? You can't imagine contentment? Picture this: The world is a honking, blaring New York City traffic jam, but in the midst of it, you feel as though you are relaxing peacefully in a canoe on a tree-lined, placid lake. That's contentment. Peace, calm, and quiet, even in the midst of chaos.

The Unwanted Gift

There's a funny thing about contentment. Most of us say we are searching for it; some are even striving for it. (Striving for contentment? Hmm . . . what's wrong with that picture?) Yet most of us pass right by contentment on our quest for more. Why? Because in our compulsive, success-driven society, we are afraid that if we ever truly welcome contentment, we will be bidding good-bye to the good life. We will be saying hello to laziness and loss of status. If we are honest with ourselves, we must admit that we think of contentment as a nice idea for those people somewhere between retirement and the rest home, or—let's face it—for those with less ambition than we have.

But contentment is not synonymous with complacency. Complacency is surrender, giving up, settling for less than you could be, not using your God-given talents and abilities to make a positive difference in the world, lacking the desire to get ahead. Complacency often sets in when a person's values are based more on what he or she has or does (or wants to have or wants to be), rather than on his or her character.

The contented person is not lazy, apathetic, or passive. On the contrary, his or her contentment frees that person to see the real issues that are worth fighting for or worth getting excited about. Contentment doesn't mean that you have no desire to better yourself, to work better, do more, or achieve more. Contentment simply frees you to enjoy life wherever you are right now.

Contentment doesn't mean that you roll over and play dead when challenges or opposition comes your way. John Hagee, a pastor in San Antonio, tells the story about the owner of a small clothing store who was being pressured to sell out to a national chain of stores. The shop owner refused.

The large national chain store bought all the property surrounding the small shop, but the "little guy" still refused to sell, and he refused to be intimidated. The representative of the huge corporation said, "If you don't sell to us, we're going to build all around you and drive you out of business."

The shop owner said, "Go right ahead. I'm not going to sell."

True to its word, the corporation built a massive store that stretched out on both sides of the small store. When the new facility was ready to open, the owners put up a large sign that announced, GRAND OPENING!

The spunky shop owner countered with a large banner stretching across the entire front of his store, which read, MAIN ENTRANCE!

Contentment doesn't turn you into a wimp. It doesn't mean that you lose your competitive edge. It just means that you don't always buy into the "bigger is better" mind-set. It means that your peace and security are not located in money or in the material things money can buy.

Discontent Can Lead to Debt

On the other hand, discontent with who you are will cause you to compensate by trying to prove your value by what you have. If you don't have nice things, or if you can't go where you want to go or do some things that, in your mind at least, cause you to appear successful, you are tempted to spend money you can't afford to put on an impressive front. When you don't have enough money in your checking account, you turn to credit to service your expensive habits. It is a downward spiral. Before long, you are head over heels in debt. The house of cards totters and threatens to plunge you into default on your loans, bankruptcy, and quite possibly divorce. And for what? To keep up the appearance that you are successful or wealthy when you are not!

What are you doing currently in your life that you know that you cannot afford, yet you continue? (Check all that apply.)

_____ leasing an automobile or purchasing it on payments

_____ spending way too much on housing

_____ buying too many expensive new clothes

_____ spending too much on luxuries such as flavored coffees, expensive perfumes or colognes, makeup, or hair care

_____ paying dues at an exclusive club

_____ keeping your children in private school when the available public education system is high in quality

_____ eating lunch or dinner at fancy restaurants

_____ spending too much on sports season tickets or other recreational activities

_____ buying new electronic or computer equipment when last year's version works fine

_____ buying junk food

_____ following expensive diet programs or getting cosmetic surgery

_____ having cellular phones, pagers, and cable television that you could easily live without

Why do you continue to do these things when you know they are harming you financially, creating discontent, and may eventually lead to your downfall?

_____

_____

_____

The Price Is Wrong!

Unfortunately, the pressures to conform to a debt-ridden culture around us are enormous. Furthermore, we live in the most "marketed-to" society ever to grace the planet. Our minds are exposed to literally thousands of advertisements on any given day. Radio, television, print ads in newspapers and magazines, banners on your computer internet service, soft-drink cups, football games, billboards, even ads in restaurant restrooms now scream for our attention on an hourly basis. We are hyped and hit with more advertisements in a week than our people were in a year's time back in the 1950s.

Now, I love marketing, and I have a tremendous appreciation for the people who have honed it to a science. But you must understand that the essence of all good marketing is to create within you a feeling of *discontent*! Somebody has something for sale that you need. And all the millions of dollars spent on those slick, shiny, appealing print and pictures are aimed at convincing you that you simply cannot live without the product the advertiser is hawking.

The result? Discontent.

Psychologists refer to the disturbance that advertising makes within us as "dissonance." It is the marketer's goal to create this dissonance in you, making you believe that you will have more pleasure or less pain if you buy the product being advertised—and not until you do!

Please understand, this process in itself is not evil. We actually need these marketers in a capitalistic society to announce to us and to inform us about new products, to stimulate our imaginations concerning what we can do with that new item, to make us aware of what is available and how it differs from competitors' products. All of this is part of the "American way." The process itself is not moral or immoral; it's just that we have been so inundated by a morass of marketing methods, we have subconsciously accepted their messages: You won't be happy until you buy our stuff!

Consequently, even people who know better periodically slip up and contract "stuffitis." This all-too-common and extremely contagious "dis-ease" frequently leads to other complications, resulting in an "I'll be happy when" syndrome. Very dangerous. It can even be fatal.

The "I'll be happy when" syndrome sometimes sounds similar to this:

"I'll be happy when I get a new car."
"I'll be happy when we live in that neighborhood."
"I'll be happy when I get my degree."
"I'll be happy when the kids are grown up and out on their own."
"I'll be happy when I have more money."
"I'll be happy when we get that new china closet."
"I'll be happy when I get a new boat."
"I'll be happy when my Sea Doo gets a sister."

"Stuffitis" and the accompanying "I'll be happy when" syndrome can be cured, but it will require radical surgery, and a reshaping of your ideas of success and what it really means to be happy in this world. Are you seriously going to allow two frogs pitching a product during the Super Bowl to define your sense of what you want out of life?

You have to understand that the one who dies with the most toys . . . still dies! There must be more to living than the mere acquisition of more stuff. Sure, having nice stuff can be fun; working to acquire more or better stuff is not necessarily wrong. But when you allow the stuff to possess *you*, instead of your possessing it, you are setting yourself up to be discontented. Genuine, lasting contentment just doesn't come on a delivery truck.

The people who are most content are those who have learned to slow down long enough to enjoy life. Rather than responding to every jerk on life's yo-yo, they have learned to relax and savor whatever circumstances in which they find themselves. They have no anxiety about living "the good life," but they have also learned the difficult discipline of saying, "No, I won't be doing that," "No, we won't be going there," "I don't need that right now," and "That isn't really essential."

Interestingly, contentment often cleanses the pallet, and causes people to lose their taste for stuff. They don't lose their taste, mind you; they still enjoy stuff, but it doesn't hold the sweet attraction that it once did. When a person is addicted to stuff, the desire works on the mind almost like a drug. But when you have discovered true contentment, it delivers you from the insatiable need for another fix. When that happens, the stuff just doesn't taste good anymore.

Growing up in the 1960s, as a middle-class kid, I didn't go out to eat very often. When my family and I did venture into a restaurant, it was a big deal for us. But about the time I turned thirteen, the fast-food revolution hit our area. Besides the usual drive-throughs, a wide variety of affordable sit-down, "semi-fast"-food restaurants dotted the landscape, one of which was Red Lobster.

I had never eaten lobster before. To me, lobster was a delicacy reserved for kings and queens, and it was always the most expensive item on the menu. But the chain restaurant brought the lobster price to within striking range of even my family's budget.

I thought I was in heaven. Ahhh, dipped in that melted butter, this delicacy tasted like food prepared by angels!

Later, when I was in my twenties, I built a significant amount of wealth, and my family and I ate out more often. Since we could now afford it, I frequently ordered lobster . . . and more lobster . . . and more lobster. Funny—if you eat enough lobster, it all begins to taste surprisingly similar to soap!

Our instincts tell us that if something is good, more of it is even better. If a television is a poor man's luxury, a big-screen television in the den, as well as an assortment of sized screens for every room, must be better! If riding to work in a car beats walking or riding a bicycle, a new luxury car—leased, of course—must be better. If eating at a restaurant is a treat, how much more of a treat is it if we eat out more frequently, at places offering more expensive cuisine! While we're at it, we can put the charges on a double-digit interest rate credit card and pay for those meals for years to come! Funny—after a while, it all begins to taste a lot like soap. . . .

How to Beat Madison Avenue

The advertising industry spends millions of dollars every day on marketing. If you think you can turn your back on it without a fight, you might as well empty your wallet and checkbook now and save yourself some time! But the truth is: There are a lot of places that Visa is that I don't need to be, and you can Discover card-freedom by cutting that high-interest credit card in two and closing the account. "American Excess" certainly wasn't there for me when I needed them (as a matter of fact, that particular company is one of the first to pull your credit card when you get behind on the payments), and you do not need MasterCard for everything else. Why? Because we don't need everything else! But the only way we can combat the influence of advertising that has consumed our society like the blob is to take some drastic measures.

For starters, turn off the television set. Ouch! I can feel your pain. Really, I can. But try going an entire week without watching television and see what that does for your attitude, not to mention your relationship with your spouse, children, friends, and extended family members. Remember, our desire for stuff is in direct proportion to the number of advertisements we see, and the marketers are playing hardball. They have meticulously studied and analyzed every possible response to those megabucks ads, and they are intent on causing you to be discontented with life as you currently know it. But the commercials are not the only threat to our contentment. If a thirty-second to one-minute commercial is designed to impact our lives, how much more is a half-hour sitcom or an hour-long movie marketing a lifestyle as well? Turn the TV off and watch your contentment level grow instead.

Second, stay out of the malls. Seriously! If you are an alcoholic trying to stop drinking, you don't go to a bar! Similarly, if you are a "shopaholic," you can't go "shop-lusting" at the malls and expect to kick the habit.

Turn the television off, stay away from the malls, and try to find your family in the house. They are in there somewhere! If you look hard enough, you'll find them. How long has it been since you and your family members spent an evening together without television or videos? Why not play a board game, or better yet, go to a park together, ride bikes together, play together. Eat dinner together. It has been statistically proven that kids who do well in school and stay out of trouble sit down at least once a day for a meal together with their families, with the television turned off. Amazing, huh?

Not really. If you are not subjecting yourself to a plethora of advertisements every day, you will be delighted to notice how quickly the "gimmes," give me this or give me that, begin to diminish in your children's speech and in your own.

Turn off the radio and listen to some self-improvement tapes. Better still, turn off the radio and tapes, and talk to one another! Now, there's a novel idea!

Cancel your subscription to the local newspaper for a month. You'll survive, and don't worry—all the bad news will still keep coming when you (or if you) decide to continue receiving the daily rag.

The point is: Do something radical to lower the impact of advertising on your family and see if your desire for stuff doesn't drop. And don't be surprised if the quality of your relationships increases commensurately. No, you probably won't decide to sell all your stuff and become a hermit, but you will be astonished at how refreshing it feels to disconnect even for a short time from the clawing, grabbing, gotta-have-it, hoarding masses. When you realize that "stuff-itis" can never satisfy you, you are ready to start looking deep within yourself for those things that bring true happiness and fulfillment to your life. The antidote for "stuffitis," you see, is rooted in your values. What really matters? What is of ultimate importance to you? What will matter to you decades from now?

Contentment will keep you from getting into debt, because you no longer have to keep up a facade of ego-based or performance-based self-worth. You can be content with what you have and what God is doing in and through your life. If you are currently in debt, a contented lifestyle will help you to get out of debt much more quickly, because you now realize that many things can be

---

Money Matters . . . but Not That Much

❖ If you are miserable with $10 in the bank, you will be miserable with $1 million in mutual funds. If you don't have contentment in your current home, you won't find it waiting in the spare bedroom of the larger one you thought would "make you happy." Real contentment is found in a spiritual life, in our faith in God, and in our trust that he will guide our paths.

---

done without and your value as a person will not be diminished one bit as a result. Building wealth can take on an entirely new meaning to you when it really doesn't matter to you anymore what anyone else thinks or says about you.

As your contentment grows, it will be even easier to build wealth because you don't need to increase your lifestyle accordingly as your nest egg grows. Contrary to popular belief, most millionaires who have earned their money by working for it do not radically alter their lifestyles when they become rich. Many of them continue to live in the same homes, drive the same cars, and wear the same style of clothing as they did when they were struggling to make it into the mainstream of middle-class America.

Moreover, as your contentment grows, you will be better able to focus on making wise long-term financial decisions which will in turn lead to more contentment. The cycle will continue as it expands your investments even further.

A sense of contentment will also cause your personal relationships to prosper. Worry, fear, and envy are unwelcome in a home filled with contentment. Relationships are bound to flourish when you have peace in your heart and in your home, which is when you are able to serve those whom you love the most. It's tough to serve and enjoy your loved ones when you are constantly drained emotionally, financially, or spiritually. Contentment serves other people out of a quiet strength.

As your contentment increases, it will impact every other area of your life, which is why I am convinced that your contentment or lack of it is the most important financial principle you will ever discover. With contentment, your vision will clear—you will be able to see where you want to go, and more importantly, you will be able to discern whether that vision is a place worth going to. With contentment, your patience will increase. You will be surprised to discover that some things just don't matter anymore. In particular, you will notice that you couldn't care less about other people's opinions about where you live, what kind of car you drive, or what name brand of clothing you wear.

As contentment becomes the overriding factor in your life, you will be amazed at how your hearing improves. You will listen and actually hear when people you trust and have given permission to speak into your life attempt to keep you accountable. Your fever for buying stuff will dissipate, allowing you to live within your means, and to hope again. Your work will become more disciplined, and efficient as you pursue your goals with a fresh diligence, drawing strength from your faith. Your sense of unity will grow stronger, as well, because you will be investing in others, not just in yourself. All of this will develop within your life a deeper strength than you have ever known before. This is why contentment is the most important financial principle of all.

Contentment doesn't come easily. Nor does it arrive instantly. No doubt, it will sneak up on you almost imperceptibly until one day, to your surprise, you realize that you are just as comfortable eating a hot dog as you are eating lobster. Or you are just as confident driving a 1984 clunker as you are driving a new Jaguar. Contentment is a continual process, not a single decision.

So as we step inside the **More Than Enough** Store, look for the long, cool, quiet aisle. The aisle on which only one item is stocked on the shelves. The small print on the label says that it is the antidote for "stuffitis," sometimes translated as selfish materialism. Either way, you know what's inside—nothing less than *contentment*.

I should give you one warning: Contentment will put you out of step with many of your colleagues and peers who are still trying to claw their way to significance. Many will not understand the peace you have found, and some may even be jealous. That's okay. There's **More Than Enough** for them too, if they are willing to pay the price to have it.

Aisle Nine—Contentment

1. Business Section

TAKING INVENTORY

In which ways does contentment affect your attitude on the job or in the workplace?

_____

_____

Describe an incident when a lack of contentment led to being lured into an unwise business decision or a "get-rich-quick" scheme in your business or company.

_____

_____

Think about the idea of being aggressive and ambitious in your business or career while being content in your life. What can you do to reconcile those seemingly contradictory ideas?

_____

_____

How is it possible for you to be extremely competitive while being content at the same time?

_____

What will you do within the next six weeks regarding your business, job, or career to improve your level of contentment?

_____

_____

_____

Your "To Do" List

List some outside influences that expose you to inordinate or unnecessary doses of advertising in your business or job, and describe how you could avoid them for a month. (For example, you could avoid reading the latest reviews, gossip columns, and product-hype promotional pieces that come across your desk frequently.)

_____

_____

_____

Commit yourself to turning off the television for a month. During that time, read some books that you have been intending to read for some time, but "just haven't been able to find the time."

The next time a business or career problem pops up, take a walk in a park for an hour rather than making a quick decision. You may find that one hour in the park saves you hundreds of hours on the job and possibly a large amount of money.

2. Marriage Section

TAKING INVENTORY

On a scale of zero to ten, how content are you and your spouse regarding your lifestyle?

0	1	2	3	4	5	6	7	8	9	10
Not content at all				Moderately content				Extremely content		

What can you do within the next six months that might improve your contentment level? (Check all that apply.)

____ Put our house up for sale.
____ Get out of debt.
____ Purchase a less expensive car.

___ Spend more time with my spouse in meaningful conversation.
___ Have more fun together.
___ Establish a regular "date night" with my spouse.
___ Work less, play more.
___ Attend church services together.
___ Attend a marriage enrichment seminar.

List three steps that you will take within the next two weeks to begin lowering the influence of advertising on your family members:

1. _____
2. _____
3. _____

Your "To Do" List

Discuss with your spouse just what it will take to increase the level of contentment in your home and particularly in your marriage relationship.

Agree with your spouse to turn off the television for one month. During that time, choose several books about marriage that the two of you can read and discuss.

Make time in your schedule to allow you and your spouse to take a walk together at least twice each week for the next six weeks. During your walk, concentrate your conversation on positive things, rather than on problems or stress-inducing subjects.

3. Parenting Section

TAKING INVENTORY

What specific steps are you currently taking to teach your children how to be content?

_____

_____

What beliefs about contentment do you hope your children will observe in you and emulate in their own lives?

_____

_____

_____

On a scale of zero to ten, how content are your children in regard to your family's lifestyle?

0	1	2	3	4	5	6	7	8	9	10

Not content at all   Moderately content   Extremely content

What can you do within the next six months that might improve their contentment level? (Check all that apply.)

_____ Turn off the television. (Caution: You may expose yourself to screaming and the gnashing of teeth!)

_____ Declare a moratorium on video games.

_____ Attend more of your children's school or church activities.

_____ Spend more time together in meaningful conversation.

_____ Have more fun together.

_____ Attend church services together.

_____ Take family walks or do other activities together as a family.

List three steps that you will take within the next two weeks to begin lowering the influence of advertising upon your children:

1. _____

2. _____

3. _____

Parents' "To Do" List

Discuss with your children the various lifestyles of some of their peers' families. Specifically discuss the peer pressure that exists because of your children's friends' material possessions or lack of them.

Declare the mall off limits for one month. During that time, plan some special family activities for you and your children. Ride bikes, go to the zoo together, or learn a new sport or some other activity.

Agree together with your children that you are going to conduct an experiment. You are going to turn off the television for one month to see how it affects your contentment level. No TV at all for adults or kids. No late-night or early-morning cheating. Each family member will keep a notebook and jot down his or her feelings and thoughts experienced during this time. Once each week, have a family time when you can review some of the insights you have recorded in your notebooks.

4. Singles' Section

TAKING INVENTORY

On a scale of zero to ten, how content are you regarding your current lifestyle?

0	1	2	3	4	5	6	7	8	9	10

Not content at all   Moderately content   Extremely content

What can you do within the next six months that might improve your contentment level? (Check all that apply.)

_____ Turn off the television.

_____ Enroll in an exercise program or some athletic activity.

_____ Seek to spend more time socializing with friends or family members.

_____ Spend less time socializing with friends or family members.

_____ Attend more school or church activities.

_____ Spend more time in meaningful conversation with key people in my life.

____ Write a note of encouragement to someone who I know is having a tough time.

____ Attend church services more frequently.

____ Become involved in a "singles" group at my church.

____ Take walks or do other activities that will get me out of the house or apartment.

____ Break off a destructive relationship.

List three steps that you will take within the next two weeks to begin lowering the influence of advertising upon you:

1. _____

2. _____

3. _____

Singles' "To Do" List

Seriously consider canceling your cable television or at least reducing it to the least possible number of selections in your area. Note the improvement that this brings in your contentment level, and the better use of your time.

Advertisers target your "single" dollars with smart precision. List some ways you can better shield yourself from the bombardment that you know is coming your way.

_____

_____

_____

One of the most difficult temptations to overcome for most singles is the idea that you will be happy only when you find "Mr. or Ms. Right" and establish a serious relationship that may lead to marriage. Plan three things within the next two months that will help you combat this temptation while cultivating contentment in your life right now.

Read one book that is outside your comfort zone each month for the next twelve months.

5. Financial Section

TAKING INVENTORY

Affluence looks so attractive, and it *can* be quite enjoyable when we use it, rather than allowing affluence to trap us. How do you plan to avoid the trap of the "golden cages" in your life?

_____

_____

List some of your basic financial needs—that if you have these needs met, your life can be comfortable and content.

_____

_____

_____

_____

Which of the above list hold the most potential to damage your contentment level if they were gone?

_____

_____

What does that tell you about your attitude concerning the relationship between money and contentment?

_____

Your Financial "To Do" List

Briefly describe the difference between laziness and contentment.

_____

_____

Recognizing that no amount of money will ever bring us peace if we are not content within ourselves, how much money, in hard dollars and cents, will you need to sleep peacefully this month? This year?

This month: $_____

This year: $_____

Think through and discuss with your spouse, a friend, or a financial adviser your ideas regarding the difference between "stuffitis" and enjoying the financial blessings God has poured into your life.

Giving—The Great Misunderstanding

When you give, you open yourself up; you allow the
dollars the freedom to leave, and the freedom to enter.
—More Than Enough

A FRIEND OF MINE was sitting in the Miami airport reading a magazine while he waited to catch a plane to New York. His attention was distracted by a fracas taking place at the ticket counter.

"But I must get to New York today!" an irate woman hotly told the clerk.

"I'm sorry, ma'am, but there are no more seats available," came the reply.

"But my eight-year-old daughter is on that plane. I can't let her fly into New York City all by herself."

"Sorry, lady. The flight is full."

"You must be able to do something!"

"Nope. Plane's full."

This exchange continued back and forth for nearly ten minutes as the frustrated woman sought every possible means of getting on that flight. Finally, her tough veneer sagging, she slumped down onto the floor and began to sob. People in the concourse could not avoid the scene, and the ticket agent looked as though he were about to call Security to have the woman removed from the premises.

My friend had been watching and listening to the woman's woeful story, and his heart was touched with compassion for her. He walked over to the ticket agent and offered to take a later flight, if it meant the woman could use his ticket to travel to New York with her daughter. The agent welcomed my friend's solution and quickly issued a revalidated ticket to the woman, and then arranged for another flight for my friend. The grateful mother boarded the flight to New York, and my friend went back to his magazine while he awaited the next flight, which was scheduled to take off five hours later.

Not long after he returned from New York, my friend opened his mailbox and discovered a letter from the airline. In the envelope was a note of appreciation for his willingness to give up his seat. Also enclosed was a voucher for a free round-trip pass, valid for any route within the airline's system. He had given up a little, and he had gained a lot in return.

That is often the way things work for a person who has discovered that giving is a key to having **More Than Enough**. Selfish people fear that they must hang on to what they have. Frequently, that attitude leads to a scarcity that becomes a self-fulfilling prophecy, and the selfish person loses even what he or she already has. It's a strange but true paradox: Give and it will be given to you. Hoard, and you will lose what you have.

Certainly, giving applies to much more than our money. For many of us, giving our time is almost more difficult than writing a check. For others, using their talent or serving in some way that is not going to enhance their financial status or career is a stretch. For most of us, however, what we do with our money is a good measuring standard for what we believe to be important.

Approximately how much money did you give away last year?

_____

Are you better at giving money or hoarding it?

_____ Giving   _____ Hoarding

What's the difference between saving and investing, and hoarding?

_____

_____

Which statements below best reflect your attitude toward giving money away? (Check all that apply.)

___ I can barely make ends meet now. How can I help someone else?

___ If I give too much, my own financial strength will be impaired.

___ Most of the charitable organizations are rip-offs.

___ I need to hold on to what I have.

___ The more I give, the more I receive.

___ I gave foolishly one time to one of those TV evangelists. Never again.

___ I know I can't outgive God.

___ Give a little, get a lot.

___ I believe that I will reap what I sow.

What is your first response when you see the images of starving children on

---

Clenched Fist or Open Hand?

❖ Often when we are scared, we clench our fists. We prepare for battle because we don't have the perception or the position of strength to avoid a fight. So while the closed fist is a sign of battle, it is born of weakness. The same thing can be seen in the realm of money. A fistful of dollars tightly held so they won't get away represents someone who doesn't know how to give. The tight-fisted person thinks that if he or she can just clutch those dollars tightly enough, he or she will be on the path to prosperity. People who are weak and insecure honestly believe that they will have more by hoarding and gripping those dollars. In fact, just the opposite is true. Those with **More Than Enough** got there by giving.

The open hand represents how you must feel emotionally and spiritually about money and relationships in your life if you want **More Than Enough.** The people who are happiest and wealthiest got that way by giving.

television advertisements or infomercials, or when you pass by a Salvation Army bell ringer and kettle at Christmastime?

_____

_____

What does your response tell you about yourself?

_____

Are you living with an open hand, or a clenched fist?

____ An open hand   ____ A clenched fist   ____ Uncertain

Don't Give to Get

You will waste what you have if you give to get. It doesn't work. Giving to get something in return is simply another form of selfishness. It will not bring you more money; nor will it bring you more love and joy in your personal relationships. Give because it is the right thing to do. Give because you will reap what you sow. Give because God is a giver and he has given to you. Give because you were created in God's image and when you give you reflect more of his character in the world. Unquestionably, that is one of the reasons why better relationships and more wealth flow to the person who gives.

As you give, you will discover that your joy increases. You will have a lilt in your step, a smile on your face, a sense of meaning in your life that was not there previously. Your creativity will be enhanced. Giving stimulates your abilities and passions. It makes you more of what you were created to be and helps you to use the gifts that God has given to you.

Giving of Yourself

The best giving involves much more than money. It is a giving of yourself. Maybe you have little money to give. That's okay. You can still be a generous giver by giving your possessions, skills, compassion, time, and service. All sorts of worthy organizations are crying out for help. Go to your local homeless shelter or city mission and help serve the men and women there. Take your children with you and allow them the privilege of serving. Besides helping others by giving, it will make you more grateful for the many blessings you have received.

Teach a Sunday school class or volunteer to help coach a Little League baseball team. Offer to serve as a room mother at the elementary school (whether or not you have children who attend it), volunteer to be a "big brother" or "big sister," or get involved in a local chapter of the Boys Scouts or Girl Scouts. Most communities have civic organizations such as the Kiwanis or Rotary Club which focus on serving rather than on being served. Your church may have other opportunities in which you can serve other people. Don't think that you are doing them a favor by offering your help; understand that you are doing yourself a favor by volunteering, because the happiest people on earth are the ones who give of themselves.

> I don't know what your destiny will be, but one
> thing I know; the only ones among you who will be
> really happy are those who will have sought and
> found how to serve.
>
> —*Albert Schweitzer*

How much time are you currently spending each week in volunteer service?

____ one hour per week
____ less than one hour per week
____ more than one hour per week

Who will you call this week to explore the possibility of serving your church or community in some specific way? _____

Ask your spouse, your children, or a friend to check on you to make sure you have volunteered for some service before the month is over.

But I Don't Feel Generous

Like so much of the **More Than Enough** lifestyle, giving has very little to do with your feelings. Giving is an act of your will. As you give, you will *feel* more generous, and you will feel better about yourself. If you need a reminder of why you should give, just pause long enough to think about how good God has been to you.

Dozens of time each day, on my radio show, people ask me, "How are you?" or "How are ya doing?" It's not that they want to hear my life story again; we all know that these questions are usually substitutes for a simple "Hello." Nevertheless, my most frequent response to the question "How are you doin'?" is *"Better than I deserve!"*

I don't say it because I have been so bad. I say it (and mean it) because God has been so good to me! He's given me a great wife, three wonderful children, good health, sufficient food (**More Than Enough**, usually!), a comfortable home, plenty of clothes, a great church family, wonderful friends, a fabulous staff, a meaningful career . . . I could go on and on! God has been good to me! How am I doin'? *Better than I deserve!*

And if I don't miss my guess, although your circumstances may be quite different, you can probably say something similar. When you are not feeling so generous, just remind yourself of God's goodness to you; remind yourself that he has promised to return to you what you sow—in bumper crops—and see if that doesn't stimulate your giving.

Examine your motives: Are you more motivated to give out of heartfelt gratitude, or are you giving out of guilt, or a desire to impress someone else?

If everyone in my town (or church, or civic group) knew my level of giving, would I be a model to follow, or an embarrassment?

If everyone else in my town (or church, or civic group) gave at the same level that I am giving, our group would be (check one):

____ prospering greatly

____ in big trouble

____ ready to close up or discontinue services

Should You Give While in Debt?

Let's face it. Getting into debt is simple. It's as easy as riding the down escalator at the mall. However, getting out of debt is like trying to walk back up the escalator that is coming down. It can be done, but it takes some real effort. While you are working your way out of debt, you will be tempted to back away from your giving or possibly stop giving altogether.

That would be most unwise. Why?

Remember, debt is rarely caused by a mere lack of money. Debt is, however, a good indicator that something may be wrong at the center of your life that has caused you to slide down the slippery slope of fiscal irresponsibility. Perhaps it was pride that led to your misuse of the financial resources God gave you; possibly selfishness played a part. Other culprits could be greed, self-centeredness, self-indulgence, impatience, fear, or lack of personal discipline. Maybe your debts were brought about through immaturity, foolishness, or lack of faith. Regardless, your first few steps toward financial peace will be realizing that your debts indicate spiritual needs as well as monetary: taking responsibility for your mistakes, apologizing to those you have hurt, making restitution where you can, and asking God and your loved ones for forgiveness.

As with any forgiveness, if it is to be effective, you must forgive any other people who might be involved in your financial problems, and you must forgive yourself, as well. You will do yourself no favors by verbally beating yourself up, saying, "How could I have been so foolish?"

Let it go, and trust God for a new start. Pray also for the wisdom to make the right choices in the future, and the courage to take the next step of obedience, as God directs you. Ask God to help you make the necessary changes that will cure the problems rather than merely assuage the symptoms.

That's where giving comes in. God will honor your efforts to get out of debt and to build wealth as you give. Not that God is going to dump a truckload of cash on your front lawn just because you give, but something does happen when we trust him enough to give in faith, believing that he will provide for our needs.

One of the more intriguing titles for God in the Old Testament is *"Jehovah-jireh,"* the God who provides. We shouldn't be surprised when God lives up to his name!

If you are not *tithing*—giving God the first 10 percent of your income—start today. Make your giving the first check you write, at the top of your budget. Have you ever considered that perhaps your failure to honor God off the top of your income is one of the reasons you have been struggling financially?

You may be thinking, *Tithe? How am I supposed to give away 10 percent of my income? I can barely pay the telephone bill!*

Then disconnect the phone, but don't rob God!

Not only do we rob God when we refuse to give; we rob ourselves. Why? Because God promises to "rebuke the devourer" for those who will put him first in their finances.

Maybe you can identify with Tom Bodett, author of *Small Comforts* and a fellow who has made a ton of money by "leaving the light on for you." Bodett observed, "After marrying each other, my wife and I discovered the principle of buy now, pay later. We sold our souls to a thirty-year mortgage and a succession of car payments with matching insurance policies. All our disposable income is calculated a year in advance and spent the year before!"

It's not my place or intent to tell you when, where, or how much to give, especially when you are working your way out of debt. All I can tell you is that you will not lose by honoring God with your giving. Instead of trusting MasterCard, try trusting the Master, not merely with your money, but with every aspect of your life. I tell audiences every day as I close my national radio show, "There is ultimately only one way to financial peace, and that is to walk daily with the Prince of Peace, Christ Jesus."

Which of the following have most often caused you to have financial problems? (Check all that apply.)

___ pride
___ selfishness
___ greed
___ self-centeredness
___ self-indulgence
___ impatience
___ fear
___ lack of personal discipline
___ immaturity
___ foolishness
___ lack of faith

If you have not been giving to God, start this week. Look at your monthly income, and determine how much you should give.

Write that amount here: $_____

More Than Enough

The diminutive black woman didn't look rich to me. But when I checked into her story, I discovered that Oseola McCarty possessed **More Than Enough** for herself and for many others.

Oseola started working in her family's laundry business in Hattiesburg, Mississippi, when she was only eight years old, helping her mother, her grandmother, and her aunt to wash and iron other people's dirty clothes. When her aunt fell sick and could no longer work, Oseola dropped out of the sixth grade to work full-time to help make ends meet. She was twelve years old and never made it back to the classroom.

To hear her tell the story, though, one would think there was something majestic about doing laundry:

When I was working, I would wake up at seven. I would go outside and start a fire under my wash pot. Then I would soak, wash, and boil a bundle of clothes. Then I would rub them, wrench them, rub them again, starch 'em, and hang 'em on the line. After I had all of the clean clothes on the line, I would start on the next batch. By the time they were finished washing, the clothes on the line would be dry. I'd take them down and pile them up in the house, on the beds, or wherever there was an open spot. Well, I would wash all day, and in the evenings I would iron until eleven o'clock.

I loved the work. The bright fire. Wrenching the wet, clean cloth. White shirts shining on the line.

From seven each morning until eleven o'clock each night, Oseola worked. Every day except Sunday, for eighty years. On Sunday morning and evening, Oseola could always be found in church, carrying a large black Bible, worshiping the Lord. She was a Christian and unashamed of the gospel. To Oseola, what mattered most in life was her faith in God, her family, and her work—in that order.

Oseola started saving money even as a child. Her first goal was to have enough to buy some candy. Later, she began saving for her future and that of her family. She lived frugally, traveled little, always looked for bargains, and spent no more than absolutely necessary on anything, although she could never pass up a bunch of pretty flowers. Each month, after taking out only enough money for basic expenses, she deposited the remainder of her money in Trustmark Bank in Hattiesburg. She never made a large deposit of money. She did not save a large amount over a short period of time. Instead, Oseola set aside a little bit, regularly, over a long period of time.

Oseola's grandmother died in 1944; her mom died in 1964, and her aunt went to be with the Lord soon after, in 1967. Their absence left Oseola alone, but she continued to work by herself until 1994, when arthritis finally forced her to "retire" at age eighty-six. It was then that Oseola revealed her secret.

Saving incremental amounts over her eighty-year career, laundrywoman

Oseola McCarty had amassed a fortune of $280,000! Now she wanted to give most of it away. She gave some of the money to her church and family members, and she gave $150,000 to the University of Southern Mississippi, a school she had never even visited. Today, there is an Oseola McCarty scholarship at USM, because Oseola wanted to make sure that other young African American students would have the opportunity to obtain the education she never received.

But Oseola received much more than a diploma. When word of Oseola's generosity got out, she received numerous national and international awards, including the Presidential Citizens Medal, presented to her personally by the president of the United States. The gentle, quiet-spoken washwoman was selected as one of Barbara Walters's Ten Most Fascinating People. She appeared on nearly every major national news network, and was featured in articles in *Newsweek*, the *New York Times*, *People*, *Life*, *Ebony*, *Essence*, and *Jet*.

And Oseola McCarty did receive a diploma—an honorary doctorate from Harvard University! Not bad for someone who dropped out of school in the sixth grade.

What so intrigued the world about a woman who spent her life washing clothes? Simply this: Oseola McCarty understood "the great misunderstanding," that by releasing what you have to give, you get more in return. She epitomizes the values of faith in God, hard work, saving, investing in the future, and giving. She reminds us that all work can be performed with dignity, and that any one of us can indeed have **More Than Enough.**

Just Help Someone Else

If you have never experimented with giving, I challenge you to try it for six months. Your life will never be the same. You will experience a whole new level of living by giving. If you are already a giver, give more. Go wild on a giving spree and see what fun you have! Just make sure that as you give, you don't attach any strings.

As I was growing up, countless times my dad and I would stop along the road to help someone who was in trouble. Or we'd pitch in with our neighbors to help lift some heavy object, or to fix something. Many times, I heard someone ask my father, "What do I owe you, buddy?"

Dad always smiled as he said, "Nothing. Just help someone else when you see that they need it. That will be our pay."

That, my friend, is **More Than Enough.**

Aisle Ten—Giving

1. Business Section

TAKING INVENTORY

List three specific ways you can be more giving in your company, business, or job.

1. _____
2. _____
3. _____

How might your giving affect your relationships at work? (For example, "My giving may impact the unity among my coworkers, and the level of teamwork in the workplace.")

_____

_____

In your opinion, how do businesses that give prosper, directly and indirectly, from their generosity?

_____

_____

Your "To Do" List

List three things that you can do to give more "materially" through your job.

1. _____
2. _____
3. _____

List three things that you can do to give more "relationally" through your job.

1. _____
2. _____
3. _____

What two things will you give this week that will affect your relationship with a client, boss, or subordinate?

1. _____
2. _____

Recognition, appreciation, and praise will be welcome additions to most work environments. Make it a point this week to "catch someone" doing something well, and call attention to it by giving a positive word of encouragement.

2. Marriage Section

TAKING INVENTORY

List three specific ways you can be more giving in your relationship with your spouse.

1. _____
2. _____
3. _____

How would you hope your giving might affect your marriage relationship? (For example, "My giving may cause my spouse to feel even more loved than at present):

_____

_____

On a scale of zero to ten, where are you in terms of giving in your marriage?

0	1	2	3	4	5	6	7	8	9	10
Selfishness					Cooperation					Giving

How can you raise that number by one notch within the next month?

_____

Your "To Do" List

Husbands, give your wife a series of small gifts, cards, and notes over the next month. Attempt to express a different aspect of your love and appreciation for her in each.

Wives, shower your husband with a series of compliments and words of encouragement over the next month. Express admiration for his strong traits. Prepare or arrange at least one special dinner for just the two of you sometime this month.

Discuss your household budget together and make sure that giving to worthy causes is a high priority.

Review your budget to find some extra money to be used for "love gifts" to each other. Make these gifts an important priority in future budgets.

3. Parenting Section

TAKING INVENTORY

Were your parents a strong positive or negative influence on your giving patterns as you grew up?

____ Positive ____ Negative ____ Indifferent ____ Uncertain

List two ways in which you are (or will be) teaching your children the importance and value of giving.

1. _____

2. _____

What have your children taught you about giving?

_____

_____

Parents' "To Do" List

Plan a family project that will lead to a giving experience; for example, helping an elderly neighbor with yard work, or helping to deliver presents to needy children at Christmastime.

As a family, make a list of worthy causes in your area in which you may wish to become involved in the near future.

Discuss with your children the feelings they experience when they give to others outside your immediate family.

Create some family traditions that involve giving and the making of special memories together.

4. Singles' Section

TAKING INVENTORY

On a scale of zero to ten, are you a giver or a taker?

0	1	2	3	4	5	6	7	8	9	10
Taker										Giver

Much of your single life revolves around yourself. If you are not careful, you can become extremely self-centered. In what ways are you attempting to break out of a "the-world-revolves-around-me" attitude by giving?

_____

_____

How much time are you currently volunteering to a charitable organization or a ministry?

_____

Is this a fair reflection of God's giving to you?

___ Yes ___ No ___ Uncertain

List two organizations that you will become more informed about within two weeks concerning opportunities to be of service.

1. _____

2. _____

In what ways are you seeking to give in your relationships with your friends or family members?

_____

_____

_____

The "Golden Rule" says to do unto others as you would have them do unto you. How does this relate to your giving patterns?

_____

_____

Singles' "To Do" List

List three things you can do that will help increase your level of financial giving. (For instance, I could cancel my cable television subscription and use that same amount of money each month to support a child through World Vision or some other relief organization.)

1. _____

2. _____

3. _____

List several of your strongest areas of expertise or your known gifts, talents, or abilities. Write out several ways that you can use what God has given to you to be a blessing to others.

5. Financial Section

TAKING INVENTORY

Giving releases more than our money, time, or resources; it releases something in our souls that causes us to feel good about ourselves. Describe briefly the last time you experienced that wonderful feeling that only comes from giving.

_____

_____

_____

In the Old Testament, a minimum standard of giving was the tithe, 10 percent. In the New Testament, there is little reference to tithing. The standard is to give as you have prospered, which for most of us is far more than 10 percent!

What percentage of your income have you given over the past year?

_____

What percentage of your income are you planning to give over the next twelve months?_____

Why have you been reluctant to give in the past?

_____

How has your attitude toward giving been affected by this book?

_____

What does having **More Than Enough** mean to you in dollars and cents?

_____

Your Financial "To Do" List

Briefly describe why you are "Better than I deserve."

_____

_____

Establish some symbol in your life to remind you that giving will always result in your having **More Than Enough.**

Discuss with your spouse or a friend how **More Than Enough** has given you hope for a fresh start financially.

More Than Enough!

TRAVELING FROM TOLEDO to Cincinnati on Interstate 75, just outside Dayton, one must pass through the community of Lima, Ohio. Looking off the highway, it's hard not to notice a large sprawling building with the name United States Plastics on the exterior. The company was founded by Stanley Tam, who first made his mark in American business when he noticed a news article in 1932. The article reported that the Eastman Kodak Company used sixteen tons of silver every week in the manufacture of photographic film emulsion, 80 percent of which was washed off by the time an exposed negative reached the final stages of producing an actual picture. To Stanley Tam, that was thirteen tons of silver literally going down the drain every week!

Stanley and a partner developed a contraption to reclaim the silver by collecting it, heating it, and skimming off the impurities, a process Stanley was sure would make money for the photo labs and for him and his partner. It didn't, and Stanley went down the drain faster than the silver. Exhausted, broke, and ready to quit, Stanley had a spiritual experience in which he said, "Lord, I will turn my business over to you. Take it, God, and if you'll make it succeed, I'll honor you in every way I can. I promise."

Stanley started again, with only $32, and through hard work, integrity, and sheer determination built a thriving silver-reclamation business. From there he spun off several other related companies. From the beginning, Tam and his wife, Juanita, both devout Christians, kept their vow to honor God with their business. They faithfully gave 10 percent of their income to their church, but they wanted to do more. They decided to make God a 51 percent owner in their business. The couple gave away more and more of their profits to worthy causes, and they continued to prosper, as did their companies.

Then, in 1955, the Tams turned over the stock in their companies, States Smelting and Refining Corporation and the United States Plastics Corporation, in its entirety to God, not just in theory or in a "spiritual" commitment with no practical ramifications, but legally, with lawyers, contracts, and the whole bit. Rather than giving God a token of *his* company, Stanley Tam became an employee of *God's* company.

Over the years, the company has funded literally hundreds of worthy projects and Christian mission programs. Through it all, Stanley and Juanita and their family never lacked for good things, although they were never ostentatious, either. They lived in a modest but comfortable home, dressed well, and enjoyed life. They taught their daughters their values, how to make money, and how to give of themselves to help others. Although they gave away more money than many people will ever make, they continued to thrive, financially, spiritually, and in their personal relationships. In fact, you might say the Tams had **More Than Enough**.

That's what having **More Than Enough** is all about.

It's not about just having enough money to pay your bills; it's about having enough to help some other people get out of debt, and build wealth, too. It's not just a matter of upgrading your lifestyle; having **More Than Enough** means that you can help other people improve their lot in life, as well. It means that you have learned to gather, process, and use information that will help you increase your wealth and improve your relationships.

Now that you have had the opportunity to work through the ten basic character qualities involved in the **More Than Enough** lifestyle, let's review briefly and see how your values, attitudes, and actions have changed.

Money Talks

Few things impact our lives as much as the "almighty dollar." For most of us, money determines where we live, where we work, what we do with our time, where or if we go on vacation, what we eat, what sort of clothing we wear, what type of car we drive, and when and where we will retire. For many people, money even dictates where and how they will be buried!

Money is much more than a means of exchange. In many ways, your money is *you!* How you make your money, how you save and invest it, or what you spend it on are some of the clearest indicators in your life regarding your values, vision, priorities, and commitments.

Money talks—but what is it saying about you? Check the statements below that best reflect your attitude toward your possessions, your priorities, and your paycheck, now that you have discovered **More Than Enough**.

____ I owe, I owe, so off to work I go!

____ I know that money can't buy me happiness, but maybe I can rent it for a while.

____ Play now, pay later.

____ Work now, play later.

____ How much money do I want? Just a little bit more.

____ If my family and I have a comfortable living, I will be content.

____ I want to make more so I can give more.

____ The one who dies with the most toys wins.

____ God owns it all and I am just managing his assets.

If your money is you, and is a symbol of what matters to you, how can you give more of yourself to help meet the needs of others around you?

_____

_____

_____

Stay Accountable

In the area of finances, as well as in their personal relationships, many people have discovered the freedom and encouragement of having another person walk with them in the journey. Certainly, you can always look to God for guidance. But sometimes it is also good to have a close friend or role model with whom you can compare notes and in whom you can confide, someone who can say, "I've been down that road before you. Here is what I learned."

We all need practical help from others who are wiser or more mature than we are, mentors who will hold us to our commitments and help motivate us to reach for our goals.

Think of a mentor who has had a profound influence on you. How can you have that same sort of impact on someone else?

_____

_____

Vision, Work, and Diligence

What motivates you to keep working so hard? (Check all that apply.)

____ So I can give more.
____ To earn enough money to get out of debt.
____ To build a bigger savings account.
____ To earn more so I can invest more for my family's future.
____ So I can feel that I am contributing something important to the world.
____ For my own sense of fulfillment.
____ Because I enjoy working in unity with my coworkers.
____ I have God-given gifts and talents that I want to use to help others.

If you had **More Than Enough** to live comfortably for the rest of your life, what work would you still want to do?

_____

Many people who have discovered **More Than Enough** enjoy their work so much, and derive such satisfaction from it, they would do it even if they were not financially compensated for it. Have you experienced that level of fulfillment in your career or community involvement?

           __ Yes   __ No   __ Uncertain

Describe briefly why you feel that way.

_____

_____

Which of the following statements most closely reflect your contentment level? (Check all that apply.)

___ I am not wealthy, but I am content.
___ I am content, but I want to build more wealth.
___ Compared to most people in the world, I am rich.
___ Relationships are what really matter to me.
___ I want to learn how to better use the wealth God has given me.

Honestly evaluate your lifestyle and goals. Which of the following statements best reflect your attitude now that you know more about having **More Than Enough**? (Check all that apply.)

___ In myself and in others, I value character more highly than cash.
___ I am content with my life. I have all that I need.
___ I have **More Than Enough**.
___ My life is colored by jealousy and greed.
___ In a conflict between character and riches, I'd choose riches.

What will it take for you to be able to relax, enjoy life, and be content?

_____

_____

In this book, we have discovered that patience and contentment can be learned. What specific steps will you take as a result of working through this book that you believe will lead to greater patience and contentment in your life?

_____

_____

_____

What do you hope to accomplish with the wealth that you are acquiring?

_____

_____

_____

Keep Giving

Rarely does God require somebody to give away all his or her money, property, or other material possessions. More frequently, God simply asks us to relax our grip on what we have so that he can use it. List some relationships or possessions that God has given to you and that he is now asking you to give back to him.

_____

_____

_____

Write a brief description of your willingness to trust God for **More Than Enough** in your life.

_____

_____

_____

The Power to Do It

Remember, the **More Than Enough** lifestyle is not self-actualized. It is value-actualized. Moreover, it is God-actualized. The abundance that God brings to your life is bound to show up in your finances and personal relationships.

Keep in mind that it all starts with a firm foundation built on your core values. Out of your core values, your vision is developed. Vision, put into work clothes, establishes your goals. Those goals, shared with those who are closest to you and with whom you are working together, will create a powerful unity. Your values, vision, and unity empower the springboard which provides you with the ability to hope. Injecting your life with hope launches your intensity like a rocket! That intensity is kept on course by people in your life who provide you with accountability and support. Yes, it will take diligence, work, and patience as you soar toward your destiny, but the contentment you will find and the ability you will develop to give and to help others will validate your values . . . and the process will keep right on repeating itself in you and in those people around you. Becoming all that God created you to be, having and doing what you were put on this planet to accomplish—that is **More Than Enough**!

It is impossible to have **More Than Enough** without God. But with God as your "Senior Partner," you cannot fail. He has all the resources that you need . . . and then some. He has **More Than Enough**. He *is* **More Than Enough**. And with God in control of your life, you too will find **More Than Enough**.

Notes

Chapter 1. Store Manager, to Aisle One, Please!

10. *the average employee:* Richard Nelson Bolles, *What Color Is Your Parachute?* (New York: Ten Speed Press, 1991), 56.

Chapter 2. Foundation Failure

37. *Press on. Nothing . . . :* Ray Kroc, *Grinding It Out* (New York: Berkley, 1978), 201.

38. *What we obtain . . . :* Thomas Paine, *The American Crisis*, no. 1 (December 23, 1776), cited in Charles R. Swindoll, *Living Above the Level of Mediocrity* (Dallas: Word Publishing, 1987), 51.

39. *"It's O.K. to be . . .":* Michael Korda, *Success! How Every Man and Woman Can Achieve It* (New York: Random House, 1977), 4.

51. *"What you do . . . ":* Zig Ziglar, untitled article, *Christian Businessman*, January 1999, 6.

Chapter 3. Vision: Binoculars Looking at Your Future

82. *money is a selfish . . . :* Dave Ramsey, *More Than Enough* (New York: Viking, 1999), pp. 57, 58.

Chapter 4. Unity—A Tangled Rope Is Just Loops

104. *"You can get . . .":* Zig Ziglar, *See You at the Top* (Gretna, La.: Pelican, 1974), 40.

113. *Separating your money* . . . : Dave Ramsey, *More Than Enough*, 85.
113. *"The two shall . . ."*: Genesis 2:18.

Chapter 7. Intensity—Move the Rock

194. *Incentives are helpful* . . . : Thomas J. Peters and Robert H. Waterman, Jr., *In Search of Excellence* (New York: Warner Books, 1982), 257.
198. *"the ability to apply* . . .": Dave Ramsey, *More Than Enough*, 160.
204. *Number of Years* . . . : Dave Ramsey, *More Than Enough*, 169.
206. *"I had the happy* . . .": Napoleon Hill, *Think and Grow Rich* (New York: E. P. Dutton, 1958), 164.

Chapter 8. Diligence—That Dirty Little Secret

217. *"If anyone will not* . . .": 1 Thessalonians 3:10 (New American Standard Bible).
223. *No, child abuse is* . . . : Dave Ramsey, *More Than Enough*, 191.
232. *"A faithful man* . . .": Proverbs 28:20 (New King James Version).
236. *Of America's current millionaires* . . . : Dave Ramsey, *More Than Enough*, 183.

Chapter 10. Contentment

279. *If you are miserable* . . . : Dave Ramsey, *More Than Enough*, 245.

Chapter 11. Giving—The Great Misunderstanding

291. *The open hand* . . . : adapted from Dave Ramsey, *More Than Enough*, 260–61.
296. *"rebuke the devourer"*: see Malachi 3:8–11.
296. *"After marrying each other* . . .": Tom Bodett, *Small Comforts* (New York: Addison-Wesley, 1987), 57.
298. *When I was working* . . . : Oseola McCarty, *Simple Wisdom for Rich Living* (Atlanta, Ga.: Longstreet Press, 1996), 3.

Chapter 12. More Than Enough

307. *Traveling from Toledo* . . . : adapted from Stanley Tam, *God Owns My Business* (Waco, Tex.: Word Publishing, 1969), 37.

Index